Sacrificing Families

Sacrificing Families

Navigating Laws, Labor, and Love Across Borders

Leisy J. Abrego

Stanford University Press
Stanford, California

Stanford University Press
Stanford, California

Printed in the United States of America on acid-free, archival-quality paper

Library of Congress Cataloging-in-Publication Data

Abrego, Leisy J., author.
  Sacrificing families : navigating laws, labor, and love across borders / Leisy J. Abrego.
    pages cm
  Includes bibliographical references and index.
    ISBN 978-0-8047-8831-1 (cloth : alk. paper) — ISBN 978-0-8047-9051-2 (pbk. : alk. paper)
1. Salvadorans—Family relationships—United States. 2. Immigrants—Family relationships—United States. 3. Immigrants—Family relationships—El Salvador. 4. Immigrant families—El Salvador. 5. Children of immigrants—El Salvador. 6. El Salvador—Emigration and immigration—Social aspects. 7. United States— Emigration and immigration—Social aspects. I. Title.
  E184.S15A27 2014
  305.868'7284073—dc23

                                                    2013036755

ISBN 978-0-8047-9057-4 (electronic)

Typeset by Thompson Type in 10/14 Minion

Para Margoth y Douglas Abrego
por su cariño y sus sacrificios

Para Carlos Colorado
porque es bello formar una familia con vos

Contents

Preface

AFTER SEPARATING FROM MY GRANDFATHER, my maternal grandmother could not bear to see her children go hungry. Not unlike many poor and single mothers in El Salvador, she had been toiling in domestic jobs for a couple of years and made barely enough for transportation but not enough for food; so she came to the United States in the mid-1960s. Penniless and driven to fulfill her responsibility to her children, she left all four of them with her mother. Initially, she worked in the United States without legal authorization to live in the country. After becoming a legal permanent resident, it took many years for all the paperwork to be processed through the complicated bureaucracy that was known, back then, as Immigration and Naturalization Services (INS). Not until she received the last piece of paper from the federal agency was she able to reunite with her children, some fourteen years after her departure. Three decades later, and although they see each other weekly, my mother, who is now in her fifties, still cannot hold back the tears when she recounts the many times in her childhood when she longed to be close to her mother. She and her sisters are grateful to their grandmother for her care, and they would have appreciated their father's presence in their lives, but it was their mother's absence all those years that continues to pain them.[1]

In general, as a society, we accept and try to adhere to the notion that parents and children reside together—at least until the children get old enough to move out on their own. Of course, families are very diverse. The social expectation, however, is that children will share a home with at least one parent (biological or not). This book is about families for whom this expectation is an unattained privilege. It is about mothers and fathers who feel that they have run out of economic options, who then make the heart-rending decision to go thousands of miles away to another country in search of jobs and greater wages for their children's survival.

In the Salvadoran immigrant community, family separation is relatively common. Everyone has a sibling, cousin, uncle, or neighbor who lives or has lived away from their children or from their mother or father—what scholars refer to as "transnational families." In conversations with youth from El Salvador, Guatemala, and Mexico about their educational trajectories in the United States, several students shared stories of painful separations and challenging reunifications with their biological parents.[2] Their narratives reveal that family separation has life-altering repercussions for countless Latino immigrant families.

Sacrificing Families draws extensively on the voices of parents in the United States—largely driven by a desire for survival—and the children who remain in El Salvador. Their narratives expose the many economic and emotional experiences of children and parents who are in the midst of long-term separation. Most notably, the stories uncover profound emotional suffering, varied economic realities (that is, not all of these families are thriving economically), and underlying structural constraints that determine how families fare.

I want to clarify a few key points about language and social constructions as I employ them analytically in this project. Throughout the book I use the categories "migrant" and "immigrant" to refer to the parents in these transnational families as seen from the perspective of their children in El Salvador versus the standpoint of someone in the United States. The word "migrant" captures movement in flux and therefore best underscores how those who stayed behind in the homeland perceive their parents. The word "immigrant," on the other hand, better captures the more long-term settlement and incorporation that often unexpectedly becomes the goal once these parents arrive in the United States. I also reluctantly call family separation a "strategy." Although the term implies full cognizance of and control over the situation, in most of these cases, parents are initially hesitant to undertake migration and pursue it only when they are convinced it is better than local possibilities for survival. Given the macro political and economic realities of the country, it is safe to assume that their chances for economic success or upward mobility are rather limited in El Salvador. This is why, in their own narratives, migrant parents take ownership of their decision to leave.[3] Also, I did not ask study participants about their sexual orientation, and nobody discussed their experiences or perceptions of family outside of the heteronormative model. El Salvador continues to be a socially conservative place where LGBT people's human rights are denied and LGBT activists' work is marginalized.[4] For these reasons, while transnational families may certainly include gay parents, this experience was not reflected in the narratives.

One of the goals of my analysis in this project is also to reveal the constructed nature of "illegality" and its consequences for Salvadoran transnational families. Some may find my use of the term *illegality* offensive because, if read superficially, it has the potential to reproduce the dehumanizing effects of terms like *illegal* to refer to immigrants and, in the contemporary moment, pejoratively racialize U.S. Latinas and Latinos.[5] I am sensitive to this form of violence and therefore consciously use the term to point the analytical lens to the structures that create vulnerability in immigrants' lives.[6] That is, contrary to using language of illegality to brand human beings, I draw on the same language to underscore how laws, enforcement practices, and discourses produce categories with grave implications for human beings.

Staying true to the stories, *Sacrificing Families* is not just about the suffering of families and individuals. What happens to these families is too complex to be portrayed only negatively. In many cases, parents are able to achieve their families' goals and children reap the rewards of separation through educational and economic gains. Others, however, suffer greatly through the lengthy separations. They feel abandoned and disconnected from the world around them. My aim is not merely to repeat their words. Instead, the focus shifts back and forth between their actions, goals, and understandings and the larger public discourses, structural barriers, opportunities, and expectations. This expanded context reveals that transnational parents' behaviors are at times encouraged or restrained, made possible or impossible by forces outside of any single person's control.

In the process of researching and writing this book, I have come to understand my own family history in that larger context. This allows me to better appreciate why any parent would seemingly willingly leave his or her children for a decade or longer and why, even when parents claim to be doing it all for the sake of their children, the children's lives do not always improve. And in conversations with my mom about my findings and conclusions, she, too, has found herself in many of these stories. It is my hope that others will be able to do the same.

Acknowledgments

THE POWERFUL STORIES THAT FILL THESE PAGES reflect the courage and hard work of Salvadoran migrants and their families. I would like to extend my most heartfelt thanks to all the mothers and fathers, daughters and sons who embraced the interviews as opportunities to bring to light experiences that they knew were not unique to them. Their extraordinary risks and sacrifices simply to secure their families' survival are compelling reminders that debates about immigration and globalization are not just about numbers; they are about human beings. By the same token, dollar figures and discussions about migration and development are also about human beings. It is their and my deepest desire that, in the hands of readers, this book will help to humanize migrants and prevent the continuation of policies that force so many to leave their children behind. I am deeply grateful for their trust in me and for their faith in this project.

This book is also a testament to the wonderful communities in my life. It was their camaraderie and encouragement that allowed me to complete it. This project was supported financially at various stages. Funds from the Andrew W. Mellon Program in Latin American Sociology, the Latin American Studies Association Section on Central America, and the UCLA Latin American Institute allowed me to travel to El Salvador to conduct interviews. I am also grateful to the Haynes and Ford Foundations, as well as the University of California President's Postdoctoral Fellowship Program for providing me with valuable time to revise the manuscript. Finally, the UCLA Faculty

Career Development Grant provided funds for research assistance and production costs.

I am fortunate to have been guided by several compassionate and thoughtful scholars. Rebecca Emigh mentored, challenged, and supported me in developing the analytical and professional tools that continue to serve me today. Vilma Ortiz and Min Zhou, with their genuine enthusiasm for my work, were central in seeing me through the first draft. My mentor, colleague, and friend, Cecilia Menjívar, deserves special recognition for her boundless generosity and invaluable contributions to academia. Her work on Central Americans in the United States has deeply enriched my thinking, and I can only aspire to be such an exceptional mentor and scholar. Ester Hernández, Arely Zimmerman, Sylvanna Falcón, Maria Cristina Morales, Suyapa Portillo, Katy Pinto, Veronica Terriquez, Cynthia Feliciano, and Shannon Gleeson are also brilliant and caring colleagues. I continue to be inspired by these women's ability to seamlessly weave together their intellectual talents with their commitment to social justice. I have also learned a great deal from Leo Chavez, whose genuine passion for scholarship and collegiality continues to inspire me.

Since joining the faculty at UCLA, I benefit greatly from the intellectual support of magnificent colleagues, including David Hernandez, Alicia Gaspar de Alba, Abel Valenzuela, Maylei Blackwell, Otto Santa Ana, Eric Avila, Janna Shadduck-Hernandez, Rubén Hernández-León, and Roger Waldinger. Ellie Hernandez, Elena Mohseni, Olivia Díaz, Nancy Dennis, and Brenda Trujillo have helped to make the Chicana and Chicano Studies Department a wonderful new home. With funds from the Penny Kanner Next Generation Grant, UCLA's Center for the Study of Women brought together a star lineup of scholars—including Pat Zavella, Maylei Blackwell, Marjorie Faulstich Orellana, Kathryn Anderson-Levitt, and Nadia Kim—who helped me tighten up the manuscript during the final stages of revisions. At Stanford University Press, Kate Wahl was thorough and kind in her support of this book. My experience with her, Frances Malcolm, and everyone at Stanford was delightful.

Many other people had large and small parts in helping me complete the book: from offering editorial advice and sharing information about the publishing process, to helping me navigate life in academia and cheering me on when I most needed encouragement. Cristina Mora, Veronica Terriquez, Sylvanna Falcón, Linn Posey, Anthony Ocampo, and Rocío Rosales took the time to read chapters and give me helpful feedback. I also benefited from the thoughtfulness of Ana Patricia Rodriguez, Roberto Gonzales, Susan Coutin, Alicia Bonaparte, Diane Yoder, Nancy Yuen, Christina Sue, Arpi Miller,

Faustina DuCros, Noriko Milman, Christina Chin, Jody Agius Vallejo, Helen Marrow, Georgina Guzmán, Gloria Chacón, and Lupe Escobar. In El Salvador, I was fortunate to rely on Oscar Ramírez, Patty Martínez, the Martínez Bolaños, and the Francia families for housing and transportation during the research phase. At UCLA, Jennifer Cárcamo, and Nathaly Fernandez provided fantastic research assistance.

I have also been graced with kind and generous friends. My life is all the better for the wisdom and support of Sandra Alvear, Roberto Montenegro, Sarah Chun, Hiyas Ambrosio, Martha Martinez, Karina Oliva, Morelia Portillo Rivas, Alicia Yvonne Estrada, Jeanette Miura, Leyda García, Maya Chinchilla, Gustavo Guerra, Hugo Nelson Chávez, Mario Escobar, Jade Sasser, Charlene Gomez, Peter Kuhns, Adrian Soldatenko, and Kevin Riley. Cheerfully, they have always encouraged and taught me to enjoy life, laughter, family, good poetry, and good food!

My sisters—Claudia, Tatiana, and Natalie—have also helped me immensely by offering welcome distractions. Aside from being great company, they are incredibly loving *tías*. As are my sisters-in-law, Claudia and Karla. My children and I are lucky to have them in our lives. I'd also like to recognize the support and understanding of my extended family—*tías y primos, abuelitas y suegra*—who always welcome me back to family gatherings. All my cousins, aunts and uncles, but especially my *tía* Paty, *tía* Mirna, Mary, and *abuelita* Juana, have consistently given me much love and many wonderful stories.

I also thank Mateo and Diego, my sons, who throughout the process of researching and writing this book have filled our lives with intensity and peace, stress, laughter, and a keen appreciation for life in all its vulnerabilities, messiness, and grandeur. Eight-year-old Mateo, who was born in the middle of the research process, has spent his entire life hearing that one day his mom will write a book. I'm thrilled not to let him down. His curiosity and love of reading have inspired me to pay even closer attention to words and their power; and I am ever so grateful that he cares enough to want to read my work. Five-year-old Diego keeps me grounded in reality with his ample imagination and passion in everything he does. His heartfelt laughs and tears, along with his amazing hugs, make me a better, more whole human being. Playing, teaching, and learning from them create great balance in my life, and I thank God every day for making me their mother. With their mere existence, both my boys have contextualized this work in a new light, helping me better appreciate the sacrifices of mothers and fathers and the suffering of children in transnational families. What an incredible privilege never to have to make the soul-crushing decision to leave them for the sake of securing their survival.

The book is dedicated to my parents, Douglas and Margoth Abrego, to whom I will always be deeply indebted. Through teenage parenthood, a civil war, the struggles of immigration, and the challenges of limited resources, they were consistent providers with high expectations. With great pride, I try to honor their experiences and accomplishments in everything I do. Inspired in part by my mom's own painful childhood experience in a transnational family and my dad's personal and professional sacrifices to provide for us, this book is a tribute to them.

Finally, I also dedicate the book to Carlos Colorado. This accomplishment, like all the others, belongs partially to you. Nineteen years and counting, and I am still convinced that there is no partner as reliable and committed as you. To say that I am incredibly fortunate to be married to you is an understatement of grand proportions. Ever since we met, you have taken each of my dreams and made it your own, all the while removing obstacles from my path—from the smallest of pebbles to the largest of boulders, both physical and mental. I am most grateful for your ability to see goodness in me at every turn. Because you never allow me to get bogged down in the pitfalls of academia, and because your humor continues to shock and entertain me, I dedicate this book to you. Como bien dice Franco de Vita, "*si me dieran a elegir una vez más, te elegiría sin pensarlo, es que no hay nada que pensar.*"

Sacrificing Families

1 Salvadoran Transnational Families

AT SIXTEEN YEARS OLD, Daniel was only about four feet, eight inches tall. His faded school uniform, bony arms exposed, was evidence of his family's dire economic situation.[1] We spoke for over an hour in an empty, dusty room in the public school he attended in San Salvador, El Salvador. Tears welled up in his eyes as he passionately described his father's many failed attempts to cross into the United States and the injustices he faced during U.S. detention. Daniel was most emotional, though, when he reflected on how the situation affected him personally. With tears streaming down his face, he admitted that he had even considered suicide. Daniel had not seen his father, Rodrigo, in years. Without the financial support the family hoped would come from Rodrigo's migration, they were overwhelmed by poverty. Unable to make enough money to eat three meals a day, Daniel, a once-promising student, was frequently going to school hungry. At school, he tried to focus on the subjects that were once so exciting to him, but stress overcame him, and high grades eluded him. And, to make matters worse, malnutrition had stunted his growth to the point that fellow schoolmates regularly made fun of him, "At your height, you should be in kindergarten!" Daniel remembered them taunting. "I feel so bad, so ashamed. I should be taller, I should be stronger, but life has been bad to me."

Across the city, in a spacious home with modern appliances, I interviewed twenty-one-year-old Xiomara. She was dressed fashionably, with dangling earrings and carefully applied makeup that complemented her reserved, yet confident personality. Her mother, who had always been her closest confidant, had migrated to the United States three years earlier, following the 2001 earthquakes. The natural disaster was devastating for her family. Xiomara's mother lost all of the merchandise in her neighborhood store and acquired an immense debt overnight. Migration became the only realistic solution to their financial problems. After three years of separation, the consistent monthly sums from her mother had reduced the debt while allowing Xiomara to graduate from a private high school and excel at a private university. She looked forward to completing a college degree in a few years and was generally optimistic about her future. But financial stability came at great emotional cost. As she reflected on the family separation, she articulated the great tension that weighed her down, "Given the context, let's say that it's going well . . . The only thing is my mother's companionship. That's something no one can replace."

The transnational family strategy is, at its core, a response to economic circumstances. Parents migrate in search of better wages to send as remittances to their children.[2] Collectively, remittances have become a mainstay of the national economies of several developing nations—including El Salvador. Migrants work hard to send sums of money that add up to relative stability for their country as a whole. At a more intimate level, remittances are also the realization of a family's survival strategy. Amid dire situations, migration became the most plausible solution for parents. They left children behind because they were hopeful that opportunities for work and higher wages would allow them to *sacarlos adelante* (uplift their families) from afar.

But not all families fare equally well. Some, like Xiomara, can thrive. They have access to greater academic opportunities and live more comfortably than ever before—even if they have to pay an emotional cost for such stability. Others, like Daniel, cannot catch a break. Here, too, children miss their parents terribly, but they have nothing concrete to show for the family's sacrifice. This book examines *why* there are disparate experiences of family separation. It uncovers some of the ways U.S. immigration policies and multiple gendered processes intersect and move fluidly across national borders to stratify transnational families, creating differential economic and emotional experiences for both parents and children.

In the twenty-first century, transnational families are not uncommon among U.S. immigrants from Latin America. Thousands of migrant parents negotiate family life and responsibilities across borders. Yet it is rare to hear people discuss the challenges openly and lovingly in shared community spaces. This is precisely what happened in May 2003, when I sat in the audience at an art space in Los Angeles to witness the coming together of several artists who, like me, are children of Central American immigrants. Among the various moving performances about ethnic identity and the ever-present search for "home," the piece titled "Prosperity"[3] was especially touching. In it, Salvadoran writer, filmmaker, and performance artist Carolina Rivera portrayed the role of an immigrant mother in Los Angeles whose children remain in El Salvador. With limited props, she transported the audience into the world of this mother who lived by herself in a tight studio apartment with few belongings. Rivera poignantly revealed the economic and emotional pain of family separation through this mother who sacrificed a great deal in the United States—a country where she felt extremely lonely. She found courage and energy in knowing that at least her family in El Salvador was doing well. But the painful separation was most evident when she received graduation photographs of her children, whom she no longer recognized. Much of the audience was in tears.

In the decade that has followed, transnational families have appeared more frequently in U.S. political discourse and been more visible in the public eye. In the spring of 2006, hundreds of thousands of immigrants and their supporters marched in cities throughout the United States advocating for immigration reform. Los Angeles, home to the largest concentration of Latin American (and Salvadoran) immigrants, witnessed two of the most massive demonstrations. In four miles spanning Pico-Union to Miracle Mile, the record-breaking multitude flowed through the city streets carrying signs calling for "Legalización para los indocumentados, reunificación familiar, soluciones humanas para problemas humanos" ("Legalization for the undocumented, family reunification, humane solutions for human problems"). The historic marches helped suspend a draconian immigration bill in Congress. But the issue of family reunification, articulated so vividly in these demonstrations, continues to be at the heart of Latino immigrants' daily struggles.

Representations of transnational families have also captured the hearts and minds of moviegoers and readers. The movie Bajo la misma luna (Under the Same Moon)[4] portrayed the heartbreaking experiences of a Mexican transnational family, and the best-selling nonfiction book Enrique's Journey[5] documents the agonizing attempt of a Honduran boy to reunite with his mother. Like these portrayals, Sacrificing Families also captures the tragedy of these families' living arrangements, but it delves deeper and uses a wider lens to situate transnational families in a larger structural context and to shed light on the patterns of inequality in their well-being. Why do parents choose to leave their children? What are these families' experiences of long-term separation? And why do some fare better than others?

Transnational Families and Inequalities

It is not immediately evident why discrepancies arise in transnational families' well-being.[6] From the work of various scholars, it is clear that most transnational families seek migration and family separation as survival strategies that take advantage of global inequalities in wages;[7] mothers and fathers practice parenting from afar through remittances, gifts, and weekly phone calls;[8] children play a role in supporting or challenging these arrangements;[9] and the bulk of the care work in both sending and receiving regions falls on women.[10] It is still unclear, however, whether and why some transnational families fare better than others.[11]

As a first step in examining inequalities, scholars have uncovered transnational families' *internal* discrepancies in quality of life and subjective experience of time apart. In her important study of Mexican transnational families, for example, sociologist Joanna Dreby[12] teases out some central incongruities within these families—particularly how time flies for migrant parents who work long hours in the United States but goes slowly for children who grow up awaiting reunification with their parents.[13] This mismatch in time leads to painful and prolonged separations when families yearn to be reunited. Sociologist Leah Schmalzbauer points to another internal inequality as seen in the class formation of migrant Honduran parents and their nonmigrant children; while parents live in poverty to remit, their children use remittances to attain more comfortable lifestyles.[14] Not willing to share the details of their sacrifices so as not to worry their children, parents inadvertently create a superficial prosperity that their children come to expect, no matter how unrealistic its maintenance. These are important details about the experience of family separation across borders, but their emphasis on inequalities *within* transnational families largely misses the structural forces that contextualize family separation in the first place. This book aims to extend the vibrant scholarly discussion on transnational families by examining inequalities *across* transnational families. What are the various patterns of inequalities and differentiated experiences of transnational families? And what processes create and sustain these?

One logical place to begin this inquiry is in the work of international migration scholars who examine why some immigrants fare better than others in the United States. Three of the most commonly cited explanations for inequalities in socioeconomic integration of immigrants are human capital, "the skills that immigrants bring along in the form of education, job experience, and language knowledge";[15] social networks;[16] and length of residence in the receiving country.[17] How much they know, whom they know, and how long they've lived here all help determine how quickly and how favorably immigrants move up economically in the United States.[18] With higher levels of education, for example, immigrants should qualify for better-paying jobs; the more friends and relatives they know in the United States, the more people they can rely on to help them find housing and work; and the longer they live here, the more they have learned about how to navigate opportunities and challenges in this country. By extension, these factors should also explain transnational family members' economic well-being.

Like other immigrants, parents in transnational families rely on economic opportunities in the United States. The difference, however, is that much of their earnings is earmarked for remittances. Those remittances, in turn, make up the majority of their families' monthly budgets in the home country.[19] One way to examine inequalities across transnational families, therefore, is to focus on variations in the flow of remittances.

In the Salvadoran case, scholars and practitioners in the field of development certainly look closely at the macro portrait of remittances. Collectively, international migrants reliably send portions of their wages to loved ones in their home countries, establishing what some see as a "migration-development nexus."[20] Indeed, some policy makers are pursuing the idea of using these monies for development.[21] This makes sense considering that, in 2012, remittances to Latin America totaled nearly $64 billion—$3.9 billion of which went to El Salvador.[22] These monies are a significant source of external funding; they exceed the combined sum of foreign direct investment and official development assistance to several Latin American countries, including El Salvador. From the perspective of government entities and aid institutions, remittances are untaxed, "free" funds that should be used more productively for national development. This book argues that part of the problem with this approach is that not all migrants remit evenly, and not all recipients benefit equally.[23] An analytical lens that focuses on inequalities across transnational families will demonstrate that the efforts of governments, the banking indus-try, and nongovernmental organizations (NGOs) to streamline the uses of re-mittances cannot presume a minimum baseline for any family. Furthermore, is it fair to expect transnational families to bear the burden of development?

Although these families often conceive of separation as mostly an eco-nomic strategy, the realities of long-term separation also have profound and undeniable emotional effects on parents and children.[24] Like most families, transnational families are expected to provide emotional support for their members, but the geographical distance between parents and children can make it very difficult to demonstrate love. Children are especially pained by their mother's absence,[25] but do other dynamics also shape their emotional well-being? What are the affective tolls on various members of these families? And under what circumstances do some children learn to cope with long-term separation? Because the emotional consequences of a parent's absence may lower academic achievement,[26] it is important to understand differences in emotional well-being and the processes that contextualize these patterns.

The work of bringing in the state to explore intimate and gendered aspects of migration is already under way. In her beautifully written analysis of trans-national Mexicans, anthropologist Deborah Boehm uncovers the multifaceted ways that U.S. policies produce and reproduce family intimacy and gendered experiences of transnational life.[27] As she traces the shifts in gender ideologies and practices with every migration and return, Boehm underscores the fluid nature of these processes, even within single families. Similarly, geographer Geraldine Pratt compellingly reveals the role of Canadian policies in forcing Filipino families apart.[28] In this case, the distance that separates migrants and their children proves to be quite painful and negatively consequential, even through what are deemed just "temporary" separations. In *Sacrificing Fami-lies*, I draw on and extend these rich insights to better understand economic and emotional inequalities across transnational families. I demonstrate that beyond the most widely cited explanations of why immigrants fare as they do, immigration policies and gender are also influential and complementary pro-cesses that complicate, amplify, and sometimes trump the effects of more tra-ditional explanatory factors (that is, level of education, social networks, and length of residency). A lens that focuses specifically on immigration policies and gender, therefore, reveals a more complete picture of why some families fare better than others.

The Production of (Il)legality

Although public debates about immigration in the United States implicitly assume that immigrants' legal status is an innate and static characteristic, the truth is that nothing about an immigrants' position within or outside of the law is natural. On the contrary, illegality—the condition of immigrants' legal status and deportability—is historically specific and socially, politically, and legally produced.[29] In its contemporary form, illegality has come to have an intimate and deep impact on all immigrants, as the potential for deportation is high, even if it is impossible to deport all undocumented immigrants.[30] With very restricted paths to legalization, undocumented immigrants and their loved ones must grapple with the fear of deportation at every turn; this is a heavy burden that millions carry.[31]

There have been moments in U.S. history when, in practical terms, undocumented status had little meaning. For various periods of mass immigration, undocumented immigrants were able to obtain a driver's license and work without the intense fear of deportation that now permeates immigrant communities.[32] But, in the last few decades, undocumented status and illegality have gained broader significance. Immigrants categorized as "undocumented" or "temporarily protected" are targets of progressively more harsh laws and ever more hateful speech, all of which work together to criminalize and dehumanize them and their families.[33]

Beginning in the 1980s, at approximately the same time that massive migration of Salvadorans began, the United States changed its contemporary immigration enforcement policies. No longer focusing only on relatively inconsequential apprehensions at the border, the Reagan administration militarized border enforcement. These changes thwarted circular migration patterns and increased the settlement of entire families in the United States.[34] For Salvadorans, who had to travel through multiple border crossings passing through Guatemala and Mexico en route to the United States, the new border policies added yet another layer of barriers between migrants and their families. The Reagan administration also gave states more power to implement immigration policies locally and, with the passage of the Immigration Reform and Control Act (IRCA) in 1986, established highly symbolic employer sanctions that for the first time made it a crime for undocumented immigrants to work.[35] These changes set in motion the production of illegality in its current form.

Immigrants were further disadvantaged through the congressional overhaul of immigration law in 1996 with the Illegal Immigration Reform and Immigrant Responsibility Act (IIRIRA).[36] Along with increasing border enforcement, the new law made it more difficult for immigrants to obtain legal permanent residence; it eliminated legal mechanisms previously available to immigrants who were fighting deportation and also made legal permanent residents deportable (even retroactively) for a vastly expanded set of noncriminal offenses.[37] As a result, deportations have markedly increased every year since.[38]

After the attacks of 9/11, legal changes to criminalize undocumented immigrants further magnified and accelerated when the Immigration and Naturalization Service (INS) was reorganized into the Department of Homeland Security with the purpose of safeguarding the country against terrorism.[39] This move explicitly linked immigrants with criminals at a time when programs such as 287(g)—in which local police are deputized to act as Immigration and Customs Enforcement (ICE) agents—and Secure Communities—which allows the FBI to communicate to ICE about anyone arrested or booked into custody throughout the country—increased their chances of deportation.[40] Indeed, such programs have led to record numbers of detentions and deportations, through sweeping workplace raids and because even routine traffic stops can quickly lead to ICE's involvement.[41]

Although undocumented status has until recently been largely a matter of civil or administrative law,[42] mainstream media images tend to portray undocumented immigrants as criminals.[43] The image of undocumented immigrants at the moment of apprehension, handcuffed and treated as dangerous felons, is common on network news. These repeated images are rather convincing to the general public, even when official statistics confirm that the majority of immigrants who are deported do not have criminal records.[44]

The record numbers of deportations, alongside the wave of hateful speech and growing animosity against immigrants, inevitably affect immigrants and their families' well-being, whether or not all members are undocumented.[45] Contemporary immigrants have made a home and settled in the United States under this cloud of illegality. Meanwhile, employers (who have little to risk under the selective enforcement of the law) willingly hire undocumented immigrants, usually as low-wage workers and easy targets for exploitation. Knowing that workers have everything to lose if they are detained and deported, unscrupulous employers threaten to call ICE as a way to control employees and undermine their rights.[46]

Beyond worksites, illegality is a central determinant of an immigrant's life chances.[47] Undocumented immigrants are marginalized by their "legal non-existence."[48] From their position outside the law,[49] they are more likely than other immigrants to earn less and work in more dangerous jobs[50] and have little access to financial and housing aid.[51] Deportations, moreover, have devastating consequences for families and entire communities.[52] And even when immigrants are not detained, undocumented status prolongs their economic insecurity,[53] while ramped up enforcement practices produce mental anguish when they know that they may be deported at any moment, in any public or private space.[54]

It is important that the *fear* of detention and deportation powerfully regulates immigrants' behavior, often impeding them from having access to their legal rights as workers and human beings and preventing them from seeking social services.[55] As policies continue to criminalize immigrants and block them from work and educational opportunities, legal statuses—as determined by immigration laws—set the conditions for vast inequalities for immigrants.[56] Over the long term, these disadvantages can prevent undocumented immigrants from thriving economically and integrating socially into the United States, while their families and communities experience the ripple effects.[57]

Drawing on research on illegality, this book examines how the production of illegality in the United States—a country that is undeniably both a regional and world center of power[58]—also determines the life chances and well-being of people beyond its territorial borders. From determining who is eligible for a visa and who can regularize his or her status to how long immigrants must wait to file a petition for their close relatives to join them in the country, policies and enforcement practices produce illegality with consequences that are not easily contained by borders.[59]

The Production of Gender

Gender is an equally important factor for the well-being of immigrants and their families. Indeed, it is a central constitutive element in all human life.[60] Gender ideologies, structures, and practices operate simultaneously to shape women's and men's opportunities and behaviors within families, labor markets, and other social institutions and spaces.[61] Fluidly, gender is produced through ongoing ever-present processes that convincingly suggest that the common and seemingly persistent behaviors considered acceptable for girls and boys, women and men at any given moment in history are natural and normal.[62] Gendered inequalities, therefore, often go unquestioned when people assume these patterns to be unchangeable. This can make deep-seated inequalities—including the uneven burden of child care and higher moral expectations for women and greater pay and decision-making power for men—difficult to erase even across national contexts.

Parenthood and its practices are heavily marked by gendered opportunities and expectations. While family practices are ever changing, motherhood and fatherhood are often defined in sharply contrasting ways. In El Salvador, motherhood is venerated as the idealized form of womanhood,[63] while fatherhood is only one of several acceptable forms of masculinity.[64] Defined culturally as morally superior to fathers, mothers are expected to sacrifice themselves in the name of their families.[65] These sacrifices can mean different things to different sectors of the population. While middle- and upper-class mothers are charged with being the main caregivers of their families within homes, poor and working-class mothers must also participate in the public sphere—through employment in the labor market, political action, or migration—to support their children.[66] Fatherhood, on the other hand, regardless of social class standing, is closely tied to authority, protection, and guidance of the family through participation in the public sphere.[67]

Structural barriers and socioeconomic inequalities can prevent poor and working-class parents from fulfilling their social expectations. In the context of economic precariousness, mothers are additionally burdened by social surveillance. Gossip and negative interactions with others can serve to police mothers into fulfilling their expected roles as self-sacrificing providers, regardless of the scarcity around them.[68] In those instances, marginalized and economically disadvantaged women may have only their own bodies, as workers, protestors, or migrants, to offer in the name of children's survival. Economically disadvantaged fathers, on the other hand, may also be targets of gendered forms of gossip, but these do not necessarily undermine their masculinity and self-worth.[69] As men, when they are structurally blocked from economic sources of masculine identity, they can negotiate and maintain their masculinity through other means, including repressing emotions, demonstrating physical strength, or signaling freedom and sexual prowess.[70]

These structural and cultural contexts help to explain why mothers who transgress gender boundaries by migrating internationally may still conform to gender norms in other ways.[71] They also suggest reasons why, despite the existence of a law in El Salvador that defines irresponsible paternity as a crime,[72] many fathers forgo their paternal responsibilities. Without strict enforcement of the law, the stakes for meeting these expectations are low.[73] Socially, it becomes acceptable for fathers who cannot provide economically for their children to establish their self-worth by performing more easily attainable forms of masculinity—including independence, stoicism, or sexual relations with multiple women. Meanwhile, migrant women face greater stigma and more meaningful punishment than men for transgressing parental gender boundaries. Unlike migrant fathers, migrant mothers throughout the world are persistently stigmatized for leaving their children's side.[74] Yet harsh and uneven economic conditions require that women continue to migrate.[75]

To be sure, migration and settlement have the potential to change women's and men's notions of what is appropriate gender behavior. Individuals may be forced to redefine their roles within families every time they migrate, as they adapt to new contexts and changing responsibilities.[76] Some immigrant women have gained independence, and immigrant men have taken on more chores at home,[77] but such gendered negotiations are fraught[78]—particularly as a result of gendered labor market opportunities and experiences.

For transnational families, labor market inequalities are particularly consequential for remittances. In some cases, migrant men—who earn more than women—send larger sums.[79] On the other hand, although women send smaller sums, they tend to be more consistent and reliable remitters.[80] Structurally, it makes sense that immigrant women remit smaller sums because they typically earn less than men.[81] Immigrant women and men have access to different kinds of jobs. Latina immigrant women are largely concentrated in menial, poorly paid jobs, in the often-exploitative service sector.[82] And although immigrant men are also disadvantaged in the labor market, immigrant women systematically earn less and are hired into less prestigious jobs than their male counterparts with similar levels of education.[83]

In the rich structural and cultural contexts that produce gendered parental expectations, remittances offer a fruitful site for the examination of gendered agency, barriers, and production in transnational families.[84] After all, remittances are more than mere economic markers; they represent a sense of obligation between family members[85] and often the expression of deep emotional bonds between relatives across borders.[86] This may explain why, in some instances, women have also been known to remit more than men.[87] Such unlikely outcomes suggest the need for a more nuanced gendered analysis. In countries like El Salvador, where women—as mothers, grandmothers, sisters, and other female relatives—continue to be held responsible for the majority of mothering tasks, mothers' migrations are likely to have far-reaching consequences in families' lives.[88] Indeed, the enormous emotional costs to family members have repeatedly surfaced as central components of the transnational family experience, particularly for families in which the mother has migrated.[89] Meanwhile, constructions of masculinity prevent migrant men from expressing their melancholy and loneliness, making it difficult to stay in touch with their families when they cannot fulfill the various gendered expectations.[90]

This book examines how gendered structures, expectations, and processes help determine the economic and emotional well-being of transnational families. In their efforts to support their families, how do migrant mothers and fathers practice agency to transgress, transform, or conform to gender expectations that mediate their family separations? Moreover, when and how does gender intersect with (il)legality during the migration decision, journey, and settlement processes to shape transnational family members' experiences across borders?

The Salvadoran Context

I chose to research Salvadoran transnational families for several reasons. Most important, this population has characteristics that help me understand inequalities across families. With a complicated history of blocked access to legal status in the United States and made up of similar numbers of men and women, the Salvadoran migration stream allows me to compare experiences across far-reaching systems of stratification—namely (il)legality and gender. This, and the fact that Salvadoran immigrants are separated from their loved ones in El Salvador by multiple national borders, makes the Salvadoran case an important one for Latin American–U.S.-based transnational families.

Massive migration of Salvadorans to the United States began in the early 1980s, mainly in response to civil war.[91] Historically, the military used repressive and violent tactics to quash popular uprisings, always in the name of "democracy," although mostly prioritizing the protection of wealth.[92] By the late 1970s, when wide-scale poverty and repression had become unbearable, leftist factions joined forces in an armed struggle to overthrow the oligarchy. Their goal was to finally put an end to the deep economic inequalities that benefited few while crippling the vast majority of the population. The U.S. role in supporting the military set the conditions for the immensely devastating consequences of the civil war.

Assuming that the armed leftist coalition represented the possibility of a much-feared "communist" victory in the region, as part of its Cold War operations, the Reagan administration armed and trained the Salvadoran military and paramilitary leaders of death squads with the goal of eliminating all opposition through any means necessary. To this end, in the 1980s, the U.S. government invested over $1 million daily—totaling $6 billion—to maintain the war against guerrilla fighters. In their attempts to suppress the popular armed movement of people who were demanding a decrease in extreme disparities and an end to government repression,[93] the U.S.-trained (and largely U.S.-funded) military indiscriminately scorched entire villages while torturing and disappearing thousands.[94] By the end of the war, at least 75,000 people were killed, while scores more were disappeared, never to be heard from again. In response, those who lost relatives, had survived attacks, lived in hard-hit zones, or simply feared imminent death fled.

While some sought refuge regionally, a larger number headed north.[95] For the first time in Salvadoran history, people migrated en masse to the United States. Based on ties with family and friends or guided by notions they had learned through television and popular culture, they imagined the United States to be a safe and politically stable place with ample opportunities for economic advancement. Unfortunately, they were met with a blocked entrance. Despite the U.S. government's role in the war, it did not recognize Salvadorans as political refugees.

According to the Refugee Act enacted by the U.S. government in 1980, individuals who are "unable or unwilling to return to their country of nationality because of persecution or a well-founded fear of persecution on account of race, religion, nationality, membership in a particular social group, or political opinion"[96] may be granted refugee status or asylum in the United States.[97] Migrants fleeing clearly recorded persecution in El Salvador, therefore, should have been accepted as refugees.[98] Refugee status or asylum would have translated into a much more welcoming and stabilizing entrance for Salvadorans, thereby increasing their chances of thriving in the United States.[99] Instead, the U.S. government failed to take responsibility for its role in the very violence and devastation that pushed so many Salvadorans out of their country, and it deemed Salvadorans unwanted unauthorized immigrants. This notably hostile context of reception, however, has done little to deter continued migration from the region.

Although the war officially ended in 1992, the lack of economic opportunities in the country, the enforcement of new neoliberal policies, and access to well-developed social networks between immigrants in the United States and their friends and relatives in El Salvador ensure a continued steady migration stream. Current estimates suggest that 20 to 35 percent of persons born in El Salvador have migrated, mainly to the United States, making them one of the fastest growing immigrant groups.[100] With a population of roughly 2,000,000,[101] Salvadorans make up the third-largest Latino group in the country and the second largest in California.[102] This trend is likely to continue, in large part due to the consequences of the Dominican Republic–Central American Free Trade Agreement (CAFTA-DR)—another U.S.-endorsed policy—that was signed into law in El Salvador in 2005. Although supporters of CAFTA-DR promised that the legislation would create jobs, increase economic investment in Central America, and strengthen the relationship between Central American nations and the United States, so far it has only exacerbated inequality in El Salvador, increased inflation, decreased jobs, deteriorated labor rights, and allowed less investment in social welfare programs.[103] Under these conditions, it should be of no surprise that people will continue to seek survival elsewhere.

Variety of Legal Statuses

Once Salvadoran migrants arrive in the United States, U.S. immigration laws and the legal statuses they confer have unequivocally extended their vulnerability.[104] The Salvadoran experience, while similar in some ways to the more widely studied Mexican case,[105] is also notably different and more reflective of similar migrations from countries like Guatemala and Honduras. To this day, the U.S. government continues to refuse to recognize Salvadorans as victims of geopolitics, making them ineligible for most legal protections but creating categories that are neither citizen or resident but also not undocumented. The largest and most long-term of these categories is Temporary Protected Status (TPS).

Temporary Protected Status is a form of administrative relief that allows otherwise undocumented immigrants to legally reside and work in the United

States for eighteen months at a time. TPS is a result of Salvadoran immigrants and their allies' organized protests.[106] Throughout the 1980s, fewer than 3 percent of Salvadoran applicants were given political asylum. Faith-based and other immigrant rights groups organized and successfully lobbied on their behalf, convincing Congress to grant Salvadorans Temporary Protected Status from deportation in 1990.[107] In that instance, TPS ended in 1992.[108] After the devastating earthquakes in El Salvador in early 2001, however, TPS was once again made available to Salvadoran immigrants present and undocumented in the United States at that time.[109] More than a decade later, the secretary of Homeland Security has continued to extend TPS to those immigrants. During each eighteen-month cycle, immigrants wait anxiously for news about the program's reapproval to then reregister and pay associated fees. It is important to note that TPS still does not provide a path to legal residency.[110] In 2010, roughly 20 percent (229,000) of Salvadoran immigrants (only those who had been continuously present in the country since February 13, 2001) were eligible for TPS.

Salvadoran immigrants who arrived after 2001 or who fell out of TPS for various reasons are categorized as undocumented. Due to the difficulty of gaining access to this vulnerable population, it is unclear exactly how many Salvadorans are undocumented; figures vary considerably from report to report and year to year. According to the most widely cited estimates, however, between 30 and 52 percent of Salvadorans in the United States are undocumented, and this proportion has grown quickly in recent years.[111]

There are immigrants who have managed, through a number of complicated and ever-changing policies, to legalize their status. In the 1980s, for example, the legalization program under IRCA was available to a relatively small percentage of Salvadorans who arrived in the United States prior to the January 1, 1982, deadline. The thousands who arrived during and after the height of the civil war were ineligible. Another pathway to permanent legal residence came in 1990 as a result of the settlement of a class action suit (*American Baptist Churches vs. Thornburgh* [ABC] legislation) against the Immigration and Naturalization Service; Salvadorans (along with Guatemalans who faced similar levels of discrimination) were allowed to resubmit asylum applications. This opened the path for a small sector of immigrants to achieve legalization. In another legal fight, some Salvadorans were able to benefit from the 1997 Nicaraguan Adjustment and Central American Relief Act (NACARA).[112]

Through all of these different measures, and especially through family re-unification laws, by 2009, an estimated 31 percent of Salvadoran immigrants were legal permanent residents (LPRs) while another 18 to 30 percent were naturalized U.S. citizens.[113]

This variety of legal statuses—undocumented, temporarily protected, legal permanent resident, and U.S. citizen—provides a spectrum that captures some of the gray areas of immigrants' legal statuses. Moreover, there are frequent and important shifts in categories; those who are in process to receive legal permanent resident status, those who are in process of qualifying for the latest round of TPS, and those who lose TPS and go back to being undocumented. Each of these categories and processes produces rights and limitations. However, academic and public conversations about immigration laws and legal categories are too often limited to "documented" versus "undocumented," thereby missing much of the complexity of the system and the associated experiences for immigrants. The variety of legal statuses in the Salvadoran migration stream makes it possible to tease out the many ways (il)legality shapes people's lives and stratifies families' well-being.

Gender

The Salvadoran case also lends itself to understanding ways that gender shapes transnational family well-being. Contrary to long-held assumptions and patterns in other countries where most migrants are men,[114] the Salvadoran migration stream includes women who lead the way and migrate almost as often as men.[115] Various factors, including the historic patterns of internal and regional cyclical migration, the high rates of female-headed households, and the increase in domestic and other service employment sectors in the United States, created the conditions that ultimately facilitated women's and mothers' migration out of El Salvador.[116]

Migration and family separation have been central to the Salvadoran experience for over a century. As aptly synthesized by the sociologist Cecilia Menjívar, Salvadorans in rural areas started practicing seasonal internal migration beginning in the mid- to late 1800s when they sought work in coffee production.[117] By the mid-1920s, landless Salvadorans were migrating internationally to work in the banana industry in neighboring Honduras, with small numbers of elites making their way to vacation in the United States through the mid-twentieth century.[118] The persistent migration patterns significantly shaped social life and relationships in rural El Salvador. As Menjívar describes:[119]

> The marginal conditions of life for these workers and their perpetual pilgrimage gave rise to a high percentage of free unions and an accompanying increase in the number of illegitimate children . . . Given a situation in which men had to move temporarily or permanently in search of work, the increased participation of women in public life and in the labor force comes as no surprise. Because of men's extremely low incomes as wage laborers, women were often left in charge of the household and also engaged in paid work in a variety of subsistence activities. Thus it was not uncommon for women to become the sole providers of a household.[120]

The political scientist Karen Kampwirth also notes that El Salvador has had high rates of female-headed households and female participation in the labor force since at least the 1950s when global consumption of coffee, sugar, and bananas increased.[121] Corrupt political leaders confiscated the land of the poor, thereby forcing impoverished men to search for seasonal work in different regions of Central America. In that process, what initiated as temporary migration often became permanent when men abandoned their families for new partners. Salvadoran families were further fractured through the devastation of the civil war. Here, too, working-class women became more likely to join the labor force for subsistence.

Historically, then, Salvadoran poor and working-class women have commonly worked outside the home, migrated to cities for employment opportunities, and become involved in organizing collectively for subsistence and social justice.[122] Indeed, there is a tradition of women leading political movements and joining collective action in pursuit of social change in El Salvador.[123] In these processes, motherhood and femininity have been negotiated and renegotiated to include not just the experience of bearing children but also "defending them and oneself against state repression"[124] and blurring public and private lines to provide for themselves and their children in the most difficult of economic contexts. These multidimensional definitions of motherhood in turn allowed poor and working-class women to consider international migration by themselves as an option for feeding their families.

Salvadoran (and other Central American) poor and working-class men, on the other hand, have historically faced structural blocks to achieving masculinity as providers. According to Nicaraguan researcher María Angé-lica Fauné, among men's limited options, "procreation represents the social legitimation" of masculine identity:

> The proof of virility to all society is that a man has the means to make a woman pregnant. . . . Since the necessary and sufficient proof of masculinity . . . is, in the strictest sense, the pregnancy almost more than the children, this explains not only the high fertility level that persists in a broad sector of women, but also the significance or meaning of the children and of paternity itself.[125]

In that context, El Salvador has the highest rate of female-headed households in Central America (31 percent),[126] suggesting that getting women pregnant is a more important source for establishing masculinity than hands-on parenting. Many men, driven by economic opportunities and gender norms, are likely to move around and become absent fathers, leaving women to be heads of households.

It is not surprising, then, that when service jobs targeting women with little formal education—such as domestic work, garment work, and hotel house-keeping—began to rise in the United States, Salvadoran women's history of working in the paid labor force set the stage for the massive international migration of women. Prior to the civil war, for example, domestic workers employed by U.S. government officials or U.S. company representatives in El Salvador were recruited to join employers on their return to the United States.[127] For male and female workers employed in U.S.-owned assembly plants in El Salvador in the 1970s, moreover, their transferable skills and knowledge about opportunities abroad made migration an attractive option.[128] Little by little, men and women trickled into the United States.

In many of these cases, Salvadoran women were leaders of migration streams,[129] and their flow remains close behind that of the males.[130] Nationally, it is estimated that the Salvadoran population in the United States consists of 52.6 percent males and 47.3 percent females.[131] Although the history of gendered migration to the United States varies across countries, as more women migrate from Mexico and Central America, the Salvadoran case sheds light on potential experiences of family separation. Given the stratified opportunities and varying expectations for male and female immigrants of any country, these gendered differences in structural barriers provide an important backdrop on which to understand inequalities across transnational families' economic and emotional well-being.

The People and Their Stories

I draw on the narratives of many people to tell the complicated stories of how (il)legality and gender shape transnational families. The pages of this book are filled with voices of children and parents who have been apart from their loved ones for long periods of time—no less than three years and up to twenty-seven years. In El Salvador, the adolescents and young adults were children of migrant mothers and fathers. In some cases, only their mother or only their father migrated; in others, both parents live in the United States. Their living situations and caregivers vary; some live with only their mother; others with grandparents, aunts, or godmothers; and others yet reside with older siblings. Their level of resources ranges greatly, and this is based almost entirely on how much money they receive from their migrant parents. Like most Salvadoran remittance recipients, many received an average of $100 each month; but there is great variation, with some receiving over ten times that amount and others receiving nothing.

During interviews, children of migrants often cried. They wanted to talk about their experiences because, surprisingly, in a country where family separation due to migration is common, they felt they had few opportunities to share their thoughts about their parents' absence. Teachers and school administrators knew about the number of students in this situation and the effects of family separation on the children's educational achievements in the short and long term, but the *institutions* did not acknowledge transnational families. The curriculum and the school calendar of events were silent on this issue, and there was no official space where students could seek support. Several students were taken aback by the number of hands (sometimes more than half) that went up in their classrooms when, during my presentations, I asked if anyone's parents lived in the United States. Many confided about missing their parents and how growing up with other relatives was their sense of normalcy; yet they did not feel comfortable discussing this with peers or teachers. Many felt deeply isolated because only siblings and the closest of friends had heard the stories they shared during conversations with me.

In the United States, the mothers and fathers worked mostly in the service sector as domestic and garment workers, hotel housekeepers, nurses' aides, street vendors, restaurant servers, cooks, janitors, mechanics, construction workers, community organizers, and upholstery workers. Most lived in the greater Los Angeles area, but four were in the greater Boston area, and a couple lived in Dallas. Although the majority of these families had few resources and lived in poor neighborhoods, some owned homes and had moved up into the bottom rungs of the middle class. They usually left their children in El Salvador with the genuine expectation that they would continue to be involved in parenting from afar. Although a few did admit that after several years they had lost touch with their loved ones, most remained in contact with their children. With few exceptions, these immigrant parents planned to live in the United States for the rest of their lives.

Unsurprisingly, interviews were often painful for parents. Many recalled in great detail the day they said goodbye to their children and the challenges they had faced since leaving. Understandably, most regarded their migration as a sound decision, particularly when they had been successful in sending money and improving their children's material lives. But even parents whose families were not faring particularly well believed that, given the dismal economic situation in El Salvador, they were still better off than if they had stayed. For many of them, even those who often talked to their co-workers and friends about their children, the interview was an opportunity to take a brief break from their strenuous lives to reflect on their trajectories before and after migration.

Gathering Their Stories

I gathered the stories of these families through casual conversations with and observations of Salvadorans in El Salvador and the United States.[132] Because of the prevalence of transnational families in Salvadoran society and their notoriety in public discourse, everyone seemed to have strong opinions about my research topic. In restaurants, stores, hometown association meetings, community organization lobbies, and various social events, whenever I mentioned my research project, people readily shared their experiences and thoughts. In El Salvador my strategy was to recruit high school and college students in diverse neighborhoods, so I also spoke to teachers and school administrators, who had much to say on this topic. They saw the ups and downs of students struggling to adjust to family separation and knew the situation to be common. But the book draws most heavily from the 130 in-depth interviews that I conducted between June 2004 and September 2006 with parents and children who are members of transnational families. In ten cases, I was able to interview parents and children from the same family. The rest of the people in the study are parents in the United States and children in El Salvador who are members of transnational families but who are not related to one another.

To capture perspectives of long-term separation, I included only families who had been apart for three or more years.

My analysis is based mostly on people's narratives. This means that I am relying on the versions of their lives as people imagine them. While their truths may have multiple interpretations, and I believe there is value in each of those individual interpretations, here I am interested in the patterns that emerge across people's narratives. These patterns are what reveal the collective understanding and construction of social categories, including motherhood, fatherhood, transnational families, remittance-receiver, visa-authorized traveler, and undocumented immigrant.

Because I was interested in comparing the experiences by gender of the migrant parent, for example, I recruited similar numbers of mothers and fathers. In the United States, I interviewed forty-seven parents (twenty-five mothers and twenty-two fathers), with various immigration statuses, whose average age at the time of the interview was forty years old. These immigrants had been living in the United States, and therefore had been separated from their children, for an average of eleven years. The single-session interviews lasted between one and three hours. To capture a variety of experiences, I recruited participants in numerous locations and through different entry points. In Los Angeles, I visited and approached potential participants at businesses, churches, union halls, day labor sites, public parks, and community-based organizations. Interviewees helped me locate other migrant parents, including two in Dallas, Texas, and four in the greater Boston area.[133]

In El Salvador I conducted interviews with eighty-three relatives of migrants. Of these, three were caregivers, and eighty were adolescents and young adult children. Through trial and error, I learned that the most effective recruiting strategy was to visit high schools and colleges in search of children of migrants. To include diverse experiences, I located and interviewed participants in a number of institutions that ranged from impoverished semirural public schools to wealthy urban private schools, in both high school and college. Here, too, interviewees helped me locate more participants, including nonstudents whom I interviewed in their homes and at their places of work. Respondents resided in different departments of El Salvador,[134] but most lived in urban areas of San Salvador. The average age of participants at the time of the interview was seventeen years old, with a range from fourteen to twenty-nine. The average length of their parents' residence in the United States, and therefore the average length of family separation, was 9.4 years.

Because gender is one of the central concerns of the book, the sample includes the experiences of twenty-nine children in families in which the mother migrated to the United States, thirty-eight in which the father migrated, and thirteen in families with two migrant parents. This allowed me to compare their experiences based on who migrated in their household. The variety in their parents' legal statuses also permitted an analysis of (il)legality. The single-session interviews lasted between forty-five and ninety minutes.[135] During semistructured interviews, we spoke about several topics, including reasons for migration, the best and worst aspects of family separation, differences in family members' lives since they had separated, and advice they would share with others who may be considering this strategy.

Although in El Salvador families of undocumented migrants were sometimes hesitant to talk to me,[136] as were a few undocumented immigrants in Los Angeles, overall, my social location as a female 1.5 generation Salvadoran immigrant in the United States helped me gain the trust of study participants. In Los Angeles, mothers and fathers often understood their participation as a way to help me attain my goal of an advanced degree. Given the low levels of formal schooling among Salvadoran immigrants, they expressed pride in my academic accomplishments and were happy to contribute. In El Salvador, people participated out of a sense of curiosity. The fact that I live in the United States indirectly drew them to me in hopes of learning more about the place where their migrant parents reside. Finding respondents was not always easy, however, and interviews brought out deep pain for many. When there was hesitation, the patterns I noticed along legal status and gender lines are what alerted me to the importance of these factors. When they eventually opened up, most respondents expressed gratitude for the opportunity to say out loud the many thoughts and aspirations they carry with them.

Learning from the Salvadoran Case: Migration, Borders, and Remittances

The Salvadoran case is interesting and important for a number of reasons. Over the last three decades, the out-migration of Salvadorans has increased so dramatically that its effects arguably reach all aspects of social life in El Salvador. For families, this has meant that in some regions of the country, as many as 16 and even up to 40 percent of children grow up without one or both parents due to migration.[137] Nationally, about 12 percent of children live this way.[138] As peripheral nations like El Salvador continue to participate in globalization through the export of its labor force, Salvadoran patterns may shed light on the increasing rates of family separation due to migration around the world.[139]

Salvadoran immigrants and transnational families are also notable for their lengthy separations. Unlike the more widely studied Mexican–U.S. case, the Salvadoran migration stream is characterized by multiple borders that separate the sending and receiving region.[140] Given the high percentage of undocumented and otherwise legally precarious migrants, multiple national borders have made circular migration almost impossible for Salvadorans throughout their history of migration to the United States. Similar to most any other largely unauthorized Latin American–U.S. migration stream, transnational Salvadoran parents may go for many years without visiting or reuniting with their children.[141]

Under these circumstances, it does not always make sense to think of transnational families as single units that happen to be spread out spatially between the destination and home countries.[142] In the Salvadoran case, to interpret transnational families as unproblematic split households that maintain communication seamlessly through electronics is to dismiss the painful reality in their day-to-day lives and in their patterned behaviors where it is evident that each individual family member is discretely present in a single and faraway space relative to loved ones.[143] Therefore, in the midst of long-term separation, even when their actions and hopes connect them to each other, they must proceed—often only tentatively—with their own lives each day while planning for the family's future. Excelling in school, building ties with local communities, making solid plans—all of these crucial activities may become quite difficult to carry out when family members feel their lives suspended by unfulfilled hopes and blocked paths to reunification.

Families all around the world are expected to provide much of the emotional and economic support necessary for children's healthy development. Likewise, immigrants would often like to rely on families for support and a sense of continuity through the migration and settlement processes. Transnational Salvadoran families are no different in these respects. Parents make the decision, within a set of limited options, to pursue migration as a way to provide for their children. They are hopeful at the outset, but not everyone is successful. In the face of increasingly lengthy and geographically distant separations, *Sacrificing Families* examines how transnational family members experience these expectations and why, in the long run, some families fare better than others.

As free trade agreements continue to expand and exacerbate global inequalities, and as nation-states open doors widely for products and profits while closing them tightly for refugees and labor migrants, these types of families are not only becoming more common,[144] but they are also living through lengthier separations. This book gives voice to these immigrants and their families and documents the inequalities across their experiences.

2 Why Parents Migrate

ESPERANZA, WHO HAS LIVED IN THE UNITED STATES for over twelve years, vividly recalls the day she last saw her daughter, Margarita. The little girl was only two years old at the time, and Esperanza had been feeling suffocated by the scarcity that pervaded their lives. Being a single mother was difficult, and, although her own mother had tried to help her, together they could not overcome the tremendous poverty that had been their reality for many years. She had been doing agricultural work in the fields for over a year but was only sinking further and further into debt. She was stuck in a cycle. Her weekly wages were gone within hours of getting paid—they were barely enough to cover existing debts at the local store—and, for the rest of each week, she begged hesitant sellers to put groceries on her tab. "You can't live like that all your life," she thought; so Esperanza finally considered more seriously her friend's suggestion that they migrate to the United States. "That's the only way we're going to make enough money to feed our children," her friend had repeated many times.

As the oldest of three, Esperanza felt especially responsible for her mother and younger siblings. Her father's untimely death during her childhood condemned her family to poverty, but she did her best to stay focused on school. When she was in the tenth grade, however, her mother informed her that she could not afford all the kids' schooling, so Esperanza would have to drop out of school to help pay for the younger kids' expenses. All of the changes were stressful for Esperanza, so she sought comfort in the company of her then boyfriend. By the age of seventeen, she was pregnant. The baby's father, also a teenager, was never involved in the child's life, and Esperanza raised her daughter as a single mother. By the time she was nineteen, she felt overwhelmed: "I felt the responsibility to at least make enough money to feed them all." She wanted her siblings to get more schooling, and she was determined not to let her daughter grow up in such misery.

Still, Esperanza was paralyzed at the thought of leaving her daughter. She struggled for weeks to make the decision and postponed the trip several days, even after her best friend had arranged for a smuggler. Through a stroke of luck, the smuggler agreed to take Esperanza without charging her for the trip up front; she could work to pay off her debt after arriving in the United States. And still, she hesitated. It was sheer desperation that ultimately pushed her to go through with her migration decision:

> My heart was boiling with sadness. I would watch my daughter play and say, "God, please give me the strength to leave." . . . One night I put my daughter to bed, and she turned to face the wall. And she always used to hug me, but she didn't that day. I think she could sense my departure . . . and I lay awake crying. And my little girl wakes up, and she tells me, "Mami, I want milk [*crying*]. I want milk, Mami [*crying*]." Those words gave me the strength to [leave]. And I told her, "There is no milk, baby, but I promise I will get you some." And she tells me, "I love you, Mami." And I tell her, "I love you too." And she fell asleep until morning. . . . That morning, the bus was coming. That was the bus that always sounded the horn loudly at the entrance to the town, and it started . . . I changed my daughter; I put on her pink sandals, and I sat her on the table, and I told my mother, "Hold her, Mom . . . I leave her in your hands. Love her as if she were your own daughter."

Esperanza sobbed intensely as she boarded that bus. In her gut, she knew it would be many years before she would see her family again. In her retelling of the story thirteen years later, she cried throughout our three-hour conversation but was especially upset while recalling the painful details of that morning when she last saw her daughter.

Esperanza's story is not unique. Mothers and fathers, at different moments in El Salvador's history, have faced great personal, political, and financial barriers and at times worked through immense hesitation before taking the steps to migrate. In every case, and for various reasons, insurmountable desperation ultimately forced them to push through their pain and leave their children with other caregivers; this with the knowledge that they may not see them again for many years. This chapter provides details about the economic and political situation in El Salvador that powerfully circumscribes these families' options—even when individuals do not personally locate the source of their hardship within this broad context. The macro conditions are woven in with the narratives of the parents to reveal how they understand and give meaning to their departure and subsequent family separation. In most cases, it is a story of subdued hope following a deep sense of despair that inspired them to leave.

Civil War

Throughout its history, El Salvador has been deeply stratified, with only a small elite benefiting from the labor of the vast majority of the population living in poverty. In response, Salvadorans—especially males—have historically migrated seasonally within the region in search of work. Thus, migration and seasonal family separation became a common strategy of survival that would later help to expand and normalize the formation of thousands of transnational families separated by great distances and multiple national borders.

Through much of the 1900s, only those with sufficient resources were able to travel—often as tourists and sometimes as laborers—all the way to the United States. It was not until the early 1980s, when the brutality of the civil war extended throughout El Salvador, that men and women and entire families began to migrate to the United States in larger numbers. Not expecting that the U.S. economic support for El Salvador's military would also mean blocked access to legalization in the United States, Salvadoran migrants headed north by the thousands. Many of these migrants—who were also parents—thought it would be safest to leave their children in El Salvador. Their main priority was immediate survival; in some cases, they would have endangered the children and their families to make contact or try to bring them along. These migrants had survived attacks or received targeted threats. For them, the decision to migrate was often in response to imminent danger.

This was the case for Jorge. He was one of four siblings who grew up in a rural area of central El Salvador. His father owned a small coffee farm where the family worked the land. They did well enough to put Jorge and his siblings through high school; as a result, they were able to acquire white-collar jobs in a nearby city. When I asked him why he chose to migrate to the United States, he responded:

It was something unexpected; well, you could call it political, because I had problems with the military. I, uh, lost almost half of my family. That night, I mean I didn't, I never thought to come to this country, never. I had my siblings, a brother and a sister were here, and they had asked me and my other brother if we wanted to come, but we never wanted to come because, well, we were not doing so well, but we were not doing poorly, either. I worked; I was a secretary for a court in [central El Salvador]. We had no reason to come here, right? We were doing well.[1]

Jorge's wife, who worked in an office setting, also contributed to their household finances, and they were raising their family in relative economic stability. When they can enjoy the fruits of their labor and feel safe from political violence, many families like Jorge's would prefer to remain in El Salvador.

Jorge emphasized several times during the interview that he had tried to remain neutral regarding the civil war. He wanted to protect his family and steer clear of the violence. As the war escalated, however, things became dangerous in their town, and his work duties changed. He was now required to accompany the coroner to identify the bodies of those killed during warfare: "They prohibited us from leaving the city. We were no longer going to identify the bodies of the people they killed outside of the city. Those people were buried just like animals. . . . And that kept increasing, increasing, increasing." By that time, he and his siblings had bought a home for their parents in San Salvador, away from the rising violence in his small town. He hoped that, with his parents in the city, they and the rest of their extended family would be safe.

Soon, two of his nephews and several of his friends joined the guerrilla movement fighting for a more fair redistribution of wealth in the country. Meanwhile, Jorge remained strong in his conviction to stay neutral. He continued in his job of identifying the deceased and thought that if he stayed out of the conflict, he would be safe. But his resolve began to waiver when he lived through a close call in his own family:

What made me, well, explode was one time that they got, they captured my father—a man who at that time was seventy years old . . . And, uh, they captured him because he would come on Saturdays to visit me at my house, right? And he would go to his farm, every Saturday. That day he had been to my house around 4 pm, he left my house, said, "Okay, I'm leaving." But around

4:30 I get a call, a woman, one of my cousins, calls me and tells me that they had captured my father, she saw them taking him in handcuffs.

Jorge and his brother contacted everyone they knew, until a high ranking officer in the military, someone who had been their childhood friend, helped them locate their father at a local prison and promised he would not be killed. Jorge realized that, had it not been for his connections, his father would have been executed that very night, even though he was not involved in the conflict. Indeed, indiscriminate violence was common, and many people were murdered senselessly,[2] sometimes because they were considered to be guilty by association, if not by actual involvement.

Jorge was shaken by his father's arrest and near execution. The incident made him begin to question his neutral position, but he was ultimately convinced to get involved after witnessing a horrific scene left by the military. Jorge received a call from his friend who owned a farm just outside the city. His friend needed help removing a dead body found next to cows that needed to be milked:

So I go get the coroner, and he doesn't want to go because it's outside the city, but I convince him that it's close enough, and that it's a favor for a friend. So I make him go, and I walk in, and I see the cadaver, just thrown there. I saw how many wounds he had and how he had been stabbed. I wrote up my report, and I turn around, and a neighbor whispers to me, "Hey, there's a hand over there." So I ask where, and I thought, the man I just saw had both of his hands intact. Well, I go, I saw it, it was, in fact, there, the hand. So I tell the coroner, and we find another body. We write up the report, and I remember heading into the house, and the door was halfway open, and I kick in the door, and I will never forget . . . I saw something that I still, to this day, it comes to my mind, and I still can't fully digest it. I see a lot of people, one on top of the other. The first one, maybe like three months old, a boy, they had cut him with a machete right here (points to his abdomen) . . . even with his bottle in hand. And then, on top of him, a woman—she was pregnant, actually—and on top of her, oh, children—the first was three months, the second was like one and a half, the third was, well, more or less, I'm guessing their ages . . . The other was like about four years old; another was around seven. Then there was the lady that I told you about, then there were three men, older, between thirty and forty years old. Nine people in one bed, but the bed didn't even have covers.

They were just there, like they had been left there that way to create terror. That's what made me change my life around, and I said, "No more. I have to do something."[3]

Jorge had several friends who were already involved in aiding the guerrillas. Their goal was to defeat the military, which only ever seemed to protect the property and rights of the wealthy elite. He decided to support the leftist coalition by providing them access to confidential information he retrieved from work. Some time passed in this way when, one day in 1982, several of his relatives were kidnapped. He learned that the assailants had come by his house looking for him, but had missed him by just minutes. Knowing that he would be caught, likely tortured and killed, any day, he decided his next step would be to take up arms and join the guerrilla fighters. Having convinced his brother to also join, they went to say goodbye to their mother, but she ultimately persuaded them to leave the country instead. Under imminent danger, they had to leave that same night, unsure of where to go. As they headed out, they decided to go to the United States to join their older siblings.

As a matter of life or death, Jorge said goodbye to his wife and their son but had no chance to look for his ex-wife and their two sons who lived in another city. He and his brother headed north without a guide, money, or concrete plans. They left El Salvador during the early stages of the war. His brother returned six years later in 1988 to reunite with his children, but Jorge remained in the United States, where he worked to bring his current wife and their child. He also reestablished ties with the two sons from his first marriage and sent them monthly remittances until they reached adulthood.

Throughout the 1980s, tens of thousands of people left the country in situations similar to Jorge's, fleeing the horrors of the civil war. Although much of the violence was indiscriminate, boys and young men were especially likely to be forcibly recruited into the fighting, making them feel more directly threatened. The U.S. government's steady funding of the military allowed the war to last as long and spread as extensively as it did. The daily violence and its sheer brutality—as committed largely by soldiers and paramilitary leaders, and to a lesser extent by guerrilla fighters[4]—made it impossible for people in certain communities and university students throughout the country to live safely there. By that period, previous migration, even though rather limited, had established links between Salvadorans and the United States—the closest country they perceived as safe, politically stable, and economically strong.

Weak Economy

Along with political violence, another source for Salvadorans' mass migration was the weak economy.[5] El Salvador is a small country with a long history of only limited economic growth, but the civil war period was especially devastating. The 1980s saw the lowest levels of growth over the last hundred years. Since the civil war ended in 1992, the level of political and military violence has decreased, but other forms of violence persist, and economic circumstances remain stagnant.[6] After a slight improvement in the early 1990s, the economy took another plunge in the first decade of the twenty-first century. During this period, El Salvador had the lowest growth rate in the entire Central American region.[7] Some speculate that dollarization of the national currency in 2001 is largely to blame for that decade's economic woes. The administration of President Francisco Flores (1999–2004) passed the Law of Monetary Integration to infuse the economy with U.S. dollars that would, presumably, attract greater foreign investment and trigger economic growth. On the contrary, however, overall inequality has worsened. Under the presidency of Antonio Saca (2004–2009), the external debt of the small nation rose to a staggering $9.8 billion.[8] And, on the streets, because it was difficult to calculate between currencies, people had to pay higher prices because merchants rounded up.

Despite the overarching failures of dollarization, the United States continues to be the most important trading partner for El Salvador. In addition, the 2,000,000 Salvadorans who reside in the United States generate, through remittances, upwards of 15 percent of El Salvador's gross domestic product (GDP). But, as the U.S. dollar loses value worldwide, there are notable repercussions in the tiny country as well. Each cycle of market loss heightens the asymmetries of the Central American Free Trade Agreement and further deepens social and economic inequalities.[9]

In such a context, only a few can truly thrive. The men and women in this study had implemented several strategies, worked in multiple industries, and commuted to different areas of the country in search of sufficient wages to feed their families or fund their children's continuing education. After feeling that they had exhausted all their possibilities, migration became the only remaining viable option. With so many Salvadorans already living in the United States, most people had relatives, friends, or neighbors with whom they could stay. Those who did not had developed the sense that, if others had made it, they, too, could be successful. Within these shared circumstances, however, there were clear gendered reasons for choosing migration.

Gendered Reasons for Migration

Regardless of whether they migrated before, during, or after the civil war, men and women had different reasons for leaving—reasons that were informed by conditions that affected men and women differently—though this was not initially evident in their narratives. When I asked mothers and fathers to tell me about what led to their migration, invariably the first response pointed to either political or economic reasons. Fathers who migrated during the period of the civil war were more likely to attribute their migration to political reasons; they or someone close to them was being persecuted, and it came down to a matter of life or death. Mothers and those who left after the official end of the war in 1992 cited economic reasons—a lack of jobs, no space for upward mobility, and a general inability to guarantee financial stability, access to health care, and basic schooling for their children. It took further questioning to uncover the gendered patterns in their reasoning and need for migration.[10]

About half of the fathers and one-third of the mothers I interviewed came to the United States before or during the civil war. The men, as most frequent targets of recruitment, were fleeing direct political violence. Like Jorge, Milton also described involvement followed by a need to flee. In the 1980s, Milton was an engineering student at the Universidad de El Salvador (UES)—the only public national university. Like many students at the time, he became involved because he was learning about the injustices that had made attending school nearly impossible for his working-class family. Though he never took up arms himself, he did attend student meetings to discuss the war and ideologically supported the cause of the leftist guerrilla movement.[11] In fact, the UES was a central meeting place for activists. They tried to connect the aims and philosophy of the guerrilla movement to the rest of the population who could have benefited from a thorough restructuring of the Salvadoran economy. When the fighting increased and the UES was attacked, Milton dropped out of school. With stories circulating of dozens of university students being tortured and killed or disappeared, he was nervous about being targeted as well.[12] His girlfriend at the time, moreover, was feeling the stress of having been involved in aiding revolutionaries to hide weapons in her home and later in giving them access to her employers' safe in a staged holdup. As the violence escalated, although she was never directly threatened, she worried about her children's continued safety in the country and contacted her sister in the United States with the intention of joining her. She and Milton had been in a relationship for several years; fearing for his life, he decided to follow her. Having lost touch with his own children's mother, he left without saying goodbye to them, only to reestablish and sustain better contact later from the United States.

Like Jorge and Milton, other men described similar stories of fleeing direct political threats during the late 1970s and throughout the 1980s.[13] For some, migration would lead to their first separation from their families, but others had distanced themselves from partners and children prior to migration. There was a different pattern, however, among the migrant women during this same time period.[14] All of the migrant women in this study who left during the war were single mothers and heads of households. The war had not played out forcefully in their towns, but they were worried about the escalating violence. Moving in search of work elsewhere in the country would put them at risk, so they felt they had no other options to provide for their children.

Gloria, for example, migrated in 1986, in the middle of the civil war. It had been several months since she had separated from or even heard from her children's father. She sold rice and beans at the local outdoor market, but her earnings were simply not enough to buy food for her four children. She was in a small town in central El Salvador where they heard much about the war but had not yet experienced local attacks. Her goal was to leave to make enough money to one day take her children to live with her in the United States away from the violence:

> Imagine that I didn't even have a place to go, but that desperation of knowing that if I didn't do anything, those kids would die. "No," I said, "I can't stay here." Besides, my mother was already older, and she didn't want to work anymore. She had it rough all her life too, right? So, by coming here, the idea was that I'd work and help all of them. I was not going to do anything there. There was nothing to gain in staying to wait for what? I had nothing to hope for.

Even when not in direct physical danger during the civil war, with the economy in shambles, single mothers like Gloria, who had no one else to rely on for financial assistance, looked to migration. In those moments of desperation, some women began to negotiate and redraw the contours of motherhood to include international migration as an acceptable path to provide for their families' pressing needs.

During the war, men in this study left El Salvador to flee the consequences of a dangerous political context, regardless of whether they had children. Unlike women's situation, men's migration was not tied to their parental responsibilities, and several of them had already distanced themselves from their children. Women, on the other hand, sought migration as an extension of their parental responsibilities in a context of economic hardship.

After the signing of the Peace Accords in 1992, Salvadorans continued to migrate in large numbers. No longer fleeing direct political violence, men and women were still unable to live up to their gendered expectations as providers for their children and other relatives. Balmore, who had lived in the United States for fifteen years when I met him, recalled that he had to make a quick decision to leave after losing his job and not having money saved up for his mother's urgent medical expenses:

> Look, I was so unsure of what to do. My mom was getting worse and worse, and I, well, I was the oldest of my siblings. I would help her however I could. The problem was when I got laid off from my job. See, I had been working there for several years at this company, and it's not that they paid me very well, but we were making ends meet. The thing was that my girlfriend at the time, she got pregnant, and that's when I felt the responsibility, I mean, I was going to be a father. And I was working and everything; we were getting ready for our son; he turned out to be a boy, right? And that's when I lost my job. There were a few months left before he was born, but then suddenly my mother got very ill, so how was I going to cover her medicines and medical expenses? That's why I had to leave.

Notably, despite not being legally married, Balmore aspired to fulfill gendered expectations and be a provider for his child and ailing mother. Later in the interview he shared that he probably would have taken his time to find another job if his mother's health hadn't taken a turn for the worse. These unexpected and dire expenses were enough to push him to migrate.[15]

Twenty-six-year-old Antonio had only been married for a few years. He was an active member of an evangelical church and a devoted family man. He volunteered to speak to me after a presentation I made about my project to his congregation, but he asked that we do the interview in a private location where he could speak freely. Although he had been in the United States for over three years, it still pained him noticeably to talk about being away from his daughter and wife. He wept through several moments during the interview: when he remembered how he made the decision to leave, when he recounted the difficult journey across borders, and when he discussed the pain of missing his family.[16] Deciding to come to the United States was not easy for Antonio. As the oldest of his male siblings, however, he represented their best hope of survival. He had already dropped out of high school and worked several years in the fields alongside his father, where he learned of the financial risks of being farm workers: When he was growing up they typically had a small margin of profits, but more recently they either had no profits at all or they ended the crop cycle in debt. In those difficult years, the sum of their earnings failed to cover the costs of the increasingly expensive seeds for their crops.[17]

As the sole provider for his own young family, moreover, Antonio felt overwhelmed by their bleak future. He had been living with his wife and daughter in his father-in-law's home, where they lacked privacy and space. Having worked full time during the week and overtime with his father on weekends for a number of years, he learned that it was impossible for someone of his socioeconomic and educational background to achieve stability and progress in El Salvador—even when he did everything within his reach to fulfill his responsibilities:

> You know how it is in one's country. I've been working since I was sixteen to help my family. The last three years before I came I was working in a factory making clothes, a *maquila* . . . I was working Monday through Friday, about eight hours a day, and then the next week I would work the night shift and go back and forth every week . . . I was making about $200 per month . . . I also helped my father work the land on the weekends . . . I was the only one working because my wife was home with my daughter, and she had to take care of her parents, too . . . So we had that conversation [*crying*], and she agreed that I had to come if we wanted to do something more with our lives—get our own house and have something to leave our daughter. Because in El Salvador it is very difficult to buy your own house. We were never going to do it if I didn't come.

Antonio's father and his younger brother already in the United States convinced him to leave. Between the two of them, his brother had said, they could ensure the well-being of their parents and their younger siblings, and Antonio would have enough to guarantee a solid future for his own wife and daughter. Hesitantly, Antonio agreed when his father and brother offered to lend him the money for the trip. He could pay them back after working in the United States. With so much pressure, he felt it was his duty as a responsible son, husband, and father to take this risk to improve his family's lot in life.

Study participants' narratives suggest that Salvadoran masculinities prescribed the role of economic provider to adult sons and fathers. This was true across different social strata and evident in men's explanations of their decisions to migrate. Fifty-year-old Felipe, for example, had lived a fairly comfortable life in El Salvador for many years. Although his brother had been disappeared during the war, never to be seen again, his family remained in the country with the hope of finding his brother one day. After finishing high school, Felipe also completed a technical degree. He worked as the leader of a nonprofit organization for many years, and although, with his and his wife Blanca's combined income, they were solidly middle class, the shrinking economic opportunities set the conditions for his migration. In 2000, he opted to migrate when it seemed that all other avenues for making money in El Salvador were closed to him:

> I would go out and teach people in the countryside how to read and teach them business skills so they could make more profits . . . But after some years, we ran out of money, and I wasn't making enough. My three kids were in private school, and my wife and I couldn't keep up with all the expenses . . . I looked into possibilities for investing some savings that we had. I tried everything. We bought some properties, we even tried to open up a small store from our house, but nothing worked. That's when I started thinking about coming to work for a while . . . It took a long time because my wife and I had to go three times to the [U.S.] embassy before they gave us both a visa.

The goal was for each of them to travel periodically, find ways to establish business ties, maybe buy things in the United States to sell for profit in El Salvador and vice versa, as they had seen others do—everything from cheese and pastries to wholesale trinkets to makeup. From Felipe's vantage point, migration had worked well for other middle-class families who could travel with visas, so they chose this option.

Unlike poor and working-class families, middle-class families had more choices about when and how they wanted to pursue migration—and this gave them some agency in avoiding the consequences of U.S.-produced illegality.[18] In the late 1980s, Amanda, who considered herself a member of the middle class, had acquired a multiple-entrance visa to the United States. This permitted her to come and go over a ten-year period so long as she did not violate the terms of the visa by staying more than a few months at a time. Her experience of choosing when and how to migrate reveals the gendered and classed processes of migration decisions:

> The reason I came last time, well, the story is that I wanted my son to come. He was fourteen at the time, and the whole thing with the threat from the guerrillas—I just wanted him to leave the country. But they would not grant him a visa because they said he had to go with an adult. So the three of us, my husband, my son, and I, went to request a visa, but they only granted me one. And you know how difficult it is to get a visa, so you have to use it so that you don't lose it, or so that you can renew it, so I had to come and make sure to use it. They told me, "The opportunity is for you; you need to go." That's the only reason I came by myself that time. I didn't want to stay because they were too young. He was fourteen, and my daughter was four. That's why I didn't stay.

During the war, her teenage son—like all boys in that age group—was under constant threat of being forcefully recruited to fight by either the military or the guerrilla fighters. Many families were desperate to get their male children out of the country to avoid the forced recruitment practices that were so widespread—boys were taken away while playing on their street, riding a bus, or leaving school. Because it is so rare for any Salvadoran to be granted a visa, visa recipients like Amanda feel compelled to travel and return to their country as a way to prove to the U.S. embassy that they can afford to travel and that they choose to return to El Salvador. This allows individuals to establish a strong record to support their case for visa renewals in the future in case they ever need to travel.

During her first trip, Amanda stayed for only a couple of weeks:

> Look, when I came in 1990, my brother would tell me over and over to stay. If I had done so, I even would have qualified for amnesty. But my children were more important to me. I knew that the war was still going on, and my son had already been threatened, so I was not going to be comfortable so far away from them.

Although she would not have actually qualified for legalization under the 1986 Immigration Reform and Control Act, popularly known as "amnesty," it is possible that Amanda could have applied for residency through other measures or, at the very least, been eligible for Temporary Protected Status.

Because she did not feel overwhelmed financially at that moment, she opted, as most parents would, to remain with her children. Unlike very poor families in El Salvador, Amanda used her privilege to prioritize her children over the economic advantages of working in the United States. She had the resources to conform to traditional constructs of motherhood and remain with her family. In so many other cases, however, family unity is not a realistic option.

In fact, just over ten years later, family unity was no longer a realistic option for Amanda either. She suddenly hit hard times, and, in that new context, she was forced to consider migration. After her divorce, she began to manage her parents' neighborhood store to make up for her ex-husband's lack of economic support. She had recently stocked the store to replace what had been sold for all the New Year's Eve celebrations, when a powerful earthquake hit the country on January 13, 2001. All bottles and containers had fallen from the shelves and broken into millions of pieces. The liquid splattered and ruined the cigarettes and other products that would have been her only source of income at that time. Devastated by her losses, she had to act quickly to get the money to pay back the companies that had recently delivered the materials. Her system was that she would receive shipments and pay for the merchandise on the sales representative's next visit when she also got to keep some profits. The earthquake, however, had destroyed most of her inventory, and the companies—including well-known global soda and ketchup brands—were inflexible. She had to pay them immediately or face stiff penalties on a sum that kept growing because of impossibly high interest rates. From one day to the next, she suddenly owed 100,000 colones (roughly US$11,400) with no possibility of further credit and no other source of income.[19]

Without delay, Amanda applied for a bank loan to cover the expenses for all the lost merchandise. She spent the following six months waiting for a reply from the bank, only to learn that she had been denied the loan. As a backup plan and only because she had run out of options, she thought to use her multiple-entrance visa to the United States. In her previous trip, she had used it to visit her family over a short stay, but this time she would use it to enter the country, stay indefinitely, and earn the money to pay off her debt.

Amanda attributed her dire situation to her divorce. Without her husband's continued economic support, she and her children would not be able to survive financially: "I would think that with a family intact, there may not have been any reason to migrate. But with the current economic situation, I think everyone thinks of leaving." As the national economy worsened for vast sectors in the country, the blocked paths to economic stability forced more and more people—including those from the middle class—to consider migration and family separation for survival. Members of the middle class, like Amanda, would be more likely to attain visas and plan out their trips. Most families I spoke with, however, faced greater limitations and negative contexts when deciding to migrate. Poor and working-class women, in particular, had few resources or support. For these mothers, most of whom had already been working outside the home, migration was the last option they wanted. It pushed them further from the already unattainable traditional gender ideologies, so they had to negotiate their definition of motherhood to include international migration and risks that endangered their lives as part of their responsibility to provide for their children.[20]

Recall the story of Esperanza, whose case opened this chapter. Her daughter's father was never present, never a source of financial support. So when she could not earn enough money to buy milk for her toddler, migration became the only option for being a good mother, the only way to earn more money to ensure such basic necessities. Several mothers described being in similarly urgent situations. Marina's case was one such example. With only a sixth grade education, she had worked selling produce in an outdoor market for years and knew that she would be limited to the informal sector where she would never earn sufficient wages. When she could no longer count on her partner's financial support, it became impossible to provide for her children on her own:

> I was married to him for seven years. But he was a sick person, sick with jealousy, and I can say that there was also domestic violence in my home. But one day I just said, "Okay, this is it." And that's the day that I left him. I left the home and went to my parents' with my two children. Three days after that, I heard that the guy who helped people cross the border to the United States was leaving on a trip, so I decided to come with him. That was the quickest way to escape my problems at home.

> LA: Did you think about staying in El Salvador?

> It's just that that wasn't an option. I had always worked in the outdoor market [mercado], since I was a child, and I barely earned pennies [unos centavos]. When he [the children's father] didn't give us money, I had to go around borrowing money, and I couldn't keep doing that all the time. My parents were getting older, and they couldn't help us much either. That's why I made that decision. Even my mother told me it was the best thing to do.

Marina's negotiation of her motherhood responsibilities was an ongoing process; at some point, it included acceptance of domestic violence, but this changed, bringing with it full economic responsibility for her children. Under those circumstances and with little reflection, she (with support from her own mother) reconstructed motherhood to also include an act of international travel in search of work. Marina's story of domestic violence, irresponsible partners, poor extended family, and a general lack of options was similar to those of several other mothers in the study.[21]

Thirty-six-year-old Angela, for example, described her situation prior to migrating the first time.[22] Although it was during the war, in 1988, she and her family did not face any direct political threat. Instead, she had to respond to constant physical attacks from her husband—the father of her three children. Growing up poor, Angela had not ventured much beyond her small town near the western city of Santa Ana. She met her partner in high school, dropped out in the tenth grade when she got pregnant, and moved in with his family; then the couple moved out on their own with their three small children, in the poorest sector of town, where they could afford to live on only his salary. Over the years, he became an alcoholic and slowly grew dangerously irresponsible.

For a long time, Angela did not leave her husband because she relied on him financially. Money was especially tight for them due to many costly medical expenses:

> It was very difficult for me because my little girl suffered from epilepsy . . . At a year old, she had started to have seizures, and I was always needing to come up with money for her medicine, doctors. And it's a great expense; those things are very expensive there. Too expensive. The doctor's visit alone was sometimes 80 colones[23] (about US$9). They would give her a small bottle of medicine that had eighty drops that would last fifteen days, and it cost, in those days, it cost 80 colones, and it was just her medicine. Aside from that we also had to buy her vitamins, because she always had to be taking vitamins. Just in her medical expenses I'd spend at least 300 colones (about $34), that, I mean, I had to come up with somehow because it was necessary to take her to the doctor every month. So that was my biggest worry . . . I always worried that I had to have that money or she would've died, or she'd still be sick.

In her experience, motherhood involved enduring violence to ensure that her daughter had the medical treatment she needed. It was the sacrifice she made for her children.

In an attempt to stabilize things when her husband started drinking, Angela went to work in his auto mechanic business, helping him with paperwork and cleaning up the place. But he began to falsely accuse her of flirting and eventually of sleeping with the clients. The beatings came more often until she could no longer tolerate the situation. Angela took her children and moved back in with her parents, who lived a fifteen-minute walk away. Her husband tried to see her; he would show up drunk at her parents' home and create great stress for her family. Though he had never tried to hurt the children or her parents, he was unwilling to let her go. So, within weeks and with the help of her father, Angela was set to leave to the United States with a smuggler:

> It was a way to distance myself from the problem, even though I was leaving my three small children, and that was the hardest part, but my father helped me in the sense that he asked if I wanted to come; he could set everything up for me, so I said yes.
>
> *LA: Did he suggest it first, or did you come up with the idea?*
>
> No, he suggested it because sometimes you stay over there, and then the children's father would not stop bothering me, and I didn't want to, and I could not return with him, so I agreed. . . . [My father] took charge, he told me not to worry about my kids, that they had a house to live in; even if they just ate beans and tortillas, they would have food, he told me. So I didn't have doubts, even though I was leaving my children, which was the hardest part . . .

Having suffered the violence for a number of years, Angela reached a tipping point. With the urging of her father and the guarantee that her children would be safe, migration represented a chance to provide for her children as a single mother. It is important, however, that Angela's migration decision was most critically rooted in her need to escape physical abuse.

Angela lived and worked in the United States for two and a half years, saving and remitting as much money as she could. She returned in 1990, just before Christmas, to spend the holidays with her children. Unfortunately, the financial situation quickly became dire; after only a couple of months, Angela once again had to consider migration:

> I saw everything around me, and I saw, I saw no future, really. I did not see a future, and, well, I don't have formal schooling; I am not an educated woman or anything of the kind, I had simply been a housewife, and I had helped my

husband in his job. So I would look around me and see the poverty everywhere. And I would see my children, and I would say, "No. I saw them, I know they are well; they saw me, so now I have to go back to the United States so that they can go to school or have something better." I decided again to leave.

As much as mothers want to remain with their children, the financial conditions, especially for single mothers, make it difficult to provide sufficiently for their families. In fact, Angela tried to leave twice but was caught by authorities in Guatemala and sent back each time. After two failed attempts, she decided to stay in El Salvador and do her best to support her children there. For the following seven years, she had multiple jobs:

> First I worked as a maid in this one woman's house; then I would help out a dentist; but the pay was too low. Then they helped me find a job in San Salvador, in the capital. I was a maid for this family; he was a military man, and his wife had been in the military, too. But they were cruel, like no one else. They were going to pay me 250 colones (just under US$30) per month. And it was a two-story house, and I was supposed to clean every day, cook, wash, iron, and take care of everything in the house. . . . she was trying to give me the workload of two people. So I quit after fifteen days; I told her it was too much work and too little pay, and I wanted her to pay me for the days I had completed, but she got mad and didn't even pay me for bus fare.

Angela's daughter's monthly medical expenses were higher than her earnings. Clearly, she would not have been able to cover her family's basic needs. She went on to work for another family for six months, but things did not work out there either because, as with most jobs for women in El Salvador, the wages were miserable. Finally, she heard about a job in a garment factory. She applied, was hired, and ended up staying several years:

> There I earned, well, with overtime and all that, like sometimes I did twenty-four-hour jobs, that they called "daylong jobs" [jornada única] when there was a very large order and they had us work twenty-four hours straight . . . Yes, dangerous, but I needed the money. So with that, sometimes I would make 900 colones (just over $100) every fifteen days. At the very least, I would make 700 ($80), and that, well, that was huge because I could pay my mom 500 (US$57), 400 ($46), and the rest I would invest in my daughter's illness because she was undergoing treatments.

Angela's job was far away from her town and required that she spend the workweek renting a room in the city to avoid a two-hour bus commute each way. She considered these to be sacrifices any mother would make because they allowed her to be with her children every weekend. As Angela's case reveals, however, poor and working-class families have little access to health care in El Salvador. Often, people simply do not earn enough to cover medical expenses, particularly when a loved one has recurring health problems. Even when employed more than full time in job sectors available to women (in Angela's case these included domestic and garment work), working-class single mothers are unlikely to make ends meet. Unaffordable health care, too, is an important reason for migration.

Her efforts paid off for several years, though she was gone much of the time and was always just a crisis away from being unable to provide for her children again. But the cost of living continued to increase in El Salvador. In that economic climate, it became more and more difficult for poor and low-income families to make ends meet. Angela, who was working in a *maquila*—the kind that have become one of the very few options for employment in the country—could not keep up with the increasing cost of living. Her daughter underwent several tests, and Angela could no longer afford her family's monthly expenses:

> There was a day when I didn't have a single cent to take her to the hospital or to pay for her doctor's visit, not even for the bus fare, because things were getting more expensive. So that day, that day the only thing I could do was get on my knees and entrust her to God, for God to do a miracle, either take her or let me keep her but in good health. And I can tell you that the miracle did happen because that's right around the time that my brother called, my brother who was here . . . It was 1998, and he said, "You know what, I have enough money for someone to come, if anyone wants to come. . . ." That is rare, but it happened.

Angela still hesitated. She "wanted to see [her children] grow . . . didn't want to miss their adolescence." Having lived for years on the brink of losing her daughter to illness because she could not afford her medical care, she decided once again to leave. In that context, work already kept her physically absent much of the week, so migration became an extension of her mothering, allowing her to meet her daughter's needs more effectively. Like Angela, many mothers resisted migration. Motherhood, as they had been taught, meant that they had to be present and reliably available for their children, taking care of their daily needs. In the face of abandonment, domestic violence, severe poverty, and a lack of educational or job opportunities and in the context of increasing cost of living and inaccessible health care, they had to renegotiate motherhood to also include migration as another acceptable path to fulfill maternal responsibilities.

What should be clear from both mothers' and fathers' narratives is that migration and the choice to come to the United States are not as simple nor as objectionable as public debates about immigration in this country suggest. Migrants do not come to the United States ostensibly to take jobs and weaken the economy. Rather, it is often the case that in increasingly unequal economic contexts and feeling unprotected from physical violence, migrants, who would rather remain with their loved ones, view migration as the only available measure to save their own lives and provide for their families. Mothers and fathers, in particular, act out of a desire to fulfill their parental responsibilities. These responsibilities are powerfully delimited by gender ideologies and class positions that inform migrants' decisions, justifications, and feelings of guilt surrounding migration.

Women, like men, who migrated after the end of the civil war explained that they were forced to leave due to economic reasons. As I prodded, however, fathers, in line with gender ideologies, emphasized a desire to provide for their families—their children, partners, and parents. This was the core of their reasoning for migration, and, most of the time, they did not have to explain further or feel apologetic because they were fulfilling expectations—setting themselves up to be better economic providers. In my conversations with mothers, on the other hand, I had to peel through multiple layers to get to the heart of their migration decisions. Women migrated only after more severe situations had forced them to go *against* traditional notions of motherhood, to leave their children instead of being present with them on a daily basis. With the support and encouragement of family and friends, women negotiated and redefined motherhood to make migration acceptable as the most viable and immediate solution for their families.

Subdued Optimism in the Face of Despair

As difficult as it was to leave their children under the care of others, many parents—both mothers and fathers—shared a sense of subdued hope when embarking on their journey. After attempting to do everything within their power to work and provide for their families in El Salvador, in a climate of rising costs and shrinking opportunities (especially for women), the United States represented the final available measure to achieve success as parents. Whether it was because they could not afford private school, had not been able to save up for college, did not have the money to pay for the required uniforms in public school, could not raise the money for costly medical care, or did not earn enough to feed their families consistently, migration emerged as the safest bet they could make to improve their family's future.[24]

Cognizant of the many dangers and unknowns that awaited them on their journey and inside the United States—a country where they did not know the language or the culture, where they would be so very far away from their loved ones and everything that they knew—migrant parents' reserved sense of hope is noteworthy. Angela, for example, had resisted leaving her children but ultimately remembered her journey in the following way:

> On the trip here, well, aside from the suffering on the road and thinking about the children you are leaving behind, about the family and everything, you don't know what you'll find on the road or what will happen, you just think about getting away from the problem, about paving the way for your children to thrive [*sacarlos adelante*], about how to survive alongside them.

Notably, Angela sees a future of mere survival for herself but accepts this as a sensible goal so long as her children are thriving. Similarly, Marina, who migrated to avoid an abusive partner and suffered tremendously on her way to the United States, says that she was able to keep going on the treacherous journey by reminding herself of her goals: "What I wanted was to give them schooling, to give them what they needed for their expenses. I was coming here because this was going to give them the opportunity to study. That's what I was doing." Balmore, who left to secure money for his ill mother and unborn son, said, "To me, coming to the United States represented a certain type of hope. To me, I was coming to work hard in whatever kind of work to send my mother money for the cost of her medical exams and to save her life." And Rafael, who left his wife and daughter, said, "I came thinking that this was the best thing I could do for them, well, in my situation." Notably, all of these parents described their migration as a choice—a moment reflecting their agency—even when analysis of the broader context demonstrates that they had few other options. In the process, they did not express optimistic or unbridled hope. Rather, they moved forward warily because their first choice—to remain in El Salvador—was simply out of the question, and, in that context, they had to prepare themselves mentally for the challenges ahead. Even when their migration decision was rooted in escaping political or domestic violence, the thought that their efforts would ultimately benefit loved ones helped propel them past the suffering.

While most wished that they could have found a way to stay with their families and still make ends meet, El Salvador—particularly as influenced by U.S. foreign and economic policies—politically or economically did not offer them those opportunities. Most parents grew up poor, unable to complete much more than elementary or junior high school, because they could not afford bus fare for their commute or the required school supplies. These parents would have preferred to stay with or near their children (in some cases, the parents had already separated prior to migration), surrounded by family and familiar culture, if they could have just had access to a dignified job that paid living wages. They would have been happy to stay in El Salvador had they known that, in times of illness and other crises, they could have had access to health care and aid for their loved ones. The reality, however, was bleak. Pervasive inequalities and widespread poverty had prevented them from obtaining the education necessary for jobs that would grant them economic stability, and the remaining jobs simply did not pay livable wages. When the most that many of them could aspire to was $200 per month and when the prices of basic food supplies and medical care were increasingly out of reach, they swallowed the pain of leaving their children and sought out the only strategy that, while difficult, would most likely lead to better results.

3 Journeys and Initial Settlement

RODRIGO, A RESPONSIBLE AND LOVING HUSBAND and father of three, had worked for years as a manager at a grocery store in San Salvador. He and his wife were thrifty, spending money only on things they considered absolutely necessary, and they had saved enough to cover their three sons' schooling expenses. The oldest had already been admitted into the university—a difficult feat for low-income families in El Salvador. When Rodrigo lost his job, he remained optimistic. He prayed with his church group and asked his neighbors for leads to other jobs, hoping to impress employers with his loyalty and hard work. During months of fruitless searching, Rodrigo and his family lived off their savings. But these dwindled, and when they could no longer afford his eldest son's university expenses on his wife's meager wages, he decided to migrate to the United States.

Rodrigo, who considers himself a law-abiding, God-fearing human being, started out by looking into the possibility of applying for a tourist visa to enter the United States. The odds, however, were against him. With such limited resources, the chances of being awarded a visa were slim, so he chose not to throw away his money on what was then the $100 nonrefundable visa application fee. Instead, he did the next best thing: He found the coyote (immigrant smuggler) with the best reputation, and the family gave their house as collateral for the $6,000 trip to the United States. Soon into the journey, though, it was clear that the coyote had no intention of keeping any of his promises: no easy route, no comfortable stays, no quick trip. Rodrigo went hungry, had to find lodging on his own in some towns, and at one point was even taken hostage by the coyote who was angry that Rodrigo stopped him from raping a woman who was traveling with them.

When Rodrigo finally crossed the border into the United States, Border Patrol agents quickly detected and apprehended him. He spent two months in an overcrowded, foul-smelling Arizona detention center where most detainees were forced to sleep on the floor, leaving little space to walk to the bathroom, where more detainees slept. From there he was transferred to a detention center in California and ultimately was deported back to El Salvador. When he arrived home, he found his youngest son selling homemade bracelets on the street and working as a baker's assistant to pay for school. After a couple of months, Rodrigo, still unable to find work, migrated again. Besides feeling the urgency to help his family, he now needed to repay the overwhelming $6,000 smuggling debt from the initial failed attempt at migration.

Undertaking another harrowing journey but traveling by himself this time, Rodrigo made it to the United States and got a job at a warehouse in Los Angeles. He worked intensely for less than minimum wage. Without proper training or safety equipment, he carried heavy loads until he hurt his back. Dismissed by his employers and unaware of his rights, Rodrigo moved on to other jobs but was quickly fired whenever his back injury prevented him from performing strenuous tasks.[1]

It may seem that Rodrigo's story is merely one of terribly bad luck. But looking deeper one finds persistent patterns that reveal that immigrants' "misfortune" is frequently the result of structural inequalities in El Salvador that are directly shaped by U.S. production of illegality. Legal statuses—the legal categories conferred to migrants that determine their legal rights or nonrights in territories outside of their home country—are important stratifying factors among migrants while en route and as immigrants in the United States.[2] The entire process of migration, moreover, also intersects with class and gender to produce patterns in men's and women's experiences and fears. As unauthorized migrant parents confront these harsh realities, the difficult conditions also affect their children's economic and emotional well-being at home. It is also important that, although we tend to think of U.S. policies and their effects predominantly within U.S. borders, this government's realm of power extends across countries and throughout the region.[3]

In this chapter, I compare the economic and emotional repercussions of the migration journey—from the home country to the country of destination—as they are shaped by the legal protections conferred to migrants while en route and during their initial stages of settlement in the United States. The migrants' experiences on the road begin to shape migrants' families' well-being right away. As the narratives confirm, legal status while en route cumulatively benefits or disadvantages migrants in their early attempts to remit to their families. Thus begin the inequalities in economic and emotional well-being of the children left behind.

The Production of (Il)legality through Migrant Visas

Although there are multiple ways to obtain legal entrance as immigrants into the United States—including through employment-based petitions and refugee status—the majority of legal Salvadoran immigrants do so through family reunification laws.[4] This option is open only to immediate relatives of legal permanent residents or U.S. citizens. Applications are costly, and petitions may take years, even upwards of a decade, to be processed. Those without immediate eligible relatives in the United States have few other paths to legal entrance.[5] In that situation, they hope to obtain a tourist visa to enter with authorization and remain past their permitted date.

Most Salvadoran migrants, however, do not qualify for U.S. visas.[6] Instead, the majority are unauthorized travelers.[7] The U.S. embassy in El Salvador, assuming that most travelers will try to remain permanently and without authorization in the United States, grants few visitor visas for business or tourist purposes. The extensive requirements for visitor visas include an often exorbitantly large sum (by Salvadoran standards) in a bank account, home ownership, and stable employment or business ownership—all of which are out of reach for the vast majority of Salvadorans. Even the application process for a U.S. visa is unfeasible for potential travelers; in 2013, the nonrefundable application fee is $140 per person.[8] With an average refusal rate of about 50 percent,[9] the chances of being denied and losing the equivalent of a month's salary are high, and most people cannot afford to take this risk. Knowing the challenges of receiving a visa, 55,000 Salvadorans per year opt for what ironically seems like a more guaranteed route and migrate without authorization.[10]

Without a U.S. visa, unauthorized travelers are not legally permitted to cross national borders.[11] Even before migrants reach the United States, they must cross Mexico,[12] where U.S. efforts in the international drug war include funding via the Plan Mérida, requiring militarization along the Mexico–Guatemala border.[13] In response, drug traffickers have diversified their

sources of income by joining forces with organized crime to target unauthorized migrants from Central America. In some cases, their goal is simply to
profit from the migrants by kidnapping and torturing them into extortion.
Other times, however, migrants are forced to also join prostitution rings or
help traffic drugs.[14] The mass kidnappings and disappearances of Central
American migrants are only the most recent in a series of perils that Salvadorans have faced along their journeys to the United States.

In 2010, international human rights organizations identified the length
of the Mexican territory as the most dangerous migration corridor in the
world.[15] Poor, disenfranchised migrants become easy targets for everyone
from thieves and police officers to organized drug cartels and military—all
of whom are also just trying to survive and thrive in structural conditions
that have blocked paths through education and the formal labor market. As
a result, Salvadoran unauthorized travelers are among the tens of thousands
of Central and South American victims who are kidnapped, tortured, and
disappeared throughout Mexico increasingly in recent years.[16]

Unauthorized Journeys and Cumulative Disadvantages

Unauthorized migrant parents felt the brunt of the criminalization and exclusion from the moment they left home. Those who traveled without visa
authorization had to undertake a dangerous and costly trip by land across
three national borders to reach the United States. Typically, these unauthorized journeys turned out to be extraordinary setbacks for them and their families. Migrants spent from several weeks to several months on the road before
finally reaching their destination. This was wasted time because, for the most
part, they could not work or send remittances while traveling.

The unauthorized trip was also exceedingly expensive. The entire trip
could cost the equivalent of years' worth of wages. Often, people gave down
payments of about $600 with the expectation that the rest of the money would
be paid in the United States on arrival. By 2013, the financial costs for an unauthorized trip have skyrocketed further; it is now upwards of $8,000 and
even $10,000 per traveler.[17] Unauthorized travelers agree to take on these ex-
orbitant debts because it would be too difficult in the current climate to attempt the dangerous journey alone. The cost of the trip, moreover, can also
vary by gender because men are often, though not always, more willing to
risk crossing the first two borders by themselves, needing to hire smugglers
only to cross the last border into the United States.[18] Although it seems that

this strategy can prolong the trip by several months for some migrants, it also creates a gendered advantage for men who can save about $4,000 compared to women. Antonio, for example, told me of his younger brother who took ten months to get to the United States from El Salvador. During that time he worked throughout Mexico to pay for short legs of the trip and saved to pay for the smuggler on the U.S.–Mexico border. Because he did not have an extensive debt to pay off, he was able to save up enough money to cover his younger brother's unauthorized trip within a year. Financially, gendered illegality privileges men through the unauthorized journey.

Equally important, the unauthorized trip by land through Mexico often involves physical and emotional setbacks.[19] Indeed, one of the devastating consequences of U.S. immigration policy is the increasing danger of unauthorized travel. Nearly all the people I met who traveled by land through Mexico recounted, without prompting, horrible tales of perils and violence. Antonio, who had been deported from Mexico twice before making it to the United States on his third attempt over three years earlier, was very emotional when telling me about those journeys. During the first trip, he was on the road for a month and three days before getting caught at the U.S.–Mexico border. The second failed attempt ended after only a couple of days in southern Mexico. His voice quivered and, despite his best attempt not to cry, tears streamed down his face as he narrated some of the torturous experiences he endured and witnessed on the trip that finally ended with arrival in the United States:

The first trailer truck, that one had air conditioning. This one didn't . . . There were eighty-seven of us, and they packed us up into a trailer truck for sixteen hours. And for all of us to fit, we had to be so close to each other, and I couldn't take it anymore; I needed to move . . . And then we started to walk across the desert. All you desire is water and food. We used our shirts to drain some muddy rainwater that remained in a plastic bag that was stuck to a tree. That's how thirsty we were! . . . And, at one point, we all had to run in different directions, and once the [border patrolmen] were gone, we went back to look for the Guatemalan man who was with us. He was already really tired, and we didn't find him. The smuggler wanted to keep going, and who knows what happened to that poor man because we still had to walk many hours, and it was so cold that night. I don't know if he survived. He probably didn't.

As his voice cracked and the pain made itself visible in each of his gestures, Antonio embodied the physical and emotional stress of such a violent process that so many unauthorized travelers endure to get through Mexico and into the United States.[20]

The hardships of the journey alone can be traumatizing, but all travelers are also targets of criminal violence as well. In recent years, cases of kidnappings and massacres have come to light as murders have skyrocketed.[21] Lydia, who traveled in a group of five led by a female smuggler, suffered a chilling experience. As the group walked along the train tracks, several thieves approached them:

> When we were on the road, they assaulted us. They were going to decapitate us. They had already made us all stand side by side along this wall. . . . So when they were about to kill us there in Mexico . . . we had to follow the railroad, and it was all shrubs and wilderness everywhere, and we walked and walked. What saved me was that I was wearing a skirt, and I was walking so much that I was bleeding a lot. So the man told me to raise my skirt and when he saw me, he told me to put it back down. He thought it was something else [laughs]. So then he got a hold of the other young woman who was with us—the smuggler's niece who was fifteen years old—and he said, "This girl is going to be my woman. You're not taking her from here." And he had a huge blade, and the girl was so scared.

Criminals may hurt or kill unauthorized migrants indiscriminately, but they rape and attempt to claim ownership mostly over women.[22] In this case, Lydia went on to explain that an ex-soldier in her group of travelers acted quickly to save them:

> And in the end I say that it was a miracle from God because one man alone against all of them, somehow he jumped on him, and the lady [smuggler] helped him, and I grabbed the girl, and we all ran. I don't even know how, I got on a bus, I don't even know where it was going, whether it was going north or going back south, but I took the girl.

All migrants are potential victims, but, beyond the most typical physical violence, women are also likely to be targeted for sexual abuse. In this case, Lydia survived with only psychological scars.

Not all women were as lucky. Another migrant mother told me the story of her older sister, Carolina. As a teenager, Carolina had traveled with a smuggler without a visa, hoping to reunite with her mother who had migrated years before. It took her over a month to get to the United States, and during that journey she was raped multiple times. Carolina had grudgingly shared this story with her sister once but refused to talk about it ever again with any family member. Her silence around this traumatic experience, however, created an emotional barrier between her and her relatives as she isolated herself to avoid the topic. Years later, the family was still fractured and hurting over the violence Carolina had endured.

Indeed, the consequences of any kind of violence during the journey can be devastating. While many are murdered, those who survive may be forced into prostitution or drug smuggling, or they may escape but with difficulty in recovering from the emotional scars.[23] Thirty-two-year-old Marta, for example, went through various traumatizing episodes when she migrated from El Salvador. After living in Los Angeles for eleven years, Marta still vividly recalled the details of the trip. It took her a month to get to the United States without authorization. Looking away in clear discomfort with the topic, she recounted some of the dangers she faced, including attempted rape, scarce food, and attacks from thieves. She was the only woman in her group of travelers, so she felt especially vulnerable, but in retelling the story she emphasized how lucky she felt to have survived the trip at all. When I asked her how she found the strength to keep going through all that hardship, she replied simply: "I just thought about my children. I would say to myself, 'I came this far to get food for them. I am going to get there. I know I am going to get there.'" Similarly, Griselda cried when she remembered her unauthorized journey from thirteen years earlier. After a long silence while reflecting on that experience, she could only muster up in a whimper between the tears, "My trip was a miracle. It is a miracle that I made it here alive." Thirteen years later, as she prepared to receive legal permanent residency, she still carried the pain of such unspeakable violence during her migrant journey.[24]

Back in El Salvador, entire families also suffer some of the consequences of illegality from afar. Spouses, mothers, and siblings of migrants are pained watching the news and knowing of the great likelihood of violence against their loved ones while en route. As one elderly mother of a migrant told me:

No, look, I really suffered. She's my daughter, and I didn't want her to ever suffer any pain. And it's that thing of wanting to watch the news because she wouldn't call, but then you see so many ugly things on television that sometimes I would say, maybe it's better not to watch anything. No, that whole time was just anguish. I wouldn't even sleep those fifteen days. That was really terrible.

Unable to do anything, even to remain informed about loved ones' whereabouts and well-being, was very challenging for relatives. In this example, the journey took two weeks, while in others, it may take one or several months. With escalating numbers of kidnappings and greater abuse of migrants, this part of the experience for transnational families is also increasingly stressful and emotionally taxing. As more caravans of Central Americans searching for disappeared migrants in Mexico attest,[25] relatives' fears are too often confirmed.

The dehumanization of migrants is so widespread that even children are targeted. In a conversation with a Salvadoran legislator, I heard the story of a Guatemalan woman who was traveling with her two children—a boy who was about ten years old and a girl who was about eight. They were heading to the United States, in search of work and opportunities that were simply not available in her rural town in Guatemala. This mother was aware of the violence against migrants, particularly against women, so, like many other women, she prepared as best she could: She took birth control pills to avoid pregnancy in case she was raped, and she cut her daughter's hair short and dressed her as a boy. During their journey, her son had asked her several times, "But why do we have to go?" And she had responded each time, "To find happiness." Shortly after crossing the border into Mexico, the group they traveled with was stopped by several gang members. They forced the migrants to take their clothes off—a common practice to locate cash and valuables migrants may be carrying. When the gang members saw that there was a little girl in the group, a number of them proceeded to rape her in front of the girl's mother and brother. As they were forced to watch, the young boy cried to his mother, "Is this happiness?" Tears welled up in the legislator's eyes as she relayed the story the girl's mother had shared with her at a migrant shelter in Southern Mexico. The depth of such pain is difficult to imagine, and I fight back tears just remembering the story. I include these details here only because these are the realities currently taking place for scores of migrants from El Salvador and various other Central and South American countries who are victims of unjust economic policies and who choose to seek out opportunities for survival elsewhere rather than stay in their country and potentially die a slow death of hunger.[26]

Sadly, these cases of horrific debasement and devalued humanity are happening daily.[27] Even before arriving in the United States, U.S. production of illegality had denied most migrants the opportunity to travel safely—even though they were fleeing political and economic conditions created directly and indirectly by U.S. enforced policies. Like this mother, her daughter, Lydia, and Carolina, many other migrants suffer at the hands of attackers who know they can get away with these crimes—including the systematic rape of women and girls. By branding them as "illegal" and when paired with hateful public discourse, U.S. immigration policy implicitly communicates that these migrants are unworthy of humane treatment either on U.S. soil or beyond. Gang members, police officers, drug traffickers, migration officers, and almost anyone who chooses to hurt unauthorized migrants are acutely aware that the Mexican federal government (along with each of the Central American governments), following the lead of the U.S. federal government, will do little to protect migrants. The impunity is so pervasive that crimes against migrants beget few to no repercussions.[28] These are perhaps undesired and unexpected consequences of immigration policy, but very real and substantial consequences nonetheless.

Initial Settlement for Unauthorized Travelers

Once migrants arrived in the United States, their journey and mode of entry—whether unauthorized or visa authorized—continued to affect their ability to remit to their children. All shared a desire to find housing and work to begin remitting immediately. Those who traveled without authorization, however, now also had to worry about paying off excessive debts; otherwise, they would be heavily penalized through harassment of their families, loss of their family home in El Salvador, or negative relations with the only people in their social network in the United States. In this context, it was often difficult to find a job and a place to live.

For unauthorized travelers, paying off the debt was the first priority, especially when smugglers pressed them for money. As Lydia recounted, the smuggler's words weighed heavily on her during those early years:

> "Well, look," she told me, "I will lend your mother the money, but she is giving me the house as collateral. I need you to sign here and write down your ID number." So I said, "Okay," and she said, "But if you don't pay this money, I'm sorry, but I will have to take your family's house and land, and I will send your

mother to prison." . . . So, imagine! I knew that I had to pay that debt off, and I didn't even have a job yet!

Knowing that her mother's life and well-being were at stake, Lydia made whatever sacrifices she could—accepting poor housing and exploitative working conditions—to pay the smuggler. Meanwhile, her children would have to wait until the debt was paid before receiving enough money to cover their basic expenses. The material consequences of illegality—in the form of severe debt—set the context for many of the migrants' options and decisions during early settlement, and in each case the disadvantages accumulated.

Unauthorized travelers were often at the mercy of relatives and strangers to help them get through initial hurdles, especially because many did not have a secure place to stay right away. Illegality shaped initial housing accommodations when migrants could not accurately plan a date or location of arrival. Moreover, because they arrived with debt and under a cloud of legal uncertainty, relatives and friends already in precarious situations had their hands tied and could not offer much help.[29] Thirty-three-year-old Griselda, a migrant who traveled without authorization, described the hardships she faced in those initial moments of settlement:

> I got here, and I had no one . . . I had relatives, but they couldn't help me, that's just how families are here . . . So, uh [long silence; she begins to cry], I found this woman, she gave me a place to stay, but just for one night. The next day, I didn't know where to go . . . I went to knock on doors . . . I met a very good woman and . . . she sees that I am young, and I just wanted to work, because I'm the type of person who doesn't give up . . . So this woman, I'm never going to forget her, she tells me: "You know what? You can stay here this week."

With limited resources and already living in crowded quarters, Salvadoran immigrants in the United States likely have little to offer newcomers,[30] especially when a migrant's unauthorized journey implies great need. In this case, Griselda was lucky to find a stranger who helped her when her family could not. Often, however, the physical, emotional, and economic disadvantages associated with illegality while en route increase the potential for further disadvantage once in the United States when others cannot help migrants due to their overwhelming need.

Unauthorized travelers are especially vulnerable when they are caught by immigration authorities. Angela, for example, traveled without a visa and was apprehended by the Border Patrol shortly after entering the United States in 1988. She already owed a smuggler $3,500, and the detention increased her debt:

> I took twenty-two days to get here, but I had problems because they caught us, the Border Patrol . . . So I was in jail [detention] for three months. . . . I had a deportation order. I had already gone to court three times. . . . So I tried my aunt's ex-husband, and he finally answered the phone that day and . . . he told me not to worry, that he would help me. He was going out with a white woman, and she helped him, and they came all the way to Texas to pay the fine that at the time was $1,500. They talked to the judge and everything, and they were able to get me out. . . . And that's how the odyssey began of this so-called American dream [laughs].

After the bumpy start, Angela wanted to pay off the debt that now included $3,500 for the smuggler plus $1,500 for her aunt's ex-husband. Her children, moreover, had gone four months without a cent from her since her departure. The disadvantages continued to accrue as her desperation led her to accept terrible working conditions, all in the name of paying off her debt. Her first job turned out to be a disaster, but she accepted it because it offered her a place to live:

> I started to work like two weeks after arriving. I worked at a house taking care of a boy, but I only worked there about three months, or maybe four, because they would barely pay me $50, I think, per week. $50 per week. So I would see that and think, what am I going to do with $50? I have three kids. . . . I lived there with the family, and I would eat there and everything supposedly, but $50? For me that was nothing because my children had to eat, drink, go to school, wear shoes, wear clothes, and I would say, $50? And then what about me? I mean, you also need to buy clothes and personal things.

By this point, it had been about eight months since Angela had last seen her children. Her initial high hopes were thwarted because of the difficult situation she found herself in. While attending English classes at a local school, she met a woman who had a lead on another job. She spent the next eight months earning $900 per month taking care of an elderly woman with muscular dystrophy. She had to move on, however, because the work was much too strenuous. She lost a significant amount of weight from the physical burden of carrying the woman around to the bathroom and all over the house until she no longer had the strength to keep doing it. Throughout that time, even when she was only earning $50 per week, Angela sent her children whatever money she could, but it was never enough to cover the debt and their expenses. Illegality's consequences, in the form of her debt for the journey and for her release from detention, weighed heavily on Angela and her family during her early settlement.

As the desperation increased for migrants, they felt they had no choice but to settle into accommodations that were less than optimal, and these often added to their cumulative disadvantage. After the first week, for example, Griselda followed the advice of her cousin, who suggested she take a live-in domestic job: "I earned $60 per week taking care of four children. Well, but that was good for me. I had $60 to send every week, and I stayed there for five months." With such low wages, Griselda had little to remit to her family, but this was her only choice that first year after migrating. Similarly, although fifty-one-year-old Jorge felt fortunate that his childhood friend welcomed him into his single apartment when he first arrived, it was too difficult to live in one room with three other adults. To avoid adding to everyone's discomfort, he took the first job he could find and moved in with co-workers who ended up stealing from him and making life difficult for the next year before he found more reliable work and better housing. Illegality makes migrants vulnerable to multiple forms of exploitation from employers and landlords.

Even when family members are able to take in newcomers, the precariousness of their own situation can merely add to the cumulative disadvantages of illegality in migrants' lives. Marta is a case in point. After a month-long unauthorized journey through Mexico, she moved in with her sister when she got to Los Angeles, and, although she initially thought this would be a good way to ease into her new surroundings, problems quickly ensued. Marta's sister, who was rather poor by U.S. standards, relied on Marta for full-time child care but did not earn enough to pay for her services. Because she was undocumented, Marta felt she had no other choice but to adhere to her sister's wishes. Unable to pay rent and still owing the money for her unauthorized trip, Marta felt uncomfortable asking her sister for wages and instead made hot drinks (*atól de elote*) to sell at busy intersections on weekend evenings. During those first two years, this was her primary source of income, and she remembers being able to send only $20 at a time, every couple of weeks, to her children in El Salvador.

Like Marta, several mothers in the study experienced similar family-related tensions when they were expected to care for kids, clean the family home, cook, and generally take care of all household chores in return for free room and board or as payment for the smuggler's debt. In these situations, contacts and social networks did not translate into great benefits. Marta's costly unauthorized trip and her undocumented status on arrival kept her locked in an exploitative and unprofitable housing situation, preventing her from sending her children sufficient remittances during the first couple of years in the United States.

Not all unauthorized travelers succumbed to the cumulative disadvantages of illegality, but they did face consequences for rejecting exploitation. In thirty-two-year-old Luisa's case, fighting for better job opportunities early on meant disturbing her fragile social network. She had been living in the United States for fifteen years when we spoke. Family friends in the United States from her hometown had offered to pay for her unauthorized trip by land. The couple had migrated years earlier and needed a nanny they could trust, so they offered to finance Luisa's $2,000 trip in exchange for her child-care services for five years. Luisa felt pressured to pay them back immediately, but it seemed unfair and much too lengthy of a process to keep her side of the deal, particularly because she was taking care of the baby and doing all their household chores but not earning money. In leaving this job, she ruined the relationship with the couple and lost the support of her only contacts at the time, but, as she described it, "I know they were bothered, but I had to do that to pay them and start making money for my daughter. For me, the most important thing was to start sending [remittances] to my family."

Even in the best of situations, when smugglers are not pressuring migrants and family members can offer safe housing, unauthorized travelers still incur large sums of debt that must be paid back quickly. Antonio, whose brother lent him the $6,500 for his trip,[31] described the sense of obligation he felt toward his brother:

My brother, he's the one who took ten months to get here because he worked in Mexico to pay for the trip; yeah, he has two jobs. He works in a [fast food restaurant] and in [another restaurant], and he shares an apartment with three other people. He works hard, and he's always saving his money, and I wanted to show him that I was very grateful for what he did for me. I don't want to be like those people who never pay. So my plan was to get two jobs

> to pay him back as quickly as possible . . . He is my only relative here, and
> sometimes money separates people and brings problems. I just wanted to
> pay off the debt.

Although not directly pressured to repay the debt immediately, Antonio was familiar with other people's negative experiences and wanted to avoid tensions with his brother. In his case, having suffered the emotional hardships of illegality while en route, he wanted to offset the cumulative disadvantages by maintaining close ties within his network, even if this required immediate repayment of debt and fewer remittances to his family at the outset.

In each of these cases, the consequences of illegality that began with dangerous journeys accumulated in ways that further disadvantaged those migrants who were too poor to afford or ever qualify for a visa to the United States. Because they had traveled without authorization and had incurred great debt, migrants had few options regarding initial housing. In turn, their difficult living conditions further blocked their ability to seek out the best jobs because in each instance they acted out of desperation to stop accruing the disadvantages of illegality. All of this becomes especially evident in comparison to the vastly different experiences of visa-authorized travelers.

Visa-Authorized Travel

Visa-authorized migrants are legally permitted and protected to cross borders and remain in the United States for a short period of time, typically ranging from a few weeks to several months.[32] Notably, the intersection of class and illegality is visible in the visa-granting process. Salvadoran travelers who qualify for a visa are part of a select group. They have the resources and, many would say, the *luck* to qualify given the stringent requirements and the highly selective application process. Among the people I interviewed, visa-authorized travelers were generally more privileged. Except for a couple of working-class study participants who qualified for a visa through their participation in international church activities or a work-related event, most visa holders came from higher social class backgrounds and had more economic resources prior to migration than did the others.

Legality and social class standing intersect to minimize disadvantages of migration for visa-authorized travelers during migration and early settlement. Unlike unauthorized travelers, migrants with visas did not have to incur as much debt. For example, Milton, who traveled with a tourist visa, saved enough money in El Salvador over several months to pay for his plane ticket. Ramón relied on his mother, who had filed for his LPR status, to also cover most of the costs for his flight. Similarly, Yajaira raised the $500 for her ticket with the help of several of her siblings. And Amanda simply put the cost of the flight on her credit card and added it to her debt.

Even when they had to borrow money for their travels, the sums were only a small fraction of the hefty price tag for an unauthorized trip by land. In Oscar's case, the only discomfort and hardship he faced during that process was the embarrassment of asking his brother-in-law in Los Angeles for money:

> I had lost my job suddenly, and we spent all our savings after that. . . . My wife told me to call her brother, to ask him to send me money for the airfare and to give me a place to stay. I didn't want to make that call, to have to ask someone else for money, but my family, we were in a difficult situation. I was starting to get desperate. I assured him that I would pay him back as soon as I got a job, and, thank God, he helped me.
>
> LA: *How much did you have to pay him back?*
>
> I think he ended up letting me borrow like $700 because I wanted to leave my wife some money for the household expenses while I found work too.

Migrants like Oscar who traveled with visas, even when they did incur debt, had small manageable sums to pay back—about one month's wages or less. Such an experience is certainly less stressful than owing at least ten times your monthly salary and more beneficial for transnational families.

In the entire study, only three migrants traveled with immigrant visas and the knowledge that they would soon be granted legal permanent residency. Their journey was the most well planned and least costly of all.[33] Ramón, for example, knew that he could legally move to the United States any time after he received word that he had been approved for an immigrant visa (the step prior to obtaining legal permanent resident status) around the Christmas holiday. He recalled waiting a few months to purchase his ticket during low travel season to save money on his flight. Similarly, although Marco's family was facing financial hardships, he chose to wait a few months until his daughter completed the school year to leave. Because they felt secure that they would soon obtain legal permanent resident status, these migrant parents were able to plan their trips to best fit their personal and economic interests. Economically, they spent only a small fraction of the cost of the unauthorized trip by land to purchase their plane tickets.[34] This gave visa-authorized travelers a great economic advantage over unauthorized travelers during the journey and initial settlement periods.

Emotionally, the repercussions for travel to the United States were also vastly different between unauthorized and visa-authorized travelers. Although the separation from family was difficult regardless of a migrant's form of entry into the United States, visa-authorized travelers were able to bypass the more dangerous and emotionally taxing aspects of the unauthorized journey by land. Amanda was one of them. She had been living in the United States for three years when I interviewed her in Los Angeles. In El Salvador she considered herself a member of the middle class. Although she had only completed the ninth grade, she got pregnant young and married into a wealthy family and lived a comfortable life in a small town in western El Salvador. Given her class standing, Amanda was one of the few to have qualified for a visa and, compared to unauthorized travelers, this allowed her a relatively easy migration journey:

> The five-hour trip was sad for me. I remember crying a lot of the time because I didn't know when I would see my daughter and my son again. But I had to come, there was no other way . . . I think that it helps that my brothers and childhood friends live in [California]. They were waiting for me at the airport and were always willing to help.

Amanda's brief, uneventful description of her journey by plane stands in stark contrast to the tales of danger and suffering among those who traveled by land through Mexico. Later in the interview, she also shared that she was able to call her children just hours after her departure to notify them of her safe arrival, thereby limiting their distress as well.

Initial Settlement for Visa-Authorized Travelers

The advantages of visa-authorized travel continued to benefit migrant parents once in the United States. Amanda's relatives, for example, were waiting for her at the airport when she arrived:

> I went to [California], and my family was very supportive. They went to pick me up [at the airport] and gave me a place to live. . . . And I had a friend . . . I went to live with her. I would go with her for a week, then come back to my brother for a week. Once I was there, that's when my nephew called me from

[the East Coast] and let me know that there was an opportunity to go work there for a family of doctors. That's why I left . . .

Amanda clearly had an extensive network, including childhood friends and family, who helped her by providing free room and board as well as work. Her nephew secured a domestic job for her with a wealthy family who could afford to pay her much more than most domestic workers make in the United States.[35] Because Amanda had entered the country with a tourist visa, moreover, the six months that she was legally protected under the visa gave her a limited but fruitful period in which to make the best use of her social networks. Legally able to travel within the United States, she moved cross-country to secure the most profitable job she could find. Unlike unauthorized travelers who typically remain undocumented on arriving in the United States, Amanda benefited greatly even from the limited protections of a six-month visa and used it to facilitate her early settlement period. In effect, the visa granted her a type of grace period not afforded to unauthorized travelers.

Intersections of legality, class, and gender, as well as reconstructions of motherhood and fatherhood, are also evident in the initial settlement experiences of visa-authorized travelers. The case of Felipe and Blanca illustrates how these intersections prevent or encourage migrants to negotiate the legal categories of migration that so deeply shape early settlement. Notably, the middle-class couple had enough savings to apply multiple times until both had tourist visas, thereby avoiding some of the harshest consequences of illegality while en route. Based on a middle-class heteronormative construction of the ideal family, they decided to take turns traveling, with one of them always present in the home, so as not to overburden their children emotionally.

Because she had relatives in the United States, Blanca was the first to go. She stayed in Minnesota with her siblings, where, unable to find work or develop business ties in the first three months, she spent the next five months working. Her wages, however, were relatively low, and she was able to send her family only $300 per month. Together she and Felipe decided that this monthly sum simply did not justify the emotional hardship of tearing her away from their three children. As Felipe explained:

Mothers have to be with their children. It was too much suffering for her every time we talked on the phone, and, at the end, she just got sick of it. The most natural thing, right, is for the mother to be with her children, so we decided that it would be best for her to go back to be with the children, then I would come to work . . . Well, I make more money than she made, and things are better this way because now she is with the kids, right?

From their class-privileged position, they were able to explore different options, all while negotiating and then reaffirming traditional notions of motherhood and fatherhood. Their decision-making processes and subsequent experiences reveal the fluidity and some of the complexities of gender ideologies that contextualized middle-class migration and early settlement. For example, although it would normally not be socially acceptable for a married woman to migrate by herself, Blanca did so because, as there is typically a gendered wage gap in El Salvador, her job did not pay particularly well, and she had relatives in the United States willing to house her. In this context, it became suitable for her, once she had been granted a visa, to leave her children in the care of their father, who had not previously taken care of the day-to-day household duties. For him, the difficult financial situation and his wife's job prospects abroad made it tolerable to take on what would otherwise be considered feminine labor in the home. With a united front to maintain the family's middle-class status, Blanca and Felipe justified their gendered transgressions through strategic adherence to some traditional gendered norms, even when their actions did not pay off.

Indeed, gendered norms influenced Blanca to migrate to Minnesota, even when it was not likely to be the most profitable destination. Without the large Salvadoran populations of places like Los Angeles, Maryland, and Houston, she was unable to find a market for the ethnic products she hoped to sell. Blanca and Felipe were aware of this risk, but Minnesota seemed like her only option—the one most appropriate for a woman traveling alone. When it became clear that Blanca's migration had not been as financially successful as they had hoped, Felipe renegotiated his position on motherhood and once again accepted more traditional norms. He explained that her return to El Salvador was necessary because "mothers have to be with their children." As in much of Latin America,[36] the idea that mothers need to be physically present with their children is prevalent in El Salvador; Felipe and Blanca's experiences and justifications, however, reveal the fluidity of gender ideologies as men and women, from their various class and legal positions, negotiate transgressions and conformity to make sense of their decisions.

After Blanca's migration did not prove to be profitable enough for the family, Felipe traveled and benefited during early settlement from a range of options and behaviors deemed socially appropriate for men. For example, unlike Blanca, who had to stay with relatives, Felipe got in touch with friends in multiple cities and, based on their recommendations, decided that New York would offer the highest wages. When he could not find a job there, after staying with friends for a month, he asked around and opted to try his luck in Boston next. Because he is a man, no one questioned his decision to go despite his lack of family ties there. On top of his male privilege, his tourist visa (a product of his class privilege in El Salvador) allowed him to move relatively freely in those early months to search for the best jobs. Moreover, he did not have to carry the burden of feeling that his absence would be harmful to the children during the initial stages of settlement.

Like Amanda, Felipe, and Blanca, all eight visa-authorized travelers I spoke with had smoother transitions into the United States than parents who traveled without a visa. Juana, for example, told a very similar story of being picked up at the airport and living in her relatives' homes where she felt secure taking her time finding a job. Ramón, who traveled with an immigrant visa, arrived at the airport, was hosted by family, and began working within days of his arrival. His family had been expecting him for months; knowing his exact date and time of arrival, they had helped line up a stable job for him. At the time of the interview, eight years after his migration, he continued to live with his brother and mother, with whom he shared household expenses while saving up to bring his wife and children.

All of the examples in this section highlight the crucial role of social networks in helping to shape migrants' initial experiences of housing and settlement. However, another important pattern related to the production of legality and illegality also emerges: Those who can escape the violent consequences of illegality, even if only temporarily by obtaining a tourist visa, are best able to make use of their social networks to ease into and facilitate their initial experiences of integration. Visa-authorized travelers, even if they eventually violate the visa's terms, not only have less debt and less emotional trauma than unauthorized travelers but are also protected throughout the duration of their visa. Although in the grand scheme of things a few months of legal protections may seem trivial, the differing experiences demonstrate that visa protections provide a notable advantage.

Conclusion

Several factors affect how quickly migrant parents can begin to remit to their children and improve their family's well-being. Although it is often overlooked, it matters a great deal how migrants travel, how long they take to get to the United States, who can help them once they arrive, and how quickly they can get a stable job. Each of these factors is also shaped by the U.S. production of migrant illegality. The impossibly difficult visa application and approval process makes unauthorized travel the default alternative for poor migrants. Although all migrants would like to qualify for a visa to travel via the safest, quickest, and most affordable route to the United States, the U.S. embassy grants these privileges to only a lucky and privileged few Salvadorans. The rest must accept that the dangerous unauthorized trip by land is their only hope to make it into the United States where they can earn the money that their families so desperately need in El Salvador.

Illegality, as it has come to be determined through U.S. immigration policies at this historical moment, means that Salvadoran unauthorized migrants risk a great deal during their journeys. Countless Salvadorans and other Central Americans are kidnapped, face physical and sexual abuse, experience extortion, lose limbs, and even lose their lives while traveling without authorization through the length of the Mexican territory.[37] Knowing that their children will not have steady access to food or schooling, that they will never have the opportunity to reach their dreams of stability no matter how hard they work in El Salvador, too many migrants see no option other than these unauthorized journeys. Illegality then follows them into the United States, where it cumulatively disadvantages these transnational families by blocking parents' ability to remit to their loved ones quickly. Instead, parents must first pay off their exorbitant smuggling debts, find a job and a place to live with few resources or connections, and likely deal with the emotional and psychological scars of the journey for many years.

Migrant parents with visas—the ones whose class standing allows them to benefit from the production of legality—typically start off with greater resources than those who travel without authorization and get to bypass many of the harrowing aspects of the journey. Because they are able to plan for their trips, purchase tickets in advance, and notify their networks before they leave, they are more likely to have family or friends waiting for them when they arrive. Moreover, they get to feel at ease during the first few weeks or months in the United States when they are covered by the legal protections of their visas. And, without a large smuggling debt, they can begin to remit larger sums to their children more quickly. So it is that the stratification created by U.S. immigration policies extends well beyond U.S. borders to stratify transnational family members in El Salvador as well.

For all migrants, the differences between traveling with or without a U.S. visa are staggering. Undeniably, however, intersections of class and gender shape migration and early settlement experiences in ways that most cumulatively disadvantage poor women. While the U.S. Department of State has the right to determine who is allowed to enter the United States, the consequences of denying visas to the vast majority of travelers from El Salvador are extremely dangerous and too often deadly. When U.S.-funded and U.S.-supported foreign policies—including civil war and free trade agreements—make life more difficult for large sectors of the Salvadoran population, more Salvadorans migrate to the United States.[38] These migrants' lives are further endangered when neither the Salvadoran government nor the Mexican government move convincingly to protect them. The complete lack of legal protection has created an environment of utter impunity, in which authorities, gangs, organized crime, and even petty thieves can easily target migrants without any repercussions. The brutal journey north communicates to the migrants that they are not welcome and not valued as human beings. If they reach the United States, they hope never to go through that process again nor to put their children through such horrors.[39] Instead, the safest option is to stay separated indefinitely across borders. For those migrant parents who are lucky enough to make it alive and into the United States, the implications of illegality while en route will soon be replaced by the implications of illegality within U.S. borders.

4 The Structure of Trauma through Separation

WHEN I MET WITH AMANDA, she had been living in the United States for over three years.[1] The forty-seven-year-old mother of two was a lighthearted woman: quick to smile, optimistic, but also emotionally burdened by the separation from her adult children. She had entered the country with a visa that granted her permission to stay for six months. Her family and friends, all of whom were very supportive, helped her locate two housecleaning jobs within the first few weeks, but when her nephew called from another state to tell her about a higher-paying domestic job with his friends, she did not hesitate to buy a ticket and travel across the country:

> [The] couple . . . had just had a baby, and they were willing to pay $1,500 per month just to take care of one baby! So I bought my ticket the next day and went out there . . . I worked with that family for thirteen months, and I would do everything for them: cook, and clean, and iron, and everything . . . It was the best job I ever had because I was able to send so much money right away to my daughter to pay off our debt and make sure she could graduate.

With a tourist visa, Amanda had nothing to fear in case anyone asked her for identification at the airport (as has been the case for many immigrants detained at airports and bus stations). Because her visa protections were limited to a few months, however, she described a very different job experience and sense of insecurity that had followed her ever since she overstayed her visa.

When the family informed her that they would be moving and cutting her pay by two-thirds, Amanda rejected their offer and found herself in a very vulnerable situation: "They were going to move to [the Central Valley in

California], from [the East Coast], and wanted to go from paying me $1,500 per month, to $500 per month. So I would ask myself, how am I going to continue to pay off my debt and send money to both my children?" Given the lower cost of living in California's Central Valley, her employers knew they could get away with paying a domestic worker poverty wages. Indignant, Amanda told them that she would not give her labor away so cheaply.

By the time she returned to California to be with her relatives, Amanda was no longer authorized to be in the country:

At that point I was scared to fly back, but it was better for me to be with my family. Since then, I've had nothing but bad jobs, where they only keep me for a few months or they just don't pay enough . . .

LA: Has your family tried to help you find a job?

Yes, they've tried, but I haven't had any luck . . . So I started cooking food a few days a week to sell to construction workers at lunch time, and that's okay, but you hear so many stories about raids these days that I get nervous going out . . . I decided to try life here . . . [but] I didn't even want to ride the Greyhound to come to Los Angeles because I know they take people and deport them off the bus, so I had to wait and get a ride from my friend who works [transporting goods] on a semitrailer.

Amanda's experiences underscore the weight of illegality in people's lives. How immigration laws are enforced either allows immigrants to integrate into the labor market or hinders their progress. For Amanda, even the minimal protections of a tourist visa were helpful at first. When these protections ended, however, so did her sense of security. No longer freely mobile, she faced the same limitations and was restricted to similar low-paying jobs as all other undocumented immigrants. Moreover, she lived with an overwhelming and constant fear of deportation—some of the gravest repercussions of illegality—that contextualized her everyday life. Even her tight social networks could not protect her from the vulnerability of possible deportation and, on realizing this, she cautiously moved to another city to continue to seek out better employment.

Illegality, as established through legal statuses, determines immigrants' level of rights (or nonrights) to reside and work in the United States for a particular length of time. Like Amanda, however, immigrants are not fixed into a single legal status category. Some who enter without a visa may eventually qualify for different forms of relief and legalization. Others who attain protections from deportation may later become undocumented.

Immigrants are labeled "undocumented" if they are in the United States without lawful status.[2] This includes unauthorized travelers who entered without inspection at the border or visa-authorized travelers who overstay their visas. Temporary Protected Status (TPS) grants beneficiaries already in the United States the legal right to remain in the country and to work during a designated period, but it does not lead to permanent resident status. Immigrants become Legal Permanent Residents (LPRs) only when they are given permission to reside (and work) in the United States permanently.[3] Immigrants with LPR status may travel internationally but may not leave the United States for more than six months at a time.[4] Finally, a naturalized citizen is an immigrant who after a period of time with LPR status (typically a five-year waiting period through an application process) gains full legal citizenship rights. Because immigrants are not fixed into these categories, it is possible—even likely—that they will move between being legally protected and unprotected in various ways and at different times in their lives.

The production of illegality as it plays out for travelers does not always neatly match the consequences of illegality as they occur postmigration. That is, the legal categories conferred to migrants while en route—unauthorized versus visa-authorized travelers—do not necessarily match the legal status categories conferred postmigration. This was evident among the immigrant parents in the study. At the time of the interview, fourteen were undocumented, nine had Temporary Protected Status, twenty-three had Legal Permanent Residency (among them, two were actually still in the process of obtaining LPR status), and one was a naturalized citizen. Although more than half of them were eventually in a stable legal status, thirty-nine had traveled without authorization and entered the United States without inspection at the border. Five had entered with a tourist visa that they then overstayed, and only three had entered with an immigrant visa to await legalization. This is an important point because it contradicts the high volume of misinformation about immigration in the United States. Public discourse suggests that immigrants are inherently "documented" or "undocumented," as if these categories were not legally produced and maintained, as if these categories and individuals' experiences were not shifting. Once in the United States, moreover, immigrants can go from being undocumented to having TPS and back to being undocumented, while others may have even attained LPR status, but were then detained and deported—treated as if they had been undocumented.[5] It is important to note that their shifts in status are also associated with shifts in job experiences and opportunities.

As this chapter reveals, legal statuses matter because they help determine both the economic and emotional well-being of all members of transnational families. Although much of the public discourse in the United States presumes that U.S. immigration policies are solely about protecting the country's national sovereignty and the rights of its citizens, these laws have notable consequences for families beyond U.S. borders as well. By opening and closing off job opportunities and pathways to family reunification, the U.S. production of illegality also determines immigrants' ability to make a living and shape how their families fare abroad.[6]

(Il)legality's Meanings and Consequences for Transnational Families

Illegality, as a legal, social, and political construct, is ever changing and can mean different things for different groups of people.[7] In the early twenty-first century, the paths to legalization for undocumented Salvadoran immigrants are very limited. Even when they have resided in the country for over a decade and whether or not they have children who are U.S. citizens by birth, immigrants do not qualify for legalization except through a family or employer petition.[8] Illegality for undocumented transnational parents, therefore, means that they will have to experience family separations that are prolonged over several years because, without a path to legalization, they cannot visit their children and reenter the United States legally, nor can they petition to bring their children to join them in the United States.

Those with Temporary Protected Status (TPS) are in a similar situation. Although TPS offers a work permit (with fees and reregistration processes every eighteen months), it does not lead to legal permanent resident (LPR) status. This automatically prevents parents from petitioning for their children's immigrant visas. Moreover, because they are required to be continuously physically present in the United States to be eligible for any further extensions, transnational families relying on a parent with TPS also experience lengthy separations.

Under current laws, illegality also involves restricted pathways to legalization,[9] especially for Salvadoran immigrants who typically cannot obtain a green card through investment or as a result of "extraordinary ability," as designated by the U.S. government. Most Salvadorans currently obtain LPR status through petitions established by immediate relatives who are U.S. citizens or LPRs (though the process is much slower when initiated by someone with LPR status instead of a U.S. citizen). Immigrants with LPR status are given permission to reside (and work) in the United States permanently.[10] For transnational families, relying on a parent with LPR status means, in part, that they can potentially reunite in El Salvador when parents return for visits or in the United States when they file for the children's immigrant visa and legalization.

Economic Well-Being

On average, Salvadoran immigrants earn low wages, but legal status further stratifies immigrant parents' long-term work experiences. These effects are especially harmful for undocumented immigrants and their families. For immigrants with even minimal legal protections, human capital, social networks, and length of residency best explain their opportunities and ability to remit.[11] However, illegality weighs heavily on undocumented immigrants, blocking the potentially positive effects of some factors while exacerbating the negative effects of others. For immigrants in this study, undocumented status trumps other benefits, no matter how many years of education they have, how many people they know, or how long they have lived in the United States. And when they have little education, know few people, or have lived in the United States for only a brief period, undocumented status makes life especially difficult. In addition to the cumulative disadvantages of illegality while en route, contemporary illegality in the United States further lowers families' chances of well-being when it creates obstacles and risks during the job search, job tenure, and overall settlement processes.[12]

In general, given the relatively low levels of formal education among Salvadoran immigrants, it is not surprising that they work in low-paying, often unstable industries—mostly in the service sector. Among other occupations, the mothers and fathers I spoke with are domestic and garment workers, hotel housekeepers, nurses, street vendors, restaurant servers, cooks, janitors, mechanics, construction workers, community organizers, and upholstery workers. For undocumented immigrants, however, finding and maintaining a stable job can be very difficult. Initially, given the great smuggling debt of many, their desperation and legal barriers lead them to terrible jobs where they do not earn enough to remit sufficiently to their children in El Salvador. As time goes by, the fear associated with illegality can also continue to prevent them from pursuing better options.

Fátima, a fifty-five-year-old immigrant mother, has lived in the United States for over eighteen years. I met her at the Salvadoran Day Festival (*Día del Salvadoreño*), where she stood in line at a booth to request information about applying for TPS. She claimed she had never had the opportunity to apply for any kind of legal protections. After toiling in factories for many years, she decided to become her own boss by selling beauty products. Although she had, on rare occasions, made up to $1,000 per month, profits varied and were unreliable. She would have liked to obtain a better job, but without papers she feared that she would only be exploited once again. In Fátima's case, her undocumented status prevented her from improving her wages and working conditions despite having lived in the United States for eighteen years. For immigrant parents like her whose employment opportunities are limited to poorly paid sectors where they are subject to exploitation, the chances of success—of socioeconomic upward mobility for their families—are slim. And although immigrants' lives typically improve after ten years of living in the United States,[13] undocumented immigrants continue to fare poorly. Like her, most undocumented immigrants continue to work for low wages and under exploitative conditions because they know that, economically, their families will be in even more precarious situations if they return to their home countries where jobs are scarcer.

Even undocumented immigrants with higher levels of education initially face limited and exploitative working conditions in the United States. Fifty-two-year-old Graciela, the only immigrant parent in the study with a college degree, fled El Salvador for political reasons three years prior to our interview. She was able to travel to Mexico with a visa but crossed the border clandestinely into the United States. Given her long history of human rights and nonprofit work, she felt comfortable approaching immigrant rights organizations, where she found a few short-term housing options, but no one could help her find work befitting her level of expertise. Desperate to make money to buy food and to send to her children, she took a retail job in the downtown jewelry sector where she was paid $20 per day for nine-hour shifts. Even though she was horrified by the high degree of sexual and labor exploitation in that sector, as she explained, "I didn't have papers or anything, and I needed to eat." It was only after Graciela won her asylum case and achieved a more stable legal status that she eventually found better work in a nonprofit organization.

Many undocumented immigrants—especially men—in the study had also experienced debilitating work injuries.[14] Sixteen-year-old Daniel in El Salvador relayed his migrant father's migration and work experiences. His father, Rodrigo, had a difficult time finding employment, and, when he did, he worked making less than minimum wage for a couple of months before he hurt himself severely. Due to his injury, he could no longer work. And because he was undocumented, he was worried about seeking worker's compensation. Based on traditional factors for understanding how immigrants integrate into the United States, Rodrigo, who had completed high school in El Salvador, should have fared better than most other parents in this study. With a high school diploma, he was on the higher end of educational attainment among the parents I interviewed. However, the consequences of illegality, including unauthorized travel and dangerous and exploitative work conditions, clearly eclipsed the potential advantages of his high school education.[15]

Importantly, Rodrigo's is not an isolated case. In fact, a number of undocumented fathers cited very similar reasons for no longer being able to work or to send remittances. Mauricio, an undocumented immigrant father who earned less than the minimum wage for backbreaking work, explained:

> You see that without papers it is very difficult to be hired just anywhere. So my brother-in-law found me a job with some Chinese owners of a company where the trailer trucks come and you pack them and unpack them. That is hard work because they don't care if you're tired, if you need to rest, or if [the weather is] too hot or too cold. And so, since they didn't even let us rest, I messed up my back, and when I told them, they pretended not to hear me; they didn't do anything. I kept complaining, and in the end they told me that if I couldn't do the work anymore, I should look for another job because they needed someone who could stay on schedule. And after that I still had to fight with them to get my last paycheck because they were saying that I worked too slowly. Up until now I still can't carry anything too heavy, so I haven't been able to find a steady job.

Because of his undocumented status, Mauricio was afraid to apply for worker's compensation or to denounce the employer who fired him when he complained of back pain. Since losing the steady job, he has spent most of his time at a day-labor site, trying to get temporary, short-term jobs. Day labor, however, has been unstable employment that did not generate sufficient wages to support his family in El Salvador.[16]

Mauricio's predicament stems mainly from the effects of illegality. While many scholars emphasize that immigrants' level of education and social networks help determine how well they fare in the United States, these factors prove to be less important in Mauricio's case. Even though he completed high school—a relatively high level of educational attainment among Salvadoran immigrants—and even though he had relatives who helped him locate his first job, it was the lack of protections associated with undocumented status that most powerfully limited him from remitting to his family. Like Mauricio, several undocumented immigrant parents in the study were no longer working or sending remittances due to injuries.

Immigration policies and legal statuses are incredibly powerful in establishing a hierarchy of well-being for immigrants and their families—both in the United States and beyond. This becomes most evident when comparing the experiences of parents across legal statuses. For example, immigrants with LPR status were generally more financially stable than those with no papers. Consider the narrative of Zuleyma, a mother who has LPR status. Even though she completed only the ninth grade in El Salvador, she had been working as a nanny all ten years of her residence in the United States and was earning $550 per week—a relatively high wage for domestic work and considerably higher than what most undocumented immigrants made.[17] As she explained it, "The employers expect to pay you $150 a week, and you say, 'No, I want to earn this much . . .' Every year what employers do [for professional workers] is give them a bonus, and they do that for me. I also get paid vacation." Indeed, Zuleyma enjoyed greater benefits and perks than most workers I interviewed. I asked her how she had managed to get such a great job as a nanny, and she explained rather knowledgeably:

> The way I saw it is, you don't know English, that's $100 less. You don't drive, that's $100 less. And if you don't speak English, you don't drive, and you're going to be a live-in, they pay you $125 a week! . . . I figured out that I had to learn English to earn a little bit more, to be able to provide for my children and give them a chance to move ahead . . . I figured out that driving was going to get me $100 more; I've got to learn to drive . . . I know that having insurance is a priority for [my employers], so I'm going to have it, but they're going to have to help me pay for it.

Her confident tone revealed a level of entitlement not evident in the narratives of undocumented immigrants. Unburdened by the repressive features of illegality, she was unwilling to let employers take advantage of her and did what was in her power to increase her salary potential: She learned to drive and obtained car insurance. In most states, however, these options are not available to undocumented immigrants. Like Zuleyma, immigrants with LPR status did not generally fear deportation and, because they had a more secure future in the United States, were more likely than immigrants with unstable legal statuses to act on the assumption that there were other possible job choices waiting for them.

Thirty-seven-year-old Cristina, who had been in the United States for twelve years when I interviewed her the first time, currently lived in Dallas. She and her husband, Cirilo, traveled without authorization and were undocumented for several years before attaining LPR status. With the shifts in their legal status also came clear shifts in their and their children's well-being. Both had completed high school in El Salvador, and they had few contacts in the United States when they first arrived. With little help and no legal protections, Cristina and Cirilo took the first jobs they could find: Cristina was a live-in domestic worker, and Cirilo worked at a nursery. They left their three children in El Salvador with Cristina's mother and wanted to remit as much and as quickly as possible. When they saw that he was earning more than she was, she left the domestic job and joined him at the nursery, where they planted and picked flowers and plants. Still, prior to obtaining LPR status, they went on to have a number of difficult, poorly paid jobs, including hotel housekeeping. Despite the hard work and even when they each worked full time, they earned so little that they were not able to afford rent on top of what they remitted to their children, so they moved around from apartment to apartment, always renting out very limited space with other people. First they paid to sleep on the floor in someone's living room. Then they progressed to renting a walk-in closet in another place. Finally, they were paying for their own room and bathroom in an apartment with another family, but they were dissatisfied with their living conditions.

Cristina and Cirilo experienced illegality as stress about their workload, their expenses in the United States, and their future, but especially as the inability to provide for their children. Luckily for them, Cristina's father—a U.S. citizen—filed for her legalization. During those six years that she waited for her papers to come through, however, because of their exploitative work conditions and poverty wages, the most she could aim to send her family was $200 to $300 per month, and even this was variable:

Sometimes I would have to call my mother and tell her that we were not going to be able to send anything that month. Then she would have to worry about how she was going to make it that month. And my mother would just tell me, "Okay, it's okay." It wasn't until years later that one of my cousins came to visit four years ago, and he told me how he would see my mother crying, wondering how she was going to make it without any money that month. I feel so much guilt for that.

Pained by the repercussions on her children and her mother, Cristina was determined to improve her life when she received her green card.[18] With the knowledge that she would eventually attain LPR status, she planned accordingly to take advantage of the better opportunities she knew would become available:

So, when I got my papers, I had to find something better. I had been taking ESL classes, and the good thing about Los Angeles is that you can take classes and learn useful skills and pay only $1 for each course . . . One day, though, I decided that now that I had papers, I wanted to bring my kids, and I would have to make much more money. So we invested, and I got loans for $6,000 for my CNA classes.[19]

The security of LPR status not only allowed Cristina to focus on safely bringing her children but also provided the encouragement to pursue better job opportunities. Although $6,000 was a large sum for the couple, who did not earn enough to pay for an apartment on their own, she understood that it was an investment in her family's future in the United States.

Having made an investment and feeling more secure in the United States, when things did not immediately improve in Los Angeles after obtaining a green card, Cristina and Cirilo did not hesitate to seek out other options in other parts of the country:

I was just never well-paid . . . That's why we decided to come to Texas . . . There's a huge difference between what I make now and what I used to make in California. The most I ever earned, even as a CNA in California, I have the check [stub] right here, is $6.90 [an hour] . . . Here, I'm almost, very close to making $14, and although we only get a raise of 4 percent every year, the benefits are really good . . . I have life insurance for each of us, I have a retirement fund . . . We've been here for six years. I drive, we have a house, and there have been lots of changes.

Unburdened by the fear of deportation that inhibits many undocumented immigrants from traveling across cities, Cristina and Cirilo ventured to another state in search of better job opportunities. Indeed, they were rewarded with significantly higher hourly wages, and their living conditions greatly improved, allowing them to increase their monthly remittance sums to $600 for her children and another $100 for her mother, who cared for them. Most important for her, they continued to take steps to ensure the upward mobility of their children and a comfortable life for them after their family reunification.

Samuel, in the United States for twenty-seven years, had been a citizen for several years before I interviewed him. A high school graduate, he migrated in the early 1970s with a visa that he eventually overstayed, but because he arrived prior to the proliferation of strict anti-immigration laws, he was able to find steady employment early on when he lived with his sister. Not engulfed by the fear of deportation that characterizes the experience of illegality today, he remarried and started another family here, all while remitting consistently to his daughter in El Salvador. He applied for LPR status as soon as he became eligible under IRCA and bought a house soon after:

> At that point, with papers, then we knew for sure that we were going to stay here, so my wife and I started saving and eventually bought our house . . .
> I took classes to learn all the new technology and equipment that auto mechanics use, so now I don't have to get that dirty, the work is easy, it's not that physically demanding, and it pays well.
>
> *LA: And it paid enough all those years to cover your family's expenses here and your daughter's in El Salvador?*
>
> Yes, well, years ago my daughter in El Salvador didn't have too many expenses. I paid for her private school and her monthly expenses. When she started going to the university, I had to send a little more. Although 150 colones ($17) sounded like a lot of money to people over there, it really wasn't a big sum for me . . .

Given the less oppressive political climate that received Samuel, he was able to make the most of his human capital and social network contacts to set his family, both in the United States and in El Salvador, on a path to upward mobility. He quickly found steady employment in a semiskilled, well-paid job, and, once he was legally permitted to remain permanently, he established deeper roots in the United States by buying a home and furthering his education to continue to move up in his field. After twenty-seven years in the country, he and his family were thriving economically.

Fifty-four-year-old Jorge had been in the United States for twenty-two years. Even though he had completed high school in El Salvador, he was only able to get low-paying warehouse jobs early on. Jorge arrived in the United States in time to qualify for legalization through IRCA. After obtaining LPR status, he hurt himself on the job but received several months of disability pay as well as physical therapy through his employment benefits:

> What happened is that I slipped. There was some water, and I didn't notice, so I fell as I was walking down the stairs, and I broke my right hand. The same people from right there, from human resources, told me to go see a doctor, and that's how I got the insurance to pay me. I didn't work for five months until it healed completely because, as a waiter, I need to put a lot of weight on that hand.
>
> LA: Were you worried about placing a complaint?
>
> No, they helped me at work to do it and everything. It took a few weeks to start getting the checks, but then it was easy.

Contrary to the experiences of the undocumented workers who were hurt on the job, Jorge did not think twice about filing a complaint, and he benefited greatly. For the past fifteen years, he had been working as a waiter in a unionized restaurant where he was generally content with his earnings and benefits. Similarly, forty-two-year-old Nelson, whose brother filed for him to obtain LPR status through family reunification laws, hurt his back while working in the trucking industry. Aware of his legal protections, he sought out workers' compensation rights and benefited from months of therapy and disability payments. He, too, had returned to work without any problems. Unlike the undocumented workers whose fear of deportation kept them from properly healing and benefiting from their rights, immigrants with LPR status could confidently seek out the legal and medical solutions they needed to continue to provide for their families.[20]

Overall, work practices such as negotiating higher salary, requesting benefits, making use of legal and medical relief for injuries, relocating for better jobs, or pursuing greater training opportunities were mainly available to immigrants with LPR status. Their higher salaries and greater benefits and protections allowed them to remit larger sums to their children in El Salvador, thereby improving their economic well-being. Notably, the traditional factors used to explain immigrant integration—human capital, social networks, and length of residency—apply most usefully for immigrants who have more stable legal status. These factors, however, tend to be less useful in explaining outcomes when applied to undocumented immigrants whose tenuous legal status undermines other possible advantages. As immigrants are sometimes categorized differently over time, a change in legal status is accompanied by changes in opportunities and future outlooks, and, in all cases, those changes affect the economic well-being of both immigrants and their children in El Salvador.

"When We Get Our Papers, We Will Be Together Again": Illegality in Intimate Lives

The labor market experiences of parents in transnational families have an impact on the emotional well-being of both parents and children. Undocumented immigrant parents, unable to find or maintain stable jobs with fair wages, are worn down by the stress. Twenty-six-year-old Gabriel, for example, had not been able to find a traditional job since migrating to Los Angeles. After several months, he opted to try day-labor work. I met him in the early afternoon, when it was clear that he would not be working or earning any money that day, so he agreed to talk to me. Feeling disappointed, he opened up about the challenges he faced, particularly because he was undocumented. When Gabriel migrated, he had hoped that his cousin, who already had LPR status, could help him find a job: "But that wasn't possible. Where he works, they don't accept fake papers (*papeles chuecos*)." Unable to get him into a stable job, his cousin asked around at other places, but they had no luck. Gabriel felt lonely and helpless: "It's hard because people expect one thing, and you come here, and you find that it's not so easy. I wish I had my family, the support of my family on the difficult days when you don't get a job or when you go for days without working."

Given his situation, Gabriel was not sending remittances back home: "I do send all the money I can, when I get it. But I know it's not a lot. It's not enough for them. Just like things are expensive here, over there it's the same thing, because remember that we have the dollar over there now, so everything costs more than before." The sums he sent varied greatly from month to month depending on how much he had worked. When I spoke to him, it had been a couple of months since he had remitted at all:

I wish I could send them more. I wish I got a long-term job and got hired someplace where I didn't have to wait around and hope to get picked every day. That stress kills you. It's a desperation that is so hard to explain. I think about my boys. I think about them all the time. I want them to know that their father is working hard, but I have nothing to show them. There's no money.

In the midst of their three-year separation and especially in the Salvadoran historical context in which absent fatherhood is a common pattern, Gabriel knew that not being able to remit to his family was sending his wife and children a strong message that he was not a hard worker or a good father.

In the meantime, Gabriel's wife struggled to raise their two boys and provide for them in his absence and without the remittances they expected. Pained by his wife's sacrifices and his inability to live up to their collective expectations, Gabriel was having difficulty maintaining a good relationship with his wife from afar:

I know that my wife has had it tough. She leaves the kids with her mother to go work. And she thinks I'm being irresponsible, but she doesn't understand it's not like that. I try to explain to her, but she's never been here, and she doesn't know how things are; she only sees that other people are getting money, or they tell her that they've received, and she doesn't know because she's never been here, and she sees, and people tell her stories about how much money others are getting, and she's not getting much.

He went on to admit that the tension was getting so unbearable that some days he drank to forget about his worries for a bit. After drinking, though, he felt even worse about the situation and more resistant to calling. The cycle would continue for several weeks, and he avoided calling them so as not to have to tell them that he had no money to send. Worried that, after three years apart, his young children would not even know him, he pondered his current situation with great sadness:

I knew it was going to be hard, but I never imagined that life in this country would be like this. I was always a responsible man, even though it's difficult to make a living in one's country. But I came here, and after years of the same thing, of not moving ahead and then your family stops trusting you, they lose faith in you, and it breaks you down.

Prior to migrating, Gabriel believed in his ability to be a good provider—after all, he had lived up to his role in terrible economic conditions in El Salvador. He knew of his cousin's story: He had also migrated without papers two decades earlier, and things had worked out well for him. Gabriel's cousin eventually got his papers, and he and his family were together. Surely the same would happen for Gabriel. Unfortunately, as I discuss in Chapter 1, however, immigration laws have changed, and enforcement practices have made life much more difficult for undocumented immigrants today. It is in this context of heightened policing and shrunken job possibilities that Gabriel and so many others like him cannot achieve their goals, even when they strongly aspire to conform to gendered expectations and family responsibilities.

The exploitation and poverty wages linked to undocumented status are problematic in and of themselves, but they also cause further damage when immigrants internalize their situation. When Mauricio, for example, was fired from his warehouse job after a back injury, he experienced not only financial strain but also emotional turmoil and a sense of helplessness. He eloquently described how his immigration status and the associated lack of protections came to define the core of his existence:

> One comes here thinking that life will be better . . . but without papers, one's life is not worth much. Look at me; I have always been a hard worker . . . but I messed up my back working, carrying heavy things without any protection . . . and I can't do anything about it. What doctor is going to help me if I can't pay? And the worst part is, who's going to hire me now? How will I support my family?

Instead of criminalizing the employers who fail to properly train workers or to provide a safe working environment, the current legal system criminalizes the immigrants who fled conditions in their countries that were directly and indirectly influenced by the U.S. government or by multinational corporations.[21] Immigrants are so thoroughly unprotected and mistreated that someone like Mauricio, who came to the United States in search of economic opportunities for his children's survival, simply feels defeated. Despite what he perceived to be his positive qualities—a hard worker who sought to improve his life—being "without papers" now meant that he was worthless if he could not fulfill his gendered responsibility by providing for his family.

Unlike undocumented immigrants who felt shunned and unprotected, immigrants with more stable legal statuses did not share these sentiments.

Whatever problems they had, they attributed them to various other issues—lack of education, lack of family support or networks, one exceptionally bad employer, or simply one episode of bad luck. In any case, they did not seem to internalize their situation in the same existential way as did undocumented immigrants. Because they had access to other opportunities, including medical services when necessary, their problems were not as all encompassing. They could compartmentalize problems and seek out more direct solutions in a way that was unavailable to undocumented immigrants.

Meanwhile, in El Salvador, children relied on remittances for their daily survival, but also, during long-term absences from parents, they came to associate remittances with love.[22] These monies not only provided vital resources but also served to mitigate the trials and uncertainty of long-term separations between parents and children. Because children of undocumented immigrants experienced illegality through limited remittances and terrible living conditions, these families were also likely to be completely distraught about the family separation. On the other hand, when parents were able to remit large and consistent sums of money, their children experienced improved living conditions, greater access to education, and, sometimes, notable upward mobility in socioeconomic status. Despite the pain of separation, they were likely to appreciate their parents' sacrifices and maintain strong, positive contact with their parents. In a sense, those who received regular sums, whose life improvements were visible and tangible—through luxury items in the home or greater access to education—had *proof* of their parents' continued commitment to the family.

On the other hand, children of undocumented migrants were much more likely to be distraught about their living conditions and the family separation. Sixteen-year-old Lucía was a student at an impoverished public school in El Salvador. Through unstoppable tears, she described the pain of not being able to justify her mother's eight-year absence: "One never really understands why a mother would abandon you, why she would leave you if nothing changes. Nothing is better. Everything is worse." Similarly, sixteen-year-old Clara said that the family's thirteen-year separation was "not worth it because I feel that I had the right to be with them, to be raised by my parents, and I didn't have that chance. And it's all because of the money, and what for? Nothing has changed." When conditions do not improve, it is difficult to justify a parents' prolonged absence, and, after some time, the dearth becomes proof that the children have been abandoned both physically and emotionally.

Children who received few or no remittances felt abandoned and resentful. In their tear-filled narratives, they lamented not having anything to show for their parents' absence. The prolonged separation, in these cases, seemed unjustified, and their impoverished conditions in El Salvador became evidence of the parents' failed commitment to the family. This was due, in part, to unrealistic expectations that many nonmigrants had about migrants' living conditions and opportunities for success in the United States. But it was mostly the effects of illegality that limited their parents to poorly paid unstable jobs that did not permit them to send money and gifts as often as the children wanted—if at all.

Length of Separation

Legal status, though, mediates transnational families' emotional well-being through multiple mechanisms; aside from determining how much migrants can earn and remit, legal status also establishes how long families will be separated.[23] Especially telling is that, beyond the financial hardships, Clara and others emphasized the emotional distress of going so long without personal interactions with their loved ones: "They call me almost every week, but it's not the same. You can't reach out through the phone to hug them, or to receive a kiss from them." Having spent most of her life without physical contact from her parents, Clara was frustrated with mere long-distance phone calls. Like her, Lucía ached just to see her mother again. In the context of harsh restrictive immigration laws, however, undocumented parents could not visit El Salvador, and these families went without direct personal contact for years—even indefinitely.

Unwilling to risk their lives again by crossing through Mexico and into the United States without authorization, most parents with undocumented status did not return to visit their children in El Salvador. This inability to travel back to their country pained them greatly. Luisa, an undocumented mother in Los Angeles, for example, had been waiting to receive her green card for eight of the last fifteen years that she had resided in the United States. During that period, her mother had passed away, and Luisa had not been allowed to see her even one last time. Her daughter, now a young lady, had grown up with Luisa's mother-in-law, and there were days when Luisa thought of nothing more than her deep desire to see her daughter in person: "The day that I get those papers, I don't care if I have to go into debt to go see my little girl. I want to know what she's like." In Luisa's experience, it was as though she had to place her relationship with her daughter and her life on hold until the imminent change in legal status. This kind of instability can weigh heavily on people's emotional well-being.

Angela, a mother in Los Angeles who had no legal pathway to LPR status, suffered profoundly while away from her children, unable to visit them. She shared how the situation affected her health:

> Well, my kids are over there, and I'll tell you this: All these years I have to take pills to sleep because I couldn't sleep, because sometimes the letters my mother sent me, "Look, the kids miss you. The kids cry for you. They don't want to eat. Look, Mireya (who is the youngest), she goes to the back of the house, and she screams out to you, and she is not doing well." So those things, they constrict my soul, and sometimes I wonder, what am I doing here?

Angela experienced illegality as an inability to see her children in person, and she felt this was damaging her health. In her deep distress and despite the physically demanding work she did as a caretaker and later as a hotel housekeeper, she could not achieve sleep without medical aids.

On the other hand, the situation was quite different for families relying on parents with more stable legal status. Immigrants with LPR status or who were naturalized U.S. citizens could come and go more freely, so long as they had the money to pay for the trip and permission from employers to take vacation time. Berta, for example, had LPR status, and when she looked for jobs, she made sure her employers would approve a month-long vacation each year so that she could travel to El Salvador to visit her children and grandchildren. Similarly, Cristina, who had recently acquired U.S. citizenship, saved up her sick days and vacation days to travel annually to El Salvador for two to four weeks to be with her children.

Children in El Salvador claimed that being able to see and interact with their parents made a big difference for their emotional well-being. Those who had seen their parents in recent years, even after a long hiatus, showed much more composure and understanding of the family separation strategy than those who had gone for many years without a visit. For example, twenty-three-year-old Javier smiled brightly when he talked about seeing his father for the first time after an eight-year hiatus: "It was a lot of time, but my father says that they gave him the [immigrant] visa today, and by tomorrow he was already on his way here. I mean, he was happy and desperate to see us, right? And it was a happy, really nice experience [to see him again]." In another example, Doris also shared her optimistic view. Even though her family was not thriving financially—Doris and her brother often had to borrow small sums from relatives to make monthly payments and cover their bills—she thought favorably of the family strategy of separation. Doris's mother was a legal permanent resident who had been able to visit El Salvador a year prior to the interview, after a five-year separation. And this is how Doris described the reunion:

> When she came, it was pure joy. When we saw her, we went to pick her up at the airport, and she didn't recognize us . . . When she left, we were little. She thought of us as small children, and, when she saw us, she didn't know it was us. I mean, she walked right past us, and when she got to my aunts, because she did recognize them, she hugged them and asked them, "Where are my children?" And my aunt told her, "Behind you." And she looked at us, and she said she didn't recognize us. She hugged us, and she wouldn't let go. It was really nice. Then we spent all month with her . . . Everything was great . . . I think that the fact that she left did not take her love for us away. I feel that it is the same because, when she was here, she was just as caring.

Being able to spend time with her mother, even after they had been apart so long that they did not initially recognize each other, allowed Doris to confirm her mother's love and continued commitment to the family. Even though the remittances did not provide luxuries for her, the physical presence and positive interaction was enough to improve her emotional well-being.

The in-person visits allowed families to reconnect in ways much more powerful than were possible through phone calls alone. Doris' mother, for example, made it a priority to visit the children's school, their teachers, and their principal to confirm that they were doing well: "She felt very proud when she saw us, how we've grown. And then she went to talk to the principal at our school to ask him how we were doing, and he congratulated her because he said that she had children who made the most of her sacrifices." In this exchange, the children witnessed their mother's interest in their well-being and their progress. Their mother, moreover, received affirmation for her efforts and sacrifices. All members of this transnational family had a chance to strengthen their commitment to each other and make the long-distance relationships more manageable emotionally—even though the migrant mother did not earn enough to greatly improve her children's material lives.

All the parents with LPR status who were able to visit their children expressed similar experiences of joy and reaffirmation of family ties. Cristina, who visited annually, even if only for one week, really cherished her time with her kids, "It's really nice. I've talked to them all year, but then I get to see them, to appreciate how much they've grown, and I pay attention to their mannerisms, and I get to know them as individuals." Cirilo, who bought his plane ticket and traveled to El Salvador the day after receiving an immigrant visa, had traveled back three times in fifteen years and also felt that the visits helped restore their sense of being a family unit, despite the long distance and the lengthy separation:

> When one can coexist and share with them, it is an opportunity to reestablish ties for the nuclear family. Here one works and sends money every month, but it is satisfying to go and see that they are well, that they are making the most of our sacrifice, and that there is still love. You forget that if you don't go, because here you just work and work without rest. So it is worth going to see how they are living.

Given the strenuous nature of many immigrants' labor and the certainty of a long separation period, these visits, even if infrequent and brief, allowed transnational family members to reaffirm relationships and strengthen bonds. Being able to witness firsthand the true fruits of their labor, immigrant parents could also commit to another cycle of hard work and continued sacrifices. Importantly, these kinds of visits that go such a long way in improving the emotional well-being of family members are only possible for immigrant parents who have stable legal status—as LPRs or U.S. citizens.[24]

Uncertainty of Reunification

Another way (il)legality shapes transnational family members' emotional well-being is by determining the certainty or uncertainty of the family's more permanent reunification. Under current U.S. immigration laws, families relying on undocumented immigrants simply do not have a legal pathway to reunification. These parents know that bringing their children, even adult children, entails great risk and almost guaranteed victimization on their way to the United States without a visa. Many of these parents left their loved ones behind precisely to avoid such risks. As the situation for unauthorized migrants crossing through Mexico continues to worsen and receive more international attention, immigrant parents are especially unwilling to put their children through this process. Without any foreseeable legal pathway to reunification, then, they face great uncertainty about when they will be reunited again—if ever.

Parents and children in transnational families have suffered tremendously through this uncertainty. In some cases, their lives have been suspended under the weight of knowing that they may not be reunited for many years, or perhaps ever. Seventeen-year-old Benjamín, for example, had been apart from his undocumented father for three years. After being used to spending their days together on the soccer field, the separation weighed heavily on him. He was especially burdened by the thought that he had no idea when he'd be able to live with his father again. Benjamín's conversations with his father, therefore, often revolved around when they would be together again:

> I wish I could see him again, because it's not the same without him . . . I mean, I wish I could play soccer or whatever with him, that he would give me advice, but no . . . I don't know when I'm going to see him. He says he wants to send for me, but I don't see any real signs [of this] because without papers it's very difficult. Right now I would've liked to go, right, to finish high school over there, maybe go to school and work to help him out, but I don't know. He says he wants me to go with a visa, but they didn't even give him one, I don't think they'll give us one. So, we don't know when we'll see each other, and I don't know if I should keep waiting or try to go to school here.

As is the case for all families with undocumented parents, Benjamín's father could not reliably plan for a permanent family reunification. The unease of not knowing when this might happen or if it was a possibility at all in some cases mediated everything else children did. For Benjamín, the anxiety prevented him from being able to focus on school some days and led to a decline in his grades: "Some days I'd like to leave, just like that, right? But I can't. And I'll be there in class, but my mind is elsewhere: Is my father okay? When will I see him again? How are we going to be together again? But there's no response for that." When only unanswered questions arise surrounding the family's reunification, it can be difficult to focus on daily activities. With no clear path to the family's future together, Benjamín's own personal goals were being muffled.

Yamilet, who had already been apart from her father for seven years when I met her, was similarly disconcerted about her family's reunification. Her father was undocumented, and although he only sent between $75 and $200 per month, he did his best to stay in touch and meet his children's desires. When Yamilet was little, she would ask him for dolls and stuffed animals, and he always obliged, even if it took months. Now, as an adolescent, all she asked of him was that he visit her in person.[25] Yamilet would be graduating from high school the following year, and she wanted nothing more than for him to see her graduate. He tried to explain that if he left, the return would be dangerous, and he wasn't sure what he'd do if he had to remain in El Salvador. At one point, she became so saddened by this that she thought maybe it would be preferable for him not to return at all:

> It's hard, and I guess it doesn't even matter because it will be the same thing all over again, to feel that sensation of knowing that he won't be here anymore and that it may be another seven years or even longer that he won't be with us again, not giving us his love and his support.

Worse than everything was the uncertainty that would follow on his departure. Once again, she would be back to not knowing when they would be together again:

> My dream would be to go live with him over there [in the United States]. If I had the opportunity, I would leave to finish high school and then go to college and graduate there, but he says that he, well, if he could, he would send for me, but since he's not there legally, then it's more difficult . . . And the truth is that by land, I mean, it's dangerous. We've already seen what they can do to people, that people even die [on their journey].

Despite Yamilet's deep longing to reunite her family, U.S. immigration laws and the way they leave unauthorized migrants completely unprotected while en route have crushed any hopes of an easy path to reunification. Unable to fulfill this desire, all of her other future goals have also been suspended in the long-term uncertainty.

Eighteen-year-old Karina, as the oldest sibling, had been solely responsible for her younger sisters for five years since her mother's departure. She had missed one year of school thinking that the possibility of leaving to reunite with her mother might come and she did not want to waste her time.[26] Ultimately, she understood that her mother's undocumented status prevented her from guaranteeing a safe reunification for all of them:

> Look, she says she can't come until she gets a visa, because she wants to come, she wants to see us, but the way things are, I think it won't be for another ten years . . . And I wish I could go and be with her. I want to be there to help her because she is by herself, but I wouldn't go unless we could all go [four siblings] because I take care of them. I'm the one in charge of them. I wouldn't leave them. But the way things are, we can't all go together. So, God willing, maybe in like ten years we'll see each other.

After five years of separation and unsure of when the situation might change, it became easier to assume that it would take at least another decade to be with her mother. In effect, without a change in immigration laws, it is unlikely that Karina's mother would qualify for legalization, and therefore it would never be possible for her children to join her in the United States. In this context, to assume that their separation will take another decade seems more bearable than accepting that it may never happen.

The situation was quite different for families of LPR or U.S. citizen parents. Not only were children in these families more likely to be thriving economically, but they also had more chances to affirm family unity during brief visits and to plan with greater certainty for the future. Cirilo and Cristina, who both had LPR status, had filed the necessary paperwork to bring their children to the United States to live with them. After filing, and during their waiting period, they bought a home: "So we decided to buy this house . . . And we have a place for my children to come to. That's really what we were thinking about when we bought it." Secure in their legal status and especially relieved at being able to legally reunite with their children, Cirilo and Cristina have continued to invest in their future in the United States, all the while establishing security for their children's future.

Their children, meanwhile, benefited greatly from their parents' legal stability. All three had completed or were in the process of completing their college degrees, thanks to their parents' consistent remittances. And, although they were unconvinced that they wanted to live in the United States, it was a relief to know that they had the option of joining their parents one day in the foreseeable future. As Javier explained:

> Their goal, besides wanting us to become professionals, is for us to go live with them over there [in the United States]. That is their goal. And their efforts to get their papers, that is one of their dreams. For example, I don't know if my

mom showed you the rooms. She tells us that there are rooms in the house, and they say, "This one is for Javier, and this room is Leonardo's, this is Laura's room," she tells us. So if they've bought a large house it's because they want us in it, they want us to be with them, and that has always been their intention.

For this family, despite their parents' unauthorized entry, their current legal stability meant that they received consistent and sufficient remittances to vastly improve their lives; they also received regular visits from their parents and, notably, were certain that they had a legal and safe path to be together in the United States in the near future.[27]

Vulnerable Stability: Benefits and Disadvantages of Temporary Protected Status

The benefits and disadvantages associated with being documented or un-documented revealed themselves clearly in the patterns I just discussed. One of the things that makes the Salvadoran case particularly interesting, however, that further reiterates the depth of the significance of (il)legality for the well-being of all transnational families, is the experience of migrants with Temporary Protected Status (TPS). Just as is clear in the name, TPS is a kind of in-between status that provides a *temporary* protection from deportation and a *temporary* work permit for otherwise undocumented immigrants.[28] It is not a permanent legal status, nor does it lead beneficiaries on a path to legalization.[29]

The fact that it gives limited relief to immigrants and their families is also evident in the well-being of the children of migrants in El Salvador. The mixed bag of limited benefits with long-term instability plays out in the economic and intimate lives of transnational family members on both sides of this migration stream. For the 20 percent of Salvadoran immigrants who have received this dispensation, the required multiple and cyclical reregistration processes have created an experience of "liminal legality" with negative impacts.[30] Unable to gain access to the rights, services, and protections that come with greater legal stability, immigrants who obtain TPS find themselves in a prolonged liminal space that can prevent them from settling and thriving.

The prolonged liminal legality of TPS holders can sometimes seem very close to undocumented status—especially when immigrants have little formal education or other resources. Lydia, a forty-seven-year-old mother of three, for example, had lived in Los Angeles and had toiled in the garment industry for over fifteen years when I interviewed her. Throughout her many years as a garment worker, she had been a victim of exploitation, largely due to her sense of insecurity based on a lack of full legal inclusion. In her case, TPS left her with a sense of powerlessness to demand rights:

> Sometimes I go for months without working, and it's not only me suffering, it's [my children in El Salvador] too. Sometimes I do have work, but the Koreans [garment factory owners] don't pay you. They give you false checks, and I have to wait an entire month before I can cash my check.
>
> *LA: Have you looked for other jobs?*
>
> I wish I could find another job, but it's not easy. It's really hard to get a job, and you always worry about the papers [legal status] . . . But I think to myself, what am I going to return for? Who will give me a job over there [in El Salvador]? If things are difficult here, they are even worse over there.

For Lydia, even though she had a work permit, the tenuous nature of TPS and the lack of a green card (only given to immigrants with LPR status) made her nervous about changing jobs. Not all employers would consider her limited documentation valid, and it was best to stay put rather than deal with worries "about the papers."[31]

Among most of the families I spoke with, however, even the limited protections associated with TPS went a long way in allowing immigrants to gain access to crucial resources. Immigrants with TPS, for example, were better able than undocumented immigrants to obtain higher-paying, more stable jobs. They were also more likely to apply for worker's compensation after an injury on the job—thereby overcoming one of the most common setbacks for undocumented immigrants—particularly among men. One of the more telling examples of the benefits of TPS comes from the narrative of fifty-year-old Felipe. Having completed some college in El Salvador, he ran a nonprofit organization promoting literacy in impoverished rural areas of the country. After several unsuccessful attempts to improve his family's situation in El Salvador, he decided to try his luck in the United States, on the East Coast where he was living when I interviewed him. Felipe's plan was to overstay his visa and remain in the country as an undocumented immigrant. But, soon after his transition from visa-authorized "tourist" to undocumented immigrant, he became eligible for the newly reinstated TPS program in 2001:

The first months were hard because you have to see who you can trust. I didn't want to be deported. But later, TPS came out, and I went to apply right away, and then things got better.

LA: For example, what would you say changed?

Well, look, at first I was just doing these landscaping jobs that didn't pay much, and I wasn't satisfied with what I made. And then, with TPS, you just show your card, and they give you a job that actually pays well, where you get days off, and you won't be fired for just any reason.

After getting TPS, Felipe had the legal status and associated protections to work and enjoy greater pay and better benefits. Prior to having TPS, he earned about minimum wage, but, feeling secure with his new Employment Authorization Document card,[32] he moved on to get a year-round job as a janitor for a large luxury apartment building, and during the summer he also did landscaping at a golf course.

Because he was able to work legally, Felipe earned about $575 per week during the winter and a few hundred more during the summer, when he worked a total of about fifty-five hours per week:

I have several jobs, depending on the time of year. Right now [during the winter], I get paid $575 per week for the part-time in the morning . . . I take the trash out of two apartment buildings with thirty-eight floors each . . . when the dumpster is full, I remove that trash with a tractor. That's what I do, I move trash around . . . I go in at 6 am and get out at 11:30. The second one, I go in at 1 pm, but there I'm a cleaner. I vacuum the lobby, clean the glass surfaces, little things like that, with a vacuum, a mop, sometimes clean stairs, pick up trash in the area outside. I get out of there at 6:30 pm . . . I only make about $220 per week at that one.

He worked and saved as much as he could because he knew that there was always a possibility that TPS would not be extended another time, and, although he would like to stay for a few more years, he thought it would be difficult to live as an undocumented immigrant:

Depending on who is elected president, the chances are that they will probably not give us TPS again, and to be here undocumented, that's not easy. Just a short time ago there was a raid, and they took forty workers from one place nearby. Some of these other guys that I live with, they don't have papers, and they just stay home, and you can see it, they worry about being deported . . . I tried to get them jobs where I work, but they ask for papers there, so we can't get them in.

Aware of the economic repercussions and fear of deportation that haunts undocumented immigrants, Felipe would prefer to return to El Salvador rather than to live without even the limited protections of TPS. The fact that TPS would not offer a path to legalization made him tentative about his future plans. He recognized that changing political tides may affect his ability to continue to work and remit. Only the high and consistent sums of money made the family separation worthwhile, particularly because, aside from worsening job prospects, undocumented status would also lead to greater instability and constant fear of deportation—he knew this from his roommates' experiences. Moreover, as much as he tried to help them by giving them access to his job opportunities, their undocumented status prevented them from benefiting in the same way he did with TPS.

Indeed, being a beneficiary of TPS provided immigrant parents with some flexibility and even a bit of stability in the workforce. Over and over, and very much like Felipe's case, families with parents receiving TPS had greater and better job opportunities than those of undocumented immigrants. Elizabeth, for example, described her mother's improved job situation after she received TPS:

[My mother] left without papers, but then, after the earthquake, somebody told her that they were giving papers, so she went to request them, and they gave them to her. And she told me that the papers helped her because before she used to work with a woman who was a bad person. The woman treated her poorly, but, with the papers, she decided it was better to leave, not work with her anymore. Because with papers she felt more secure that she could get a better job.

Elizabeth's mother, much like Felipe, benefited from TPS. Even though it is not a long-term solution, it allowed her to move from a hostile work environment to a better situation—a rather meaningful change in any immigrant's life.

This temporary stability, however vulnerable, made a clear difference in the lives of immigrant parents and their children in El Salvador. Immigrant parents with TPS were often in better financial situations than undocumented parents; not only could they seek out better, more stable jobs, but they could also change jobs in search of better options when they hit a roadblock. Children in El Salvador also benefited. In a consistent pattern, children relying on parents with TPS received higher and more consistent remittances than children relying on undocumented parents; sometimes they received as much or more than children relying on parents with LPR or U.S. citizen status.

Felipe, Elizabeth's mother, and all other immigrant parents with TPS were certainly appreciative of the work opportunities and the bit of protection this status granted them and their families. Many of them, however, also noted its limitations. Guillermo, a father in Los Angeles, described his feelings around the legal status in the following way: "TPS, you know, it's a good thing because you can work, but that's all it gives you. I don't complain, but you just never know when they're not going to renew it again, and then one is left with nothing." It was precisely that feeling of liminality—that prolonged vulnerability—and the knowledge that it could all be pulled out from under them at any moment that weighed heavily on beneficiaries of TPS.

Families in El Salvador did not seem to understand this vulnerability well. For them, TPS generated confusion that sometimes protected them from the harsh reality that their economic well-being was based on a temporary, easily revocable status but sometimes also caused great suffering. Interestingly, although 20 percent of Salvadorans are estimated to have TPS, and they have had it for over a decade, the status continues to be poorly understood. Salvadorans in the United States and in El Salvador are much more familiar with the statuses associated with "*tiene papeles*" ("has papers") or "*no tiene papeles*" ("does not have papers"). Children, for example, understood that, without papers, their parents typically could not return to visit nor could they apply for legalization for the family. On the other hand, with papers, they knew that it was possible for parents to travel safely out of and back into the United States, and they could file for papers to guarantee a family reunification. It was interesting, then, to hear how they talked about parents with TPS. It was as though they did not understand or simply made it up along the way. Along with creating a prolonged period of insecurity and instability, TPS also generates confusion and complexity that has affected transnational families' emotional well-being.

Particularly confusing for many was that migrant parents with TPS seemed able to demand their rights. In previous examples, Elizabeth noted that her mother used the security of TPS to leave an abusive employer, and

Felipe left jobs because of pay that he deemed unsatisfactory. Others had received unemployment and disability benefits when they were not working. In the minds of children of migrants in El Salvador, undocumented migrants were not supposed to act in these relatively empowered ways. So when they heard their parents say that they securely sought out a better job or that they were working "with papers," they incorrectly believed their parents had LPR status.

In an earlier excerpt, for example, Elizabeth assumed that because her mother was working legally, because she had the perceived luxury to look for an employer who would treat her well, that she must be documented. "The papers," in this case, gave her enough security to move in search of better opportunities. But Elizabeth did not understand that, beyond legal employment, TPS granted little else. As she expressed: "I'm waiting for her to file for me so that I can go over there, to live with her, to go to school and work there." In her incorrect understanding of the consequences of TPS, Elizabeth had developed impossible hopes on the assumption that her mother could seek legal pathways to reunification.

Such incorrect understandings were common. The more familiar experience was that people who had work permits were also allowed to come and go easily across borders. So children also expected this from parents with TPS. Keny, for example, described her shaky understanding of her mother's legal situation and what this meant for their family's future:

> I mean, [my mother's] legal, yes. She's kind of legal, because she has papers and she can work legally there. But to be honest, I don't really understand much about it because she says she has permission to work legally, but, at the same time, she can't come here. She says they don't let her come here. And we're still waiting for her to file for us, so we can go there and live with her.

After years of such false hopes, many children in these families grew tired and felt abandoned because the day of their reunification never came.[33] Emotionally, then, despite the fact that they were often thriving financially, children in these families suffered. It was difficult to understand why, if their parents could work legally, they could not also return to visit them. Why, if they did not fear being deported, were they not already filing the necessary paperwork to grant the children legal status in the United States?

Meanwhile, in the United States, although most immigrant parents understood clearly that they were not on a path to legalization, some maintained a great sense of hope that TPS would eventually lead to LPR status. Lydia, for example, expressed:

> Well, I think that since we, right, we've been living here so many years, we've been working, and we've been paying [for TPS applications], they should give us the papers already. With so many years, give us the papers because we've completed the time and we've been paying. They should recognize that, right?

Salvadorans with TPS have qualified for this in-between status since 2001. Over a decade later, they have gone through multiple reregistrations, paid hundreds of dollars in renewal and processing fees, repeatedly proved that they were of "good moral character," and worked consistently to establish their lives in the United States. In their minds, these long-term contributions and experiences should serve as proof that they are deserving of a more stable legal status in the country, but, without any possibilities for legalization, many also get frustrated.

Moreover, as the cyclical fees increase, some eligible immigrants are unable to reregister, thereby losing their protections and transitioning into undocumented status. Such was the case for Milton who, after obtaining TPS during the first round it was available, failed to reregister during the brief window of the second round of applications. Unemployed at the time, he simply did not have the means to pay the required fees. Having lost TPS, he lived in continual fear of being detained at home because USCIS had acquired all of his information in the process.

With all of these repercussions, TPS created a sense of liminality for immigrants and their families on various levels. It granted them only limited rights, enough to make a difference in employment but not enough to improve other key areas of families' lives. They were able to live and work legally in the United States for a temporary period, and the legal protections allowed them access to better jobs and better pay relative to undocumented immigrants. In the mixed bag of associated consequences, however, TPS also led children in El Salvador to misunderstand their migrant parents' realities and possibilities. Immigrants with TPS were unable to leave and reenter the United States, and they were also uncertain about when they would see their families again. With no path to legalization, they could not bring their children legally, and they were at the mercy of legislators who could potentially expel them at any given moment. Therefore, children certainly received some of the financial benefits of more stable legal status but not the emotional advantages of visits and a legal pathway to reunification. With limited protection against deportation and an ongoing sense of instability, then, most immigrants with TPS fared better than undocumented immigrants but certainly worse than immigrants with more stable legal statuses.

Conclusion

Increasingly tighter immigration laws in the United States affect immigrants and their families. The families' narratives in this chapter provide evidence for the often overlooked but important point that U.S. immigration policies—and illegality, in particular—effectively have an impact on people's life chances and levels of happiness beyond U.S. territory. More than this, U.S. immigration laws establish the inability of families to migrate together, the potential for physical violence and even death during journeys, the space for total impunity during and after migrants' journeys, and hierarchies that powerfully help determine how well or how poorly a family will live. In this sense, inequalities and divergences in experiences across transnational families can be traced in large part to U.S. immigration laws.

Intuitively, it makes sense that legal status helps determine families' economic well-being. Indeed, immigration laws and their implementation unequivocally affect transnational families' consistency of remittances. Relative to other statuses, stable legal statuses (LPR and naturalized U.S. citizenship) provide immigrants with the possibility of the most legal protections, the best jobs, the highest pay, and the most secure future in the United States. Comparatively, undocumented migrants have fewer legal protections, worse jobs, lowest pay, and highest incidence of debilitating injuries than migrant parents with TPS or LPR status. Although TPS grants migrants only temporary protections, these are enough to provide them access to better jobs and better pay than undocumented immigrants in most cases, though with less stability than immigrants with LPR or citizen status. Those cumulative effects in turn shape immigrants' economic resources, thereby determining how much money they can remit to their children.

Perhaps less obvious, but equally important, (il)legality also shapes people's emotional well-being. First, how families fare financially also informs their emotional experience of separation. In the context of multiyear separations, children left behind try to make sense of the situation and look for cues from parents about what they hope is a continued commitment to them. Children who are faring well financially can justify their family separation by pointing to concrete gains, while children who are faring poorly have no way to justify the family separation. As a result, children of undocumented parents experience compounded suffering; besides the pain of their parents' absence, they are also likely to endure dire poverty.

Regardless of how families are faring financially, long-term separation is more bearable when parents and children can see each other in person, even if only infrequently, and when they have a legal path to reunification. These possibilities are established by a migrant parents' legal status. Parents with LPR status can best maintain family unity through in-person visits that help children cope emotionally with the separation. Undocumented parents, on the other hand, cannot leave and legally reenter the U.S. safely. Because of legal restrictions, they cannot risk visiting El Salvador, so they go many years without seeing their children. Legal uncertainty also pervades a family's future plans. Because undocumented immigrants cannot apply for legalization for their children, they have no legal pathway to reunification. For these families, illegality translates into an overwhelming sense of uncertainty about when and if they will ever live together again—and this weighs heavily on the children. Children who rely on parents with greater legal stability, on the other hand, feel greater comfort in knowing that they will eventually reunite.

Finally, the repercussions of Temporary Protected Status further substantiate the primacy of legal status for transnational families' well-being. This in-between status, with its limited protections and rarity in an otherwise binary understanding of legal statuses (as documented or undocumented), very tellingly has mixed consequences for families. Even with its rather limited protections (relative to undocumented status), TPS opens up the possibility for notable improvements in immigrants' and their families' lives, particularly in an economic sense. That said, I cannot stress enough that TPS provides only a very fragile kind of stability. The prolonged fragility creates confusion and uncertainty that weighs heavily on immigrants and their families. Ultimately, TPS does not go far enough in setting the conditions for families' positive economic and emotional well-being.

Overall, the comparison across legal statuses demonstrates that greater legal stability has the potential to foster opportunities and upward mobility for immigrants in the United States and their families. Rather than further restricting and criminalizing immigrants, immigration policies should serve to integrate people who are already here. Under the current immigration system, the great hope that led parents to migrate is often met with legal restrictions that prevent so many of them from fulfilling their goals. Their intentions to improve their children's living conditions through migration may never come to fruition due to strict legal barriers that end up creating unequal experiences of well-being for transnational families.

Immigration policies, however, do not explain the full variation of experiences for transnational families. Another important pattern of stratification quickly emerged, and this one was based on migrant parents' gender. I explore gendered experiences of well-being in the next chapter.

5 Gendered Opportunities, Expectations, and Well-Being

EVEN THOUGH THEY ALL DEPART with the same desire to pull themselves and their families out of poverty, women and men have very different migration experiences. Women are more vulnerable than men, not only during the journey north but also once they arrive in the United States, where they continue to face significant structural barriers. Most notably, immigrant mothers in transnational families are disadvantaged in the U.S. labor market. These realities, in turn, stratify their children's well-being. Beyond the consequences of U.S. immigration policies, this chapter demonstrates that economic inequalities and emotional variations of separation also depend a great deal on migrant parents' gendered opportunities and approaches to parental responsibilities as they negotiate and subscribe to shifting gender ideologies.

Gendered Jobs

Salvadoran immigrants generally earn low wages by U.S. standards, but men, who have access to different kinds of jobs than women, tend to earn an average of $6,000 more per year.[1] In all of the most common occupations for Salvadoran women, workers earn meager wages, even after years of being on the job. Undocumented mothers, moreover, face greater hurdles than fathers in sending money to their children.

Immigrant parents were aware that women generally earned less than men.[2] Marta, an immigrant mother, explained how she understood this inequality. I interviewed her on the street, next to her vending cart for an hour and ten minutes on a hot summer day when few people walked by and not a single person bought anything from her. After eleven years of living in Los Angeles, Marta, whose family in El Salvador was not doing well financially, provided this analysis of gendered structural inequalities:

> I would say that things always go better for the men because you know that there are a lot of jobs that only men can do, and those jobs almost always pay better than the jobs for women. For example, my co-worker's husband worked in construction, and he used to make good money in that. I know a lot of men who can make like $8, $10 per hour, and that's really good. And my partner now, he works as a gardener, and he makes like $325 per week! When do you think I'll be able to make even $300 a week?! So yeah, they have it much better.

Because Marta's points of reference were the lowest end of the U.S. labor market and the limited opportunities in El Salvador, she interpreted her partner's monthly wages of $1,300 to be a considerable amount of money when, in reality, this sum was not enough to cover rent and other basic household expenses for families living in an expensive urban area like Los Angeles.[3] Regardless, her gendered analysis of wages by and large proved true in the experiences of study participants.

Female Workers

Indeed, many immigrant mothers corroborated that labor exploitation was rampant, especially among undocumented workers.[4] For women, the three most common occupational sectors were domestic, garment, and hotel housekeeping work.[5] Besides low wages, they described various forms of exploitation in each of these sectors. Given the lack of regulations and the private nature of their jobs, women who performed domestic work were especially vulnerable. They typically earned between $60 and $550 per week, depending on their immigration status, but most earned about $250 per week. And even when they were supposedly hired solely to provide child care, their duties typically also included cooking, cleaning, and laundry. The patterns revealed that illegality intersected with gender as undocumented women tended to earn less than women with legal permanent residency.[6]

Consider the case of Adela, a fifty-five-year-old mother of three and grandmother of four who had been living in the United States for ten years when I spoke with her. In El Salvador, she had worked in electronics manufacturing in a U.S.-based multinational corporation for twelve years, but she felt forced to migrate when the factory closed shop and she was unable to find another job to support her children and grandchildren. Even though she qualified for Legal Permanent Resident status through family reunification provisions soon after arriving in the United States, she had obtained only a series of live-in nanny jobs with several different employers. At her first job, she was a live-in nanny and housekeeper working an average of fourteen hours per day, five days per week. She endured difficult living conditions:

> During the week I'd have to take care of the girl, and on Fridays I'd do the cleaning. The first week I came, and I even developed a fever [after doing all the arduous work] because it was such a tremendously big house, and they had so many little things, and let's just say that they hadn't been taking care of the house. They hadn't had anyone to clean it for them. It was too much work. And they paid me $150 a week.

Adela was much happier in her current job where she was a live-in domestic worker for a family with only one toddler. She was hired to care for the boy but had taken on several more responsibilities—first out of fear that her employers would think that she was not doing enough and then out of loyalty to them. Although she cooked all three meals, cleaned, did laundry, ironed, attended to the employer's elderly parent, and cared for the toddler twenty-four hours a day (she even shared a bedroom with the boy and woke up throughout the night whenever he needed anything) from Sunday through Friday evening, she earned a meager $250 per week. Cases like Adela's, in which her legal permanent resident status cannot explain her stagnation in poorly paid domestic work, demonstrate the need to also consider gender as a central explanatory factor of immigrant integration. The gendered devaluation of domestic work makes it possible to expect a single female worker to take on so many responsibilities for such limited pay.

Many other mothers had similar work experiences as those of nannies and housekeepers. Araceli and Aura went through difficult times and minimal pay with families who expected them to put in ten- to sixteen-hour days. Esperanza spent five months caring for four children for only $60 per week. After several similar nanny jobs, she was hired as a full-time housekeeper for a couple who continually mistreated her:

> I have many friends who work as domestics, and they all have the same opinion: [the French] are exploitative people. They are good when it comes to food, but their treatment . . . I go with this woman, and I put up with a lot. The last

day that I put up with her was, that house was like a mirror, it shined because it was so clean—I love cleanliness—but there, wow, it was horrible. She gets there one day, and, you know, there is always some dust, so she slides her finger on a painting, she grabs some dust, because you can't avoid *some* dust, and she tried to rub [her dirty finger] on my face! I said, no, this is it . . . I had worked for her for a year, living there, going to sleep at 10 every night, making $100 per week . . . So I lost that job.

Esperanza's story revealed the extent to which, in domestic employment, women could be routinely humiliated because they had little recourse. Her experience was by no means unique—several women shared stories about similar types of humiliation, exploitation, and labor injustices.

Women's experiences with exploitation were not restricted to domestic work. Garment workers were also exploited.[7] Their inconsistent, poorly paid employment confined even seasoned workers and their children to poverty. Many garment workers who had been in the industry over a decade still earned as little as $100 per week working full-time. These poverty wages, in turn, blocked their ability to help their families.

Lydia, who worked in the garment industry for fifteen years, described it as inconsistent, poorly paid work. Even when she did have steady work, the factory owners did not reliably pay her in a timely manner. For example, she and her peers at other factories regularly received checks without sufficient funds for work they had already completed. In those cases, they had to wait a month for funds to come in. When I asked her how she foresaw her future in this industry, she responded:

Well, the future that I see, now that I have been working there for so long, in my old age, which is when I most need work, they want to give me less work. I came in sewing collars, sewing zippers, waistbands. Those are the things we do that pay better. Now they just want to give me things that pay the least. It's just because God is great that I was able to make $105 this week. I'm not lying! Imagine, what am I going to do with $105?

Due to age discrimination against older workers (particularly as their eyesight worsens) and because of the piecemeal nature of garment work, it is structurally very difficult to secure fair, livable wages.

Hotel housekeeping also paid relatively meager wages, despite being physically demanding. Housekeepers, including longtime workers, earned between minimum wage and $12 per hour[8]—too small of a sum to maintain a household in the United States, let alone guarantee economic stability for employees' families in El Salvador. Cristina, who had worked several different kinds of jobs, described her experience at a nonunionized hotel housekeeping job in Orange County, California:

> I think that the hardest job that I've had to do is cleaning hotel rooms. They told us we had to clean eighteen rooms during each shift. So, when my shift was done, I had to clock out, but I would simply go back up to finish cleaning. My husband always remembers how he would be waiting for me in the car, and I would come out crying. . . . The wages were miserable. I don't remember exactly, but it was less than $6 an hour.

Thirty-two-year-old Luisa, who labored in the garment industry for thirteen years, had been working as a hotel housekeeper for about a year when I spoke to her. She was young and thin and seemingly healthy. But, like Cristina, she agreed that this was the most physically demanding job she ever had:

> At the end of the day, I don't even know how I do it. You should see me—I am shaking, not able to walk straight. I just barely get the work done. They expect you to do sixteen rooms in eight hours . . . Vacuum, clean, make the beds perfectly, nothing can be in the wrong place, the tubs, the mirror, everything has to be shining. . . . I'm always the last one to finish with the rooms. It is heavy work.
>
> LA: And do you make enough there for your expenses?
>
> No, I'm telling you I have to go from there to my second job. I go in at 8, get out at 4, then I start my other job at 5 and get out at 9 or 11. And the next day I do it all over again . . . I tell my husband that I'm not that much of a bad-ass [*chingona*]; I can't keep this up much longer with two jobs.

Despite the physically demanding nature of hotel housekeeping work, and like the other fields restricted to women, the wages were insufficient to maintain a household in the United States. This made it even more difficult to guarantee economic stability for workers' families in El Salvador.

Parallel forms of labor exploitation were also prevalent in other fields dominated by women. For example, Graciela, a college-educated fifty-two-year-old woman who worked in retail (selling jewelry in a shop in downtown Los Angeles) described the extreme exploitation in this industry:

The first days were really hard because you have to learn everything over here . . . I started to work downtown, but there was a lot of harassment . . . and I cried because it was too much harassment. It was horrible.

LA: Who was harassing you?

The owner. They, the majority, prostitute the women there. The man wanted to touch me, wanted me to touch him. It was very painful because I would think about the thousands of women in the world going through similar and worse situations . . .

LA: What do the women do in that area? Sell clothes?

The majority, yes. Selling jewelry . . . for those women, a work contract doesn't just mean during work hours, but it often means having sex, too . . . And I would say, "Wow, and I'm not even young!" I would see the young women and think, they are pretty, they must get harassed. And sure enough, in the evenings you would see the Arabs [sic] driving around and their bosses pushing them toward cars, and one time I counted like twelve men driving around, picking up the girls.

LA: And why did you work there?

Because I needed the money. They paid me $20 for the day, and I worked from 9 am to 6 pm . . . I didn't have papers or anything, and I needed to eat.

As Graciela noted, these structural realities are especially harmful for undocumented women when they first arrive in the United States; they become easy targets for multiple forms of labor and sexual exploitation. Making only $20 per day for nine-hour shifts, women in this informal industry earn roughly $2.22 per hour. Most difficult for Graciela, however, was the sexual exploitation that she and her female co-workers faced at the hands of unscrupulous employers. The complexity of these experiences suggests the need to examine immigration through an intersectional lens, to include a focus not only on race, immigration status, or gender, but also on several aspects of a person's social location at once.[9] As will be evident later in the chapter, these social locations and their associated experiences in the labor market help shape parenting practices and children's well-being in El Salvador as well.

Male Workers

Although the majority of immigrant fathers in the study did not necessarily earn high wages, they tended to make several more dollars per hour than immigrant mothers. This is consistent with patterns nationwide.[10] On the lowest end of the spectrum for men, day laborers typically made about $10 per hour. Day labor, however, is inconsistent and unreliable. Further along the spectrum, construction workers and janitors make between $10 and $12 per hour, while one contractor I interviewed makes about $50,000 per year. Soon after migrating and starting a new job, however, immigrant men were able to earn close to or just more than $300 per week in landscaping, dishwashing, or painting. Construction workers, auto mechanics, waiters, truck drivers, and upholstery workers made between $450 and $600 per week. This was especially noteworthy when contrasted with Marta's comments; after eleven years of toiling in several jobs, she wondered, "When do you think I'll be able to make even $300 a week?"

One of the reasons men earned more than women is that in occupations traditionally restricted to men, workers are able to translate their educational attainment and work experience into greater wages—particularly when they had attained legal permanent residency. Structurally, men are more likely than women to work in sectors that provide opportunities for upward mobility. For example, Milton, a construction and upholstery worker, was promoted multiple times when he was allowed to use his engineering knowledge. In upholstery, he earned about $600 per week; in multiple jobs, he had been given chances for promotion:

> Ever since I got here in 1985, I started working in upholstery. I was very lucky that I only spent a week without a job. From that point on, I've always been working. I had never worked in upholstery before, but because I had studied some engineering at the university before I came, I knew about blueprints (*planos*) . . . I noticed that there was a mistake in one of the blueprints and I pointed it out to the boss . . . So the boss noticed right away that I had more knowledge than the other workers, and he moved me up so that I was earning more than the other people. I also had the opportunity to work in construction. There again, I was able to use my knowledge . . . For the first two weeks, I did a regular construction job like anybody else, but as soon as they realized that I could read the blueprints, they moved me up.

Unlike the immigrant mothers, Milton was able to translate some of his premigration educational attainment into higher status and higher pay in the United States because, structurally, sectors more open to men have room for some upward mobility.

Samuel and Cirilo, both of whom worked as auto mechanics, described similar experiences of achieving promotions in their jobs. Cirilo made about $30,000 per year, while Samuel earned about $35,000 (roughly $575 and $675 per week, respectively). Ongoing advances in car technology provided them with opportunities for updating labor skills, and mechanics could get certified in new areas relatively often, thereby increasing their hourly wages with more certificates. As Cirilo detailed:

> The good thing about my job is that there is always new technology and new things to learn, because cars always have new features. I can take classes, get certified in something new, like fixing a part of a hybrid car, and then I can make more money by the hour with that certificate. With all of those, my pay has gone up a lot since I started.
>
> *LA: And is this the kind of work that you used to do in El Salvador?*
>
> No, I had never fixed a car until I came here. I heard that you could take some classes at an occupational center to start working in that. I figured it was stable work because people always need to use their cars. And once you're in it, if you work for a big company, you always have the chance to keep getting certificates, and they have to raise your pay.

Especially significant is the fact that Cirilo and Samuel had a clear sense of the available path to upward mobility in their line of work. This stands in stark contrast to the experiences of most domestic workers, garment industry employees, and hotel housekeepers, who reported spending many years in those industries without opportunities for significant upward mobility.

Labor experiences, however, are also informed by legal structures. Undocumented immigrant fathers reported debilitating work-related injuries that prevented them from continuing to work. In effect, gendered experiences of illegality put immigrant men at high risk. Sixteen-year-old Pablo, for example, described how this happened to his father: "Two years ago, he had an accident. He fell and broke his back, so I think he's been paralyzed for too long. That's why he says that he can't really help us out anymore." This is not surprising, given that many of the jobs restricted to men are so physically demanding. Even though immigrant mothers in the study complained of back pain, loss of eyesight, and carpal tunnel problems resulting from their repetitive work, the men reported broken backs and other serious fractures. In fact, it is not uncommon among Mexican and Central American immigrants to experience work-related injuries that lead to "serious or permanent health problems, including the inability to work in the future."[11] In the women's cases, however, they endured the pain (that was perhaps more manageable than the men's) and continued to work.

Given the undeniable gendered disparities in the U.S. labor market, I expected to find that children in mother-away families would not be faring as well as children in father-away families. However, a different pattern emerged.

Perspectives from Children in El Salvador

Despite the unequal labor-market opportunities for men and women in the United States, in El Salvador many children in mother-away families could count on consistent remittances. And although a third of children in father-away families were similarly thriving, given the consistency of mothers, it was notable that not more families relying on migrant fathers fared as well. Many families relying on fathers said that remittances were insufficient and inconsistent and tended to decrease over time.[12] Following only economic markers, these findings are paradoxical, but they make sense when analyzed through a gender lens.

More than half of children in mother-away families received relatively large and consistent remittances from their migrant mothers. Twenty-four-year-old Sofia, for example, was thriving economically with funds her mother earned as a domestic worker. She could name various tangible economic benefits resulting from her mother's migration three years earlier: "Yes, economically life is much better since my mother left . . . She sent me enough to pay for my driver's license [$125]; I was also able to buy a laptop. My friends notice how many more things I have since my mother left." Sixteen-year-old Emilio similarly lived in a household that was thriving economically. His mother migrated eight years earlier and was working as a nanny. Although he did not know exactly how much she remitted because she sent the money to his father, he was aware of all that her consistent remittances afforded him and his family:

> Well, she pays the $45 a month for [tuition for private] school, she sends another $50 or $60 a month just for me to cover any other expenses, and she sends my father and my grandfather all the money for the household expenses . . . There has never been a time that she didn't send us money.

Sixteen-year-old Alex was also thriving with funds from his mother's cleaning job. His mother migrated when he was only one year old, and, despite the length of their separation, he said, "My mother sends between $300 and $500 every month . . . She's consistent with the $300, but when we need more, we tell her . . . And that pays for tuition and food, and my sister's university expenses." Regardless of the length of the separation—in these cases, between eight and fifteen years—mothers continued to remit sufficiently and consistently to their children. With that money, children were able to reliably eat, attend school, and cover various education-related expenses.

There were also mother-away families who were not faring as well. In these cases, although they did not receive sufficient remittances to substantially improve their living conditions, children reported that they received small consistent sums. That was the experience of eighteen-year-old Karina. Her mother, who was undocumented and had been doing various odd jobs, had migrated five years earlier and remitted money monthly, but the sum did not cover all household and school expenses: "I know she sends money every month. She does not fail. But you could say that it's not enough because sometimes I don't have money for the homework assignments, and I see that my grandmother has to borrow from my aunts." Despite the struggles, her life had improved noticeably as a result of the remittances:

> Yes, for me it was worth it [for my mother to migrate] because thanks to her I'm in my junior year in high school. Otherwise, I probably wouldn't be in school anymore. My mom used to earn money by doing people's laundry and sometimes they didn't pay her, and when they did, it was very little. And my father sometimes didn't work either. . . . Now we always have food. It's not like it used to be . . . Now we can eat, thanks to her.

Although Karina was only able to afford attendance at an impoverished public school, she was grateful to attend consistently and to know with certainty that she had enough funds for food. Given the structural barriers women migrants faced in the U.S. labor market—especially when they were undocumented— Karina's mother, and others like her, were doomed to minimal wages and limited remittances. In these cases, despite consistent remittances, children were faring poorly.

Children relying on remittances from migrant fathers were also often thriving. Just over a third of them,[13] too, had benefited from their fathers' consistent remittances through higher education, improved housing, and increased comforts. Given the higher wages of migrant fathers, however, it was interesting to hear children express other patterns, as well; about two-thirds of them received relatively small or infrequent sums. Seventeen-year-old Dalia relied on her father, who had TPS and was a gardener. She said, "Every month, I would say [my father] sends like $100 . . . it's not constant. Sometimes he doesn't have money, and he sends $75, and every once in a while he tries to make up for it and sends us $200 that month." Pablo described the process they went through to receive remittances from his father, a former warehouse worker, "We have to ask him, but only if we really need it. The first time we ask for $40, let's say. But in the whole year we only ask him three times, so he sends us a maximum of $120 [per year] . . . If we asked for more, it would bother him." And twenty-six-year-old Adrián shared a similar story. His father, Milton, who was undocumented, had migrated eighteen years earlier; although he earned over $600 weekly in upholstery, remittances had declined throughout the years: "When we were little, he would help us, sometimes. Based on what I can remember, he would help us once every three months or so . . . As we got older, we received much less." Similarly, other fathers became less consistent remitters over time.

In the context of structural barriers that disadvantaged migrant mothers through low wages, it was notable how many children in mother-away families were faring well. Despite men's greater earnings, only about one-third of father-away families was faring similarly well.[14]

Contexts and Processes Behind Gendered Inequalities in Well-Being

The findings about economic well-being are particularly interesting given the economic and labor market context of Salvadoran immigrants in the United States: In 2000, Salvadoran men earned an average of $22,600 a year compared to women's $16,000.[15] Not surprisingly, 15 percent of men and 22 percent of women lived below the poverty line.[16] How, then, did these gendered disparities lead to so many women's and fewer men's families faring well financially in El Salvador?

A closer look at the overall picture of the parents I interviewed did not immediately provide clear answers. Mothers' and fathers' experiences varied greatly, with no consistent patterns of discrepancy in level of education or access to social networks. Moreover, there was little difference between how long mothers and fathers had resided in the United States. On average, fathers had been apart from their children twelve years compared to mothers' ten years. Immigrant parents had various legal statuses, though a larger proportion of women were undocumented (36 percent of mothers compared to 23 percent of fathers), while more men were legal permanent residents (55 percent of fathers compared to 36 percent of mothers).

Instead, a detailed examination of the narratives suggests it was parental expectations conforming to gender ideologies that informed differences in remitting. Mothers, who had already transgressed gender boundaries by migrating internationally, felt extra pressure to then conform more closely to other gender norms, including being selfless.[17] Being so far away from their children, one of the only ways to prove they were worthy mothers was to live up to high moral standards and consistently provide for loved ones.[18] Given their meager wages, this involved many and extreme sacrifices to remit. Fathers, on the other hand, though they are expected to be economic providers, have multiple options for keeping their masculinity intact.[19] When they cannot send sufficient remittances, working-class men can maintain their masculinity by repressing emotions or signaling freedom and sexual prowess.[20] As a result, among transnational families, the mothers' almost palpable sense of obligation to remit and their strict approach to parental responsibilities were more frequently evident than in the fathers' narratives. These social expectations seemed to travel transnationally with mothers and fathers who continually negotiated and redefined their roles to justify migration and inform how much and how often they would remit.[21]

Expectations and Sacrifices

Feeling as if they had already pushed the boundaries enough by leaving their children's side, especially over such long periods of time, mothers seemed especially intent on fulfilling their parental responsibilities. In line with strictly policed ideologies of high moral standards, mothers in the study never failed to send their children money, if they had it. Even when their earnings were limited, they deprived themselves and sent higher percentages of their wages. Esperanza recalled the hardships she underwent to ensure her family's economic well-being in El Salvador during the initial stages of her settlement in the United States:

> I've always sent $300 [monthly] to my mother, and I would get paid $100 weekly [working as a live-in nanny]. I would end up with $90 because I also had to pay the fee to wire the money . . . It was horrible . . . Each week I would buy a dozen ramen noodle soups that I don't even want to see anymore, really.

I would think, you're supposed to enjoy the weekend here, no? At least go out to eat. For me, it meant a ramen noodle soup three times a day because since I had the day off, I couldn't eat [my employers' food]. I had to eat my own food, and so my food was the ramen noodle soup. But I was the happiest woman in the world because my daughter had something to eat!

Keeping only a quarter of her meager monthly earnings for bare necessities, Esperanza willingly limited her own spending and suffered the consequences. Over a decade later she remembered the details vividly, suggesting the depth of her suffering. Yet, despite the sacrifices, she emphasized that she was "the happiest woman in the world" because her daughter was benefiting. Being able to provide for her daughter proved her to be a worthy mother whose gendered transgression was forgivable.

No longer physically present with their children, over and over, mothers did their best to live up to most other social expectations by accepting challenges and taking on sacrifices to send as much money as possible to El Salvador. Cristina described that, in her case, "I just get my check, and I go almost directly to the mail to send it. And you know, I'm a woman; I would like to go shopping for things, but I just can't give myself that luxury. I just need enough to eat here, and the rest is for them." Drawing on the notion that femininity is about being a consumer of personal things, Cristina is able to signal that instead she chooses to be a worthy mother who sacrifices for her children. Similarly, Lydia, who worked in the garment industry, recalled the sacrifices she made to quickly pay off her debt and to support her family in El Salvador:

When I first got here, that year was hard. I worked as hard as I could, Monday through Saturday almost all day long. When the boss saw how quick I was, she gave me the best pieces, so at one point I started to earn $250, $300, even $450 [weekly] . . . I would send [my mother and my kids] everything I could. I would just keep enough to pay the rent and to eat . . . Back then, you could eat with $25 a week, and I was paying a lady, she was charging me $150 for rent . . . per month. But I lived there for almost a year, sleeping on the carpeted floor in the living room; I would just roll out my blanket, and I'd put my purse down, one of those cloth ones; I would use it as a pillow and sleep there.

Even when she was making between $1,000 and $1,800 monthly, Lydia was keeping only about $250 for her housing and food expenses. Her physical discomfort and all the details of her sacrifice were still important to her years later because they proved that, despite her physical absence from her children's lives, she was still fully devoted to their well-being from afar.

Strict adherence to gender norms created problems for mothers who were already disadvantaged in the labor market. In particular, immigrant women accepted labor exploitation and difficult working conditions that, when viewed through the lens of gendered expectations, they dismissed as minor sacrifices to support their children. For example, Adela had a series of negative experiences with employers; they humiliated her, expected her to put in sixteen-hour work days, and paid her $100 to $150 per week as a live-in nanny. In the face of such adversity, however, she resisted portraying her work situations in a negative way. Instead, she emphasized the benefits of her earnings. When I asked her how she kept going, she responded, "The only thing is that I have the satisfaction that I haven't let [my children] die of hunger." In another example, Angela described in great detail the difficulties she faced working as a caregiver to three children, earning $50 per week:

> I started to work there; I worked for like six months, and the only thing I cared about was that there was money to send to the people over there . . . I mean, I had food, which was the most important thing. What I needed was money to send them because I knew there were three mouths to feed over there.

Many female immigrant workers, like Angela, intent on proving their worthiness as mothers, choose to interpret exploitation as sacrifices worth making for their children in their road to gendered redemption.

Working so hard to prove that they were worthy mothers, these women subscribed to gendered expectations that set them up to accept exploitation. Employers in domestic, garment, hotel housekeeping, and other industries that hire immigrant women already function in the context of limited enforcement of labor regulations. Structurally, they run only a very minimal risk of getting caught for such violations as paying workers less than minimum wage, demanding overtime work without pay, or not providing clean, safe environments. As workers in these conditions (especially if they are undocumented or only temporarily protected), immigrant mothers are unlikely to protest. In their worldview, the sacrifices were useful in helping them signal to others that they had not fully transgressed from their roles as commendable mothers, even when they had not seen their children in years. Simultaneously, moreover, viewing their experiences through this gendered lens made their conditions bearable. Transnational mothers survived the challenges by focusing on their ability to feed and maintain their family with their earnings.[22]

Transnational fathers, too, negotiated and redefined their parenting roles from afar. Some men in the study shared stories of sacrifice and pride in maintaining gender roles by consistently sending remittances to their children. They spoke of hard work and sacrifice, though rarely in such extreme ways as women. Joaquín, for example, was very committed to his two children in El Salvador:

> It depended on how it was going for me, that's how it was going for them . . . I never sent them anything less than what I thought they absolutely needed to pay for clothes, adequate food, and I never, as far as I can remember, I never sent them less than $100. Never. When I first got here and things were difficult, I still sent $100 or $150, and then later, as I told you, as my earnings increased, they did better also.

Like Joaquín, some fathers were unwavering remitters, covering at least the bare essentials for their children. They felt secure in their ability to maintain their masculinity by providing consistently for their children, even when the sums of remittances were relatively low compared to other parents.

For some, migration and new sources of economic stability provided for the first time in their lives opportunities to fulfill their roles as providers to their children and partners. In these cases, women in El Salvador noted the shift. Sonia, whose husband, Ramón, had cheated on her numerous times and become increasingly violent before leaving to the United States on an immigrant visa, experienced a dramatic shift in him: "I was worried about that, that he was going to go and forget about us. But being over there, it's as if he changed his way of thinking, as if he really missed us, and he was really desperate to see us." It took some time for Sonia to believe that Ramón had changed, but, unlike his irresponsible behavior prior to migrating, when he only earned about $130 per month and they never had enough for food, now he was sending them $250 every month. For the first time, they had enough money to send their kids to private school after paying their bills on time. In trying to explain his transformation, Ramón said, "What happened is that here you realize what you have." Being able to provide sufficiently for his family—to noticeably improve their living conditions through his earnings—raised his own sense of masculinity and self-worth so much that he felt comfortable sending love letters, even when he had never done so before.

Such newfound economic stability similarly informed the remitting practices of other men who had dissolved ties to their children prior to migrating. Jorge and Samuel, both of whom had separated from their first wives in El Salvador and did not say goodbye to their children when they migrated, found stable jobs in Los Angeles that allowed them to fulfill their role as economic providers to those children. Jorge, in a unionized waiter position, and Samuel, as a mechanic, earned enough to provide for their new families in the United States and the children they left behind. In effect, the structural conditions in the United States helped them fulfill their aspirations to conform to a sense of masculinity that valued paternal responsibilities, even from afar. In this new context, they renegotiated their fatherhood roles to reestablish ties with children they had previously abandoned.

Because their masculinity was tied not only to their role as providers for their children, however, fathers in the study had multiple ways to establish their sense of self-worth. In this context, and unlike the more limited options for mothers, sending remittances to their children did not have to be their top priority. Milton, for example, had a job in furniture upholstery where he earned about $600 weekly. Despite the stable employment and available paths to promotion, he described his remittance practices in the following way:

> I don't have an exact date to send money, nothing on the calendar to remind me. I simply send them when there is a need. That's why I say that [my children] are good people, because they don't expect me to be sending them money for everything they want.
>
> *LA: During the past year, how much money would you say you sent?*
>
> . . . The truth is, I couldn't tell you how much I send each year. There have been years in which I did not send them anything.

Milton's relaxed attitude about the timing of his remittances suggests that remitting was not a high priority. Not internally or socially motivated to remit, he went as far as to label his children "good people" because they did not demand money from him. Presumably, this freed him up to maintain his masculinity in other ways. Indeed, in another part of the interview, he admitted to having some regrets about his decisions; "If I could, I would go back and do things differently, drink less, invest my money in a house or something." Unlike mothers who expressed a strong desire to conform to gendered expectations by sacrificing themselves, Milton spent money on leisure activities in the United States. In his case, conforming to a notion of masculinity that endorsed independence led him to unproductive spending habits. Un-burdened by expectations of self-sacrifice, several men uncritically prioritized themselves above their children. When juxtaposed against mothers' unflinch-ing commitment and consistency, immigrant fathers' gendered attitudes and behaviors were quite striking.[23]

Even in the cases where men sent consistently large sums, fathers negoti-ated their masculinity and class background in shifting ways that informed how much and how frequently they would remit. Felipe, for example, sent his family a monthly average of $1,500—the highest in the study. As a man and a recipient of TPS, he made a significant amount compared to other immi-grant parents. Because he lived in the northeastern United States, he had even more work during summer months when the weather permitted outdoor ac-tivities. During the winter he made almost $800 per week—more than double the earnings of many immigrant mothers. Of the roughly $3,000 he earned monthly, he only spent $350 on rent (because he shared expenses with three roommates), sent his family $1,500, and still kept over $1,000 for himself. Al-though $1,500 was a large sum for his family, his remitting behavior did not reflect the same kind of extreme sacrifice that mothers practiced.

Felipe was saving much of the money that was left over each month. He suspected that TPS would not last forever, and he wanted to be prepared to return to El Salvador with a large enough sum to maintain his middle-class status and start a business when the time came.[24] He had no problem admit-ting, however, that he also used some of his surplus money on drinking and entertainment. As Felipe described, "I work so much and do little else in this country. You have to have a way to break the monotony . . . I drink from Fri-day night, almost straight through Sunday afternoon. That's my routine." He never missed work due to the drinking, but he also did not feel pressured to save or send every last dollar to his children. He prioritized his own needs in a way that was not apparent in the women's narratives. Coming from a middle-class, well-educated background in El Salvador, Felipe understood that he was temporarily sacrificing his masculine and class privileges by doing service work in the United States, to eventually return to his middle-class status in El Salvador. Given his sacrifice of transgressing middle-class masculinity, he al-lowed himself indulgences that were in line with other aspects of Salvadoran masculinities—including independence to do as he pleased.[25]

Considering mothers' extreme sacrifices, it is noteworthy that not all fa-thers who earned high wages remitted large sums. Contemporary Salvadoran gender ideologies—while they restrict mothers' options to prove their worthy womanhood—include various paths to masculinity that made it acceptable for fathers to be less consistent remitters and even absent fathers.[26] When structurally blocked from hegemonic forms of masculinity, men found meaning in establishing their independence and maintaining a sense of control over their free time and their earnings.[27]

Household Compositions

Migrant mothers and fathers also varied by whom they left behind and who cared for their children.[28] The different household compositions also shaped remittance practices and children's well-being. This was most evident when parents reflected on their children's living situations and their levels of gratitude toward children's caregivers.

In a few cases, migrant mothers left children with different extended relatives or under the care of the eldest daughter but most commonly with maternal grandparents. Because migrant mothers could rarely count on the support of their children's fathers in El Salvador, in most families, nonmigrant fathers were absent from or only minimally present in their children's lives.[29] The children, therefore, were being raised by grandparents or extended families whose resources were often pushed to the limit with extra children to feed. Consequently, mother-away households had less direct parental involvement and fewer resources than their male-headed counterparts.[30] Fully cognizant of the dire situation, mothers expressed a great sense of responsibility toward their children and their children's caregivers.

Cristina, whose children resided with her widowed mother, explained the responsibility she felt toward her mother. Her thoughts reflected what many other immigrant mothers shared:

> My mom has raised them, and she's been with them through everything . . . my children have suffered being away from us also. But I think the person who's suffered the most is my mother . . . Those kids are my responsibility, not hers. I have to provide for them and for her because she is with them every day.

Still negotiating her own transnational motherhood, Cristina alleviated some of her guilt by prioritizing her children's and their caregivers' well-being. Centering their roles as mothers, in women's eyes, their transgression had required them to forgo the responsibility of being present with their children, so they were supremely grateful (and often felt guilty) for the work of caregivers.

Similarly, Esperanza described the debt she felt she owed to her mother for raising her daughter, Isabel, for the last thirteen years:

> My mother is the best mother in the world . . . I've wanted to imitate her, but I'm a long ways away, a long way . . . She fulfilled her promise to me [cumplió conmigo]. I have stayed here with nothing; I have gotten into debt, and I don't care, because it's for my mother . . . I often stop and think, who would have taken care of my daughter the way my mother has?

Transnational mothers understood caregivers to be meeting responsibilities that they had not been able to fulfill in person. To make up for their own absences and out of deep gratitude to caregivers, they made sacrifices in the name of their children and the caregivers' economic well-being.

There was little variation of household composition among father-away families. In a few cases, the men left their children with paternal grandparents once the marital relationship had dissolved. However, most migrant fathers left their children with the children's mothers, in what was initially an intact marital relationship. Drawing on traditional gender ideologies, men expressed great satisfaction in knowing that the children were with their mothers and therefore presumably in the best care possible. Felipe exemplified this attitude. He strongly believed that "the most natural thing, right, is for the mother to be with her children. . . . That's why my children are with my wife, and that is the best way to do it."

Similarly, Joaquín, who had left his children with their mother twenty-two years earlier, said that, in general, children were best off when they resided with their mother: "Well, think about it. Who is the best person to care for children? Their mother, of course. Even though I left, they stayed with the person who took care of them every day, so I always knew that my leaving would not affect them." Revealing the deep-seated gender ideologies that place most daily caregiving responsibilities on mothers, Felipe and Joaquín provide some insight into the social pressures that make transnational mothers feel guilty while absolving transnational fathers of the very same guilt. As a result, fathers felt less pressure than mothers to remit consistently.

Families with Two Migrant Parents

Many of the same patterns and gendered justifications were evident among families in which both parents migrated. Children's narratives confirmed that when couples had dissolved and parents lived in different U.S. cities, mothers were more reliable remitters than fathers. And even when they still resided together, mothers set forth greater efforts to remit than fathers. Luisa and Rafael, for example, lived together in Los Angeles. They worked to support their daughter, who lived in El Salvador first with Luisa's mother and, after her passing, with Rafael's mother. To pool their resources, they took turns sending money every month, but both admitted that Luisa sent larger sums and more enthusiastically than Rafael. Luisa, following the logic that she had forfeited her most important daily responsibilities, felt that "every penny is worth it because they [her in-laws] are doing the work that I should be doing." Rafael, on the other hand, was hesitant to send more than was absolutely necessary for his daughter because he worried that his mother and younger siblings would misspend the money. He felt strongly that "I didn't come here to sacrifice for my brothers. Let them go out and work for themselves. My only responsibility is my daughter."

Luisa and Rafael disagreed heavily about how much and who should benefit from the remittances produced by their hard work in the United States. From Luisa's perspective:

I have sent as much as $500, and I never asked my mother-in-law how she spent it because I am grateful that she cares for my little girl. For me, that is very special. Even if I don't save any money, but if they are well over there, look, I will work for that money here, and they will enjoy it over there, and that makes me happy. That is how I am . . . She is a mother, too, and if she wants to use that money to give to her children, then she can do that. I give her that money with all my heart.

Even when Luisa knew it was likely that some of her remittances would help more than just her daughter, she preferred to signal her own sacrifices as a mother and allow her mother-in-law to fulfill the full motherhood role. Meanwhile, Rafael was very critical of Luisa's approach. At times, he felt resentful that so many people wanted to benefit from his work:

They are always asking for money, only money, everything is money. And who am I going to ask for money? . . . It's all the time. They want $100: "Can you send me $100 for my stepdaughter's graduation?" Let them try to find a job and earn that money. I already sent the $200. The $200 is enough.

In Rafael's mind, he is meeting his responsibilities as a father by sending $200 monthly. Beyond the role of economic provider to his daughter, he is uninterested in providing for others.

These gendered attitudes were equally true for Cristina and Cirilo. In separate interviews, they voiced their sentiments on the matter. As a couple, they pooled their resources together but divided their responsibilities: Cirilo was in charge of paying the mortgage and all bills, while Cristina sent remittances and paid for groceries. Cirilo's understanding was that the couple sent $500 monthly—and even this, he felt, was too large a sum for his children's needs. Whatever was left, they placed in a savings account. Cristina, however, admitted that she kept Cirilo in the dark about the number of hours she worked overtime and the true sum of monthly remittances she sent:

> That has been constant . . . I send $600 each month for my children, and, separate from that, I try to send my mother another $100 or whatever she might need for emergencies—sometimes $200. For example, a few months ago, there was construction on the house, so I had to send $1,000. And that's how it goes.

Cirilo had no idea that Cristina was sending $200 to $300 extra each month, and she kept it a secret because she knew he would not approve. Instead, she made it a point to work one extra day per week for the supplementary earnings that she sent immediately after being paid.

New Relationships

Mothers' and fathers' remitting practices also differed in another notable way: When parents began new relationships abroad or in El Salvador, father-away families tended to suffer, while mother-away families benefited economically. Immigrant mothers were consistent remitters, regardless of their own or their ex-partners' relationship status. Immigrant men, however, tended to decrease or discontinue remittances due to their own or their ex-partners' new relationships.

Certainly some fathers continued to remit despite starting new families. Samuel, for example, remitted to his daughter in El Salvador consistently for two decades despite beginning a new family in Los Angeles. When he married, the remittances continued: "My wife also worked, and she knew from the beginning that I was going to be supporting my daughter and filing for her papers, and she accepted that." He was honest and upfront about his responsibilities, and his partner accepted his priorities. Unfortunately, Samuel's example was uncommon among the people I interviewed.

In total, seventeen father-away families in the study shared a pattern confirming one of the common discourses in El Salvador about transnational families: Fathers migrate and forget about their wives and children when they begin new relationships in the United States.[31] Some of these families were headed by migrant fathers who, when they left, had intact marriages but, soon after migrating, started new families in the United States. Although the mere act of starting a new family did not guarantee an end to remittances,[32] participants claimed it was very difficult to maintain two families—one in the United States and one in El Salvador—and therefore had to curb their remittances. Nelson, an immigrant father who had been living in the United States for sixteen years, sent his children money only for emergencies. When I asked about how much money he generally remitted, he explained:

> [A]t first I would send them money often. I would try to send $100, $200 a month . . . Later on, that's when I met my wife, the one here. And since we became a formal couple, well, one has to see what one can do to avoid causing any problems between the couple. And besides, my children's mom in El Salvador found herself another man soon after that, so I didn't worry anymore because she also had someone to help them.

Having constituted a new family in the United States, Nelson's efforts to keep his new family intact included diminishing most forms of contact with his children in El Salvador. Not only was it difficult to maintain two households on his low income, but a new partner's jealousy added another barrier. His current wife, who was probably trying to guarantee her own family's survival in the United States, opposed the idea of him providing for his ex-wife. Despite the overall social distancing between Nelson and his family in El Salvador, like other fathers, he still sent remittances to his children during crises and emergencies.

Other immigrant fathers stopped remitting to their children when their partners in El Salvador began (or were rumored to begin) new relationships. These immigrant men said they were uncomfortable sending money to a household that now included another male. For example, Jorge, a business owner, admitted that his two daughters in El Salvador grew up in terribly poor conditions. He justified his decision to stop remitting by citing the gossip that his ex-partner had become promiscuous in his absence:

> What is the point of maintaining a family where the woman is providing such bad examples to the daughters? My parents-in-law, I told them to let me know if they ever needed anything, but, aside from that, I was not going to be supporting the woman so that she could go around doing crazy things with other men.

Unlike mothers who stopped remitting only when they simply could not afford to, Jorge and others like him felt justified in basing their remittance behavior on what they perceived as their ex-partner's moral character. In Jorge's mind, as in the minds of other immigrant men, a woman who did not adhere to gendered moral expectations—an unworthy mother—did not merit economic support. Gender ideologies, therefore, informed and justified their decision to distance themselves from their children.

Other fathers also cited their wives' improper behavior (or, in some cases, the *potential* for improper behavior) to justify either a decision to stop remitting or a decision to move the children to the paternal grandparents' home to avoid the possibility of supporting their ex-wife's new partner. As Edgar described:

> She [the mother of my children in El Salvador] heard that I had moved in with another woman here, and she was not happy. So her next step was going to be to find herself another man. Before that happened, because I didn't come here to be sending money to her new partner, I gave my kids the option of coming to be with me here. We could all work and live here with my new partner. But only the two oldest boys came, so they benefited. But I wasn't going to be sending the others money because they were with their mother, and who knows who else was living with them. So the other five kids, I sent them money when they asked me for it, and that's it.

In these cases, immigrant fathers cut ties not only with their former partners, but with the children they shared as well. Guided by notions of masculinity that prohibited providing for other men or for unfaithful women, their partners' (potential) new relationships were more morally reprehensible than their own lack of support for their children. Notably, these justifications also reinforced idealized notions of motherhood when men's behavior undermined women who (potentially) transgressed all traditional gendered norms.

Mothers, on the other hand, continued to remit to children regardless of their partner's or their own relationship status. In line with the idealized notions of motherhood, mothers continued to prioritize their children even after joining new partners. Mothers explained that new relationships allowed them to increase monthly sums to their children because they could share household expenses with new partners. As one mother, Juana, explained:

> Because both of us work, we split the expenses, and I am able to send my daughters more money now. The money that I used to spend on rent and bills,

that's only half now, because my husband pays the rent every month. That leaves me with a lot of money, and I'm happy that it can go to my daughters.

In fact, immigrant mothers in the study created stable partnerships in the United States only with men who would help them support their children. Both Zuleyma and Gloria, for example, began new partnerships after migrating. In each case, they first made it clear to their new partners that their children's well-being was their top priority. Gloria described, "I told him, before we moved in together, that I had to save at least $300 a month for my kids. I wasn't going to hide that because that is always going to be the same."

A couple of women went so far as to admit that their new partnerships were a strategy to save and remit more money to their children, even if they had to put up with physical and emotional abuse from their new partners. Marina said, "Well, he's not a bad man, and I would say that I've come to care for him, but, in the beginning, to be honest with you, I just wanted to move in with him because he could pay for the rent, and that way I could send my sons more money." Sometimes, however, these decisions proved to be harmful. Juana, for example, accepted a violent relationship in the name of economic stability for her family in El Salvador:

> Look, I'm embarrassed to admit it, but as a mother, you come here, and you know that there are mouths that are waiting to be fed with the money that you make, so you do what you have to do to send them money. I can at least say that I never did prostitution or stripping, but aside from that, I've done it all.
>
> LA: *Among the sacrifices you've made here, what would you say has been the most difficult?*
>
> [long silence] The worst part was that I stayed in a relationship for six years with a man who used to hit me. The problem was that he was an alcoholic, and when he was drunk, he was one of those people who was a violent drunk; he had a terrible temper. [silence] I stayed because at least he would pay rent and most of the bills. That was the only way I could have enough to send to my daughters. Otherwise, my whole family would go hungry over there. They were counting on me.

In a distanced tone, Juana recalled that when multiple jobs in different industries were not enough to provide for her daughters, she also endured physical violence from her partner for six years. In her retelling of her experiences and decisions, being a victim of domestic violence was more acceptable and in line with traditional gender norms than earning money as a sex worker. Violence, therefore, became a tolerable sacrifice she willingly made for her family's economic well-being; under those circumstances, the drive to fulfill her motherhood role made a six-year violent relationship acceptable: "That was the only way I could have enough to send to my daughters."

Like Juana, mothers did not try to negotiate away their parental responsibilities, even when they began new unions and regardless of their relationship with their children's father. Interestingly, Juana was also one of the few women in the study who migrated with her relationship intact. Her husband at the time—the father of her daughters—actively encouraged her to migrate because she had siblings already living in Los Angeles. Their plan was that she would work and return after a couple of years, but, within a year of her migration, he had started a new relationship with the nanny. In stark contrast to the men's behaviors, however, even when her husband fathered a child out of wedlock and moved his new partner into the house, Juana continued to remit to that household. She explained her thinking on the matter: "They were not doing well, and he was, after all, the father of my daughters . . . I was angry, yes, but my daughters would tell me that they barely had enough for the baby's food, so I started sending a little more for them too." Unlike fathers, then, immigrant mothers (whether they strategized about it or not) *increased* remittances when they formed new unions. Regardless of the circumstances or of their partners' behavior, they did not negotiate away their own parental duties.

Economically, families relying on migrant mothers were faring well more often than families relying on fathers. Despite wide inequalities in pay, women bypassed their economic disadvantages by sacrificing greatly in the name of their children's well-being. Acting selflessly to make up for their transgressions, they remitted large percentages of their earnings more consistently and over a longer period of time than many immigrant fathers. With more options to maintain their sense of masculinity and self-worth, fathers felt less pressured to prioritize their children's needs as consistently as mothers. Financially, children reaped the rewards in the form of concrete improvements in their lives when they relied on mothers, or they saw little improvement over the long run when relying on fathers.

Emotional Well-Being

The gendered patterns of economic well-being played out in uneven and sometimes contradictory ways for children's emotional well-being in El

Salvador. Even when families fared well financially, a mother's absence caused greater emotional distress than a father's absence. Children of migrant mothers always emphasized their unhappiness with the separation, regardless of how they were faring economically. And although all children of migrants expressed great sorrow resulting from their family's separation, the narratives revealed patterns of more emotional language and greater suffering for children whose mother, as opposed to father, migrated.

The children's emotional experiences were heavily contextualized by cultural practices and traditions that reinforced idealized notions of masculinity and femininity. Society and daily household practices cyclically and frequently reminded them of their mother's absence. Children repeatedly spoke of cultural festivities—such as Mother's Day, Christmas, and New Year's[33]—and the daily contact and care work that centrally involved mothers to reinforce the notion that a mother's love is unique. Both boys and girls, for example, made reference to the time lost and particularly to the uniqueness of a mother's love. More than one also described feeling as if they had a hole in their heart due to their mothers' absence. In this way, they were always enveloped by a sense of longing.

Mothers in El Salvador, as in many cultures, were expected to be caring and present on a daily basis.[34] It was in remembering these details about the daily things they missed about their mothers that children were especially prone to choke up or cry. In fifteen-year-old Nadia's case, for example, both her parents had migrated. Her living conditions had improved with her parents' remittances, but Nadia's demeanor reflected a deep sadness. When I asked her to explain her feelings to me, even though both her parents were gone, she focused on the pain resulting from her mother's absence:

> They left when I was twelve, so I was in the most difficult stage because, I mean, you're so close, too close. Plus my mother was very caring. I would fall asleep with her, she always rubbed my head, the way I liked to be rubbed. When I'd wake up, she was caressing my face, and I miss all that.

Similarly, 15-year-old Fabián recalled the details that made him miss his mother most often. Though his mother had been gone for five years, he still cherished his memories of her, especially when she cared for him individually: "I almost always carry that inside me, right? But it affects me the most when I get sick because she's the one who used to care for me. She would make me soups or she would cook for me, so that I could feel better. Nobody else does that. Not like her." On the verge of tears, he recalled that, although the pain of her absence was always present with him, those details of her individual acts of care were especially painful. From that point on, he could no longer look me in the eye during the interview.

Children were especially pained when mothers remitted insufficiently. Fifteen-year-old Catalina, for example, recalled the many times she wished her mother could be by her side:

> I always think about the times that I needed her. Every Mother's Day and Christmas, you're supposed to be with your family, and I don't even have one memory of that with her. And I know that some kids get excited when [their parents] tell them that they're leaving. The kids think, "Yeah! Now I'm going to get everything I want!" But look at me. I don't have anything; I barely have enough to pay for transportation to come to school, and some days I can't come because I just don't have money for the bus fare. *And* I don't have my mother.

Her mother's prolonged absence from key cultural celebrations only heightened the pain of her financial problems adding to her sense of abandonment.

Even when they were thriving economically, children in mother-away families were often distressed about their mother's absence. Twenty-one-year-old Xiomara, for example, used remittances from her mother to attend and graduate from an expensive private high school. She was a college student when I met her. Although she was a confident young woman, she could not hide that she missed her mother terribly. She recognized that her mother's remittances had vastly improved her life but also insisted, "The only thing is my mother's companionship. That's something that no one can replace. It's unique." Although she kept busy with school and part-time work, she often broke down and cried unexpectedly at the deep sense of loss she felt since her mother's migration. For Xiomara, as for many other children of migrants, the financial advantages of receiving remittances did not make up for the emotional void of living without her mother.

Twenty-four-year-old Sofia was similarly pained by her mother's absence, despite her new economic stability. The monthly sums allowed her to attend a private university, and she relished all her new privileges, but when I asked Sofia whether the family separation was worth it, she said:

I can have all the money and the degrees in the world, and, yes, life is much better than before. My mother sacrificed everything for us, and we talk on the phone often. I don't want to sound ungrateful, but you do live with a hole in your heart. Nobody can replace those years that she didn't take care of us . . . A mother's love is unique, and we didn't have it.

LA: *What kinds of things are most difficult?*

It's been difficult not having her here because she used to take care of me when I was sick, and she used to do more of the work around the house. Since she's left, the times that I've been sick, no one has looked after me, and I have to figure out how to get better and still take care of the house . . . The economic help is the only advantage to having her over there.

Although she wanted to underscore her gratitude toward her mother—"I don't want to sound ungrateful"—and she made the connection between her mothers' sacrifices and her own educational success explicit—"Life is much better than before"—Sofia nonetheless emphasized the emotional hardships of her mother's absence. Economically, the separation had been an "advantage," but, like other children who miss their mothers, Sofia employed vivid imagery, "a hole in your heart," to express the pain of separation.

Transnational mothers certainly felt the consequences of these gendered expectations—to the extent that their situation could lead to clinical depression.[35] In many cases, in their pain, children exacerbated their mothers' intense suffering by purposely hurting them with their words. This was the case of Lydia, a mother of three, who worked tirelessly as a garment worker in Los Angeles to provide for her children. Despite her many sacrifices, they grew up resenting her:

I would call them on the phone and not understand why they had so much anger toward me. The boy, he wouldn't ask, he *demanded* that I send him money. . . . He tells me that he looks forward to the day, because he has all those emotions, he just waits for the day to come and tell me in my face, to create a war against me, so that I can feel all the pain he felt when I left . . .

LA: *Does he feel the same way toward his father?*

No . . . his response is that the man can do as he pleases, but the woman can't . . . He still says that it would have been better for me to be there and to eat rice and beans, but to have someone there. But the resentment is only toward me, not his father.

Lydia's eighteen-year-old suffered through the absence of both parents but directed his anger and resentment mainly toward his mother, with the gendered justification that "the man can do as he pleases." In a society that demands so much from mothers, children felt justified in being more hurt about or, in this case, more angry at mothers who migrated. Fathers, on the other hand, can "do as they please," and this attitude helps explain why so many children were better at coping with a father's absence.

Indeed, emotions were less intense in the narratives of children whose fathers migrated. Although no child expressed happiness at his or her parent's absence, those relying on fathers generally seemed to be coping better. These children implicitly accepted gender ideologies that deemed fathers as economic providers but also just regular men who had the prerogative to do as they pleased. After all, they lived in a society with high rates of mother-headed households where it was relatively common to grow up with an absent father—whether through migration or neglect. As a result, these children tended to sidestep the emotional repercussions of a father's absence to instead focus on economic conditions—whether these were positive or negative.

Focusing on their economic conditions was easiest when families were faring well financially with fathers' remittances. This was the case for María Elena. In thinking about her father's absence, she stated, "Economically, I can't complain because I'm very conscious that if he went, it was in search of a better life for us." She understood his reason for migration and benefited economically from his work. So, while she certainly missed him dearly, unlike children in mother-away families she seemed less consumed by her father's physical absence because he was still being a good father in living up to his expectations as a provider. Similarly, sixteen-year-old Iván responded in a neutral tone that he understood the need for his father's migration and, although he missed him, "The sacrifice that he has made for us is very much appreciated." He understood that the absence, while labeled a sacrifice, was also the reason for his and his sister's privileged educational opportunities. In cases like Iván's, when children's lives had improved significantly with their fathers' remittances, they could more easily interpret the separation as a successful financial strategy. And, unlike children missing their mothers, those relying on fathers justified the separation and looked past their emotions to instead focus on the benefits of this arrangement.

Children had a harder time emotionally when fathers did not provide for them economically. But, again, they were not consumed by their fathers' absence in the same ways as children missing their mothers. Seventeen-year-old Tanya, for example, said about her father's migration that "it has definitely not been worth it. He never gave us the life that we deserve, that he promised. I always tell him that I would have preferred that he were here; he would have seen me grow up, and he could have fought to maintain the relationship with my mother." After explaining how tired her ill-stricken mother was from working hard, Tanya said she regretted having an absent father:

> Let me give you an example; Okay, during Christmas and New Years, when all the kids spend time with their fathers, whom am I going to spend time with? I only have my mother. A mother's love is unique; it is really unique, but a father's love is also important from time to time . . . But I'm grateful that I have her here. It would be more difficult if she weren't here.

Tanya missed her father and noticed his absence, particularly during holidays, just as others missed their mothers. Interestingly, though, in her description of how she missed him, she quickly turned back to the notion that a mother's love is actually "unique" and that, in the end, it was preferable to have her mother by her side.

Whether they were doing well economically or not, children talked in ways that suggest they had learned to cope with being separated from fathers. For example, in many cases, when the family was barely subsisting, children pointed to the lack of remittances as a reason to distance themselves. In one such case, Sandra described the relationship she and her brother had with their migrant father, Milton, who (even by his own admission) only rarely sent remittances:

> We would talk to him, ask him for things, and he would agree to everything. And then we never saw anything of it. So it was uncomfortable to be in that position, and you end up opting to not know anything about him instead and just not call him. Of course you always want to know something, at least know if he's still alive, but I opted not to call him anymore. And now, I don't care if he calls or not. He didn't care about us.

When fathers, like Milton, were not consistent remitters, when they promised money and gifts but failed to send anything, children experienced this as proof that their fathers were no longer committed to them. Unlike children missing their mothers, however, these children were able to develop narratives, informed by traditional gender ideologies, that allowed them to cope with their fathers' absence and failure as providers. I am not arguing that children of migrant fathers did not also experience great pain; rather, the pattern in the narratives suggests that society signaled to these children that they need not be as consumed by the pain of family separation when it was their father who was absent.

Conclusion

For parents in transnational families, remittances to their children are a central responsibility.[36] After all, they represent the economic goal that most often fueled their migration and family separation. But the results are rather uneven, and the economic inequalities of transnational families play out powerfully along gendered lines. This chapter reveals that immigrant parents in transnational families act within the context of macroeconomic structures while negotiating and abiding by societal expectations. Even though both mothers and fathers migrated with the same hope and intentions—to improve the living conditions of their children—once in the United States, they faced the structural reality of gender-stratified opportunities and persistent gender ideologies that harmed them in multiple ways.

Immigrant mothers were much more vulnerable to blocked mobility than immigrant fathers, yet they were more reliable remitters. Having transgressed the part of their traditional motherhood role that required their physical presence next to their children, they were especially committed to fulfilling the rest of their parental responsibilities by remitting consistently over many years, regardless of their relationship status. In the process of conforming to their working-class motherhood roles, these women accepted labor exploitation and domestic violence because they understood these to be necessary sacrifices that would prove their worthiness as mothers despite their physical and prolonged distance from their children. Fathers, on the other hand, had multiple ways to achieve a sense of self-worth and masculinity. While many took advantage of their higher earnings to fulfill the role as economic providers, others also sacrificed less and were more likely to remit inconsistently. Fathers relied on the presumed higher morality of mothers and acted on the assumption that they could afford to be more lenient in defining their parental responsibilities, having already established their masculinity through virility or continuing to seek it through independence.

Social expectations and images of motherhood and fatherhood so deeply informed mothers' and fathers' remitting practices that when I shared with a few respondents the patterns I found, none seemed surprised. As Graciela, a college-educated mother, expressed, there is a common assumption in Salvadoran society that mothers and fathers behave differently. She provided the following analysis for the divergent parental behavior:

> It's a contradiction. The topic of motherhood is like a thorn [among Salvadorans]. A woman has worth when she is a mother; otherwise she is not valued as a woman. But, in the end, the woman is alone. No one is with her if she is a single mother. Because the men, they *choose* whether they want to be responsible as fathers, while we, because of our biological nature, I don't know, we keep our responsibilities—here and there.

Graciela's analysis reinforces and naturalizes gendered parental behaviors. Like her, many Salvadorans come to believe that gendered parental behaviors are normal.[37] The social act of remitting, therefore, takes place under these social expectations; real women are good mothers and good mothers are to do almost anything to care (and provide) for their children, while fathers who fail as providers and caregivers have other ways—including virility, sexual prowess, and independence—to perform and maintain their sense of masculinity. In this way, the possibilities for transforming gender ideologies in transnational spaces seem to dissipate when women are cumulatively disadvantaged in the labor market, as well as by gendered structures and expectations.[38]

This very same social context then shapes children's experiences so that they tend to be more lenient and emotionally distant from fathers whether or not they receive remittances, while they suffer more when separated from their mothers, regardless of economic circumstances. In these ways, gender, in its various structural, cultural, and social forms, powerfully determines inequalities and uneven experiences of well-being for transnational families.

6 How Children Fare

GIVEN THE FAR-REACHING CONSEQUENCES OF (il)legality and gendered disparities, how do children of migrants in El Salvador experience family separation? Scholars and policy analysts there need to continue seeking answers to this question. To date, much of the emphasis has been on the economic aspects of migration, particularly surrounding national remittance sums and yearly flows.[1] This is arguably with good reason. With a full 28 percent of "the adult population report[ing] that they personally received remittances from a family member living abroad,"[2] El Salvador has one of the highest rates of remittance reception and family separation in the region.[3] So researchers speculate on labor market participation and economic investment rates; they watch the figures closely and look for patterns from year to year. This is certainly important because it reveals the overall economic survival of the country, but the national-level figures tell only part of the story—one that misses the microsocial realities of family separation. This chapter examines more systematically what these figures mean to children in El Salvador.

Because transnational families are common in El Salvador and among Salvadorans in the United States, everyone believes that he or she already knows what family separation and remittances mean for the children and the country. Based primarily on dominant public discourses and the most visible examples of transnational families, three prevailing assumptions inform Salvadorans' understanding of family separation through migration—none of which considers the legal and gendered disparities shaping inequalities. People fortunate enough to have avoided long-term separation are often quick to judge. Most common is the discourse that "those kids are ruining it for everyone else" because they receive money from their parents abroad and spend it irresponsibly on unnecessary luxury items such as clothes, shoes, electronic gadgets, and entertainment. This behavior, many believe, drives up market prices and harms other consumers. The second discourse addresses issues of parenting from a distance: "Those are the kids who join gangs in El Salvador because they feel abandoned," because their parents cannot keep a close eye on them from abroad, and their grandparents are too old to be effective disciplinarians. As gangs and organized crime continue to proliferate in the country, this discourse shortsightedly blames transnational families for this national crisis. And the third prevailing public discourse maintains that migrant fathers "say they're leaving for their kids, but as soon as they step on U.S. soil, they forget that they ever had a family." In these cases, people discuss how fathers abroad are quick to start other families in the United States.[4]

Although these assumptions certainly capture a few of the possible experiences for transnational families, they exclude a wide range of complexities. In fact, a closer look quickly reveals that the parents' and children's experiences are often in direct conflict with the prevailing public discourses. I spoke to children of migrants in different places and across a broad range of schools. Unsurprisingly, given the consequences of illegality and gendered disparities among migrant parents, I found stark inequalities in children's well-being. Students in public schools in very poor neighborhoods shared stories of dire poverty, while students in private schools in wealthier sectors of the city clearly had more resources. In this broad spectrum, there was much variation of experiences, but a few patterns emerged. This chapter lays out the categories that were especially meaningful in capturing the children's lived experiences since their parents' migration. In the first section, I focus on their economic well-being as shaped primarily by their parents' remittances. Toward the end of the chapter, I shift gears a bit to describe another important aspect of being apart from their parents—their varied experiences of emotional well-being resulting from long-term separation.

Children's Economic Well-Being

Based on the parents' narratives of migration in search of better access to food and schooling for their children, I developed three categories to describe the general patterns of children's economic well-being: (a) barely subsisting, (b) surviving, and (c) thriving.[5] Because remittances could vary greatly from month to month and year to year, rather than focusing only on sums and consistency of remittances, I found it more useful to highlight children's access to food and schooling. As I will detail in this chapter, children whose families are "barely subsisting" are unable to eat or attend school regularly. Toward the middle of this spectrum, children whose families are "surviving" can usually cover basic household necessities and attend school but have no surplus money for other expenses. Finally, on the far end of the spectrum, children whose families are "thriving" often attend private school, easily cover household expenses, and have enough money for savings, investment, or luxury items.

Importantly, these categories are fluid, and some of the people I interviewed described economic situations that matched different categories at different times—particularly as migrant parents lost or changed jobs or started new relationships. For analytical purposes, the categories reflect the patterns as the children of migrants described them at the time of the interview. I use them here because, despite their potential for fluidity, they often represent persistent economic experiences for the children, and they help me make comparisons that reveal indisputable economic inequalities across transnational families. To complement their words, I also took note of clues about economic well-being in the places where I interviewed them and indications about emotional well-being in their gestures and internal logic of their stories. In ten cases, moreover, I was able to interview parents and children in the same families, and in all cases—including children who were thriving and those who were barely subsisting—their accounts of the family's economic and emotional well-being experiences were consistent.

Barely Subsisting: Deprived of Food, Schooling, and Health

Out of 130 participants, twenty, or roughly 15 percent, described conditions of subsistence for family members in El Salvador in spite of, or in some cases because of, their family's migration strategy. Nationally in El Salvador, 10 percent of children and adolescents with migrant parents do not receive remittances.[6] Another 26 percent of households that receive remittances are similarly living below the poverty line.[7] Although the figures in this study do not match representative national statistics, the personal narratives illuminate the experiences of these most destitute families.[8]

In 2004, when I conducted many of the interviews for this project, it was estimated that the *canasta básica*, or the minimum food and household items required for a family over a one-month period, in urban areas of El Salvador was equivalent to $129.50.[9] Families who did not meet these standards struggled to buy food and may not have eaten regularly, or they faced difficult decisions that often included keeping children home from school.

Public schooling is compulsory in El Salvador. Up until the ninth grade, Salvadoran children are legally required to attend free public schools; from the tenth grade on, students also pay a nominal fee to attend *bachillerato* (the equivalent of high school). But very poor families face considerable barriers to education. Throughout the country, and much as in other developing countries around the world, families aspiring to send their children to school simply cannot afford the required uniforms, shoes, and school supplies every year.[10] Moreover, when children live too far away from the nearest school to walk, attendance also involves paying for daily transportation. For families that are barely subsisting, this all adds up to make continuous schooling or solid nutrition prohibitive.

Although families receiving remittances typically have greater access to education than families who do not count on these monies,[11] not all transnational families benefit equally. In particular, access to education is greatly limited for children whose families are barely subsisting. Choosing to buy food, instead, many parents are forced to remove children from school or let them attend only inconsistently. In many of these cases, children also exit school or skip for extended periods of time while they work to help support their families. In fact, I came across many youths who had fallen several grades behind, eventually dropping out due to shame of being older students still completing elementary school.

In this context, I classified families as "barely subsisting" based on two key measures: (1) children did not consistently have enough money to cover all meals, or (2) they could not afford to attend school regularly. All of the youth in this category were notably thin and possibly malnourished; they faced various challenges in trying to remain and thrive in school. This was certainly the case for Ana, whose father was an injured undocumented worker in Los Angeles.[12] At the age of twenty-four, she was still finishing up the last year of high school. Previously, she had been forced to exit school for several years when her family could not afford to send her. She described how she was budgeting her money to allot enough for school-related expenses by limiting her food intake:

I do limit myself. I have to be careful because otherwise I will end up without enough money to go to school, because I have to spend one dollar daily on transportation and everything. So with food, sometimes I try to just have three pupusas for the day, because bus fare is 35 cents each way.[13]

For Ana, as for the other young people in El Salvador who were barely subsisting, food that would typically constitute one meal had to be spread out throughout the day. She made this sacrifice because, at her age, she wanted desperately to finish high school.

Another high school student, Francisco, also depended on limited remittances from an injured undocumented father. Francisco attended school regularly despite being a member of a family that was barely subsisting. He described the strategy that his mother practiced for feeding him and his sister on a regular basis, even with minimal resources:

> With food, well, yes, you could say that we do have food. Even if it's only beans every day, all three meals, you know, but we do have food. Sometimes we can only eat in the morning and at night, but you can say that we do have food.
>
> *LA: How often do you have meat?*
>
> Meat? No, it's very rare. That's a whole other thing, you could say, maybe for one of our birthdays. That's how it is.

Among the sacrifices Francisco's family made to ensure regular school attendance for him and his sister, they refrained from a variety of foods and subsisted on two to three meals per day of beans—one of the most affordable and filling staples in the Salvadoran diet. Similarly, Daniel's family had to subsist on tortillas and *curtido*, a pickled cabbage salad usually used to garnish pupusas and other main dishes.

The levels of scarcity varied across families that were barely subsisting. In the case of sixteen-year-old Tanya, for example, the situation was so terrible that she had stayed out of school for two years when I met her. She had reentered that year to finish up the ninth grade, but she knew that this would be the last year she could afford to attend:

> It's just not enough. We don't have enough to cover our expenses . . . We pay for electricity, and we, well, we pay for the land [on which her home lies], but we are behind with the monthly payments. We haven't paid those in over

two years because we just don't have enough. And the situation is only getting worse . . . This is the last year I can go to school because high school, I
mean, the expense is greater, and my mom has two younger daughters still
in school.

Tanya's father was never present in her life; he had sent remittances only
on rare occasions, and now her family's financial circumstances were so restricted that she had to forgo further schooling just to be able to cover elementary school expenses for her two younger sisters, ages seven and ten. In this
bleak situation, the family's aspirations were forcibly limited to free public
schooling only through the ninth grade for each of the children.

Along with malnutrition and great stress, families who were barely subsisting also experienced greater frequency and severity of illness that further
exacerbated their difficult situations. Children and caregivers in these families suffered from malignant tumors, loss of eyesight, epilepsy, and general
symptoms of weakness.[14] It is likely that because these families lived in poor
sectors of El Salvador where public services, including trash collection, elec-
tricity, and running water, were unreliable, the unsanitary living conditions
coupled with poor nutrition lent themselves to greater incidence of sickness.
With limited access to medical services, the situation could quickly become
dire. Tanya, for example, cried most forcefully when discussing her mother's
illness:

> I just want to be able to help my mother because, I mean, the main thing is
> that she's sick. She gets constant headaches, her hands hurt so much that she
> can't sleep from the pain, and what we are thinking is that she might have
> cancer. Or whatever she has, it's serious. And what's more, she's tired. She's
> tired from helping us so much, from working so much.
>
> *LA: Can she get medical care?*
>
> Well, the thing is that you need referrals to get into the health units for these
> things. She can't stop working to go spend the day, several days, to be seen.
> Then we wouldn't eat.

Access to free or affordable health care is so restricted and the process so
bureaucratic that patients would have to spend one or multiple days waiting to
be seen by specialists. Poor people like Tanya's mother cannot afford to miss
a day or more of work, so they neglect their health over prolonged periods of
time. This is just one more way in which poverty, hunger, blocked opportuni-

ties, and family illnesses are all severely taxing for young people who faced structural barriers at every turn.

The various stressors inevitably affect young people's chances of success in El Salvador. Daniel's situation, for example, poignantly captured how all of these challenges—many initiated through his father's experiences of illegality as he traveled to and lived in the United States—intertwined and multiplied in his life to block him from thriving:

> Look, I have worked as a baker, as an assistant, I've worked as a packer . . . since before my father left [because we were all trying to contribute so that he wouldn't have to migrate], and even now, I was working as a baker's apprentice. But I wasn't able to keep working. . . . I couldn't; it was so much stress to turn in homework, it was stressful to study. . . . The problem is that, what is difficult for me, and I still can't adapt, is that I was not like this. I mean, I'm shocked, and so were [my classmates] because prior to that, I never got below a 9 or a 10.[15] But the problem was that I began to miss school and to fail. And it's because sometimes I have no energy to study because I have so many problems, so I became neglectful. Since last year I've had this problem of low grades, because of so many things, not just the problems, but it's that sometimes I start to think about how I'm going to pay for my schooling because there were times when it was my responsibility; sometimes, with the little bit that I earned as a baker's apprentice, that's what I used to go to school, with 50 cents, with 75 cents. I didn't ask [my parents] for much [so as not to stress them out more] . . . The truth is, you can't live like this.

As I witnessed young Daniel reveal the intensely stressful details of his life, his testimony spoke powerfully against the common misconceptions about the financial excesses of transnational families. His father, who suffered grave injuries and indignities on the road to and within the United States, had not been able to live up to the family's high hopes—not because he was irresponsible but because of the consequences of illegality while en route and in the United States. Instead, Daniel and his family fell deeper into debt, and they saw their access to food diminish along with their energy and ability to thrive as students. It was often too much to handle for the young man:

> It has been three or four months that [my father] hasn't worked. He wants to send us money, he used to send us whatever he could, but he only sends letters now . . . It's just been such bad luck . . . Look, there are days—that's why I'm

going to church now—because there are days when I just want to climb up to the roof and I want to hang myself . . . Because when I see so much that is happening to us, the situation is really terrible. I just start to think, I say, man, if they take the house, what's going to happen? What will happen if we have to live on the streets? It's really terrible. That is my fear, losing everything we have. I wouldn't wish for anyone to be in my situation.

Despite his father's best attempts, the lack of consistent remittances was a heavy economic and emotional burden that put Daniel's life at risk.

For families that were barely subsisting, the expectations of greater access to schooling and other resources did not pan out. Despite migrant parents' hopes when they initiated their migration journeys, the consequences of illegality and of gendered inequalities—as they played out differently for undocumented mothers and fathers—prevented them from fulfilling their promises of remitting to their families consistently. Contrary to one of the most common popular assumptions about transnational families—that they receive exorbitant sums of money and waste them carelessly on luxury items of consumption—families that are barely subsisting prove this to be untrue among a notable sector. And when migrant parents do not live up to their families' financial expectations, it is not always merely because they opted to forget their children.

Surviving: Just Enough for Food and Schooling

Twenty-nine-year-old Sonia recalled her mother leaving at the break of dawn one day, when Sonia was only eight. She remembered crying with her older sister and two younger siblings because they wanted so desperately to go with their mother. Their grandparents, who now cared for them, reiterated over and over that this was a necessary sacrifice for the family; her younger twin siblings had been born with an illness that prevented the proper development of their hands and feet, and without the support of their father, who had disappeared years before, migration was their mother's only chance at earning the money to pay for their surgeries while also feeding the other children. Despite her mother's migration as a strategy of survival, twenty-one years later only one of Sonia's siblings had prospered significantly in El Salvador. Although, after about a decade, Sonia's mother had been able to obtain LPR status, gendered inequalities evident in her meager wages in the garment industry had never allowed her to save, and she had been unable to apply for her children's immigrant visas. But the family's life had certainly changed as a result of Sonia's mother's departure:

> Before she left, when we could, we would eat, and if we couldn't, we didn't, right? But then, since there were five of us, when she went to work over there [in the United States], she sent us money, but it was just a little bit, right? But it was enough for school and food. We didn't dress well or anything, we just recycled the same clothes over and over, right? So, but yes, there was always money for food and for school . . . Every month she would send $150.

Unlike families who were barely subsisting who only rarely if ever received remittances, Sonia and her siblings received consistent remittances. And yet, contrary to the common assumptions about transnational families in El Salvador, the sums were not enough to pull them into the middle class or even to guarantee economic stability. Instead, the extra money allowed them to pay for her siblings' multiple surgeries and survive on a day-to-day basis, with just enough to cover their most basic nutritional and educational needs.

Throughout El Salvador, whenever I shared the topic of my research with people, they had similar reactions. As one man told me, "Those people receiving remittances from the United States, they're the ones keeping the big malls open. They just have to sit back and get their check every month. The kids don't appreciate the money; they don't know what it is to have to work for anything, and they haven't even finished cashing the check, and they've already spent it on things they don't even need." This narrative is ubiquitous in El Salvador, particularly among people who do not receive remittances from a relative. According to half of the people I interviewed, however, this assumption does not accurately reflect their experiences.

At the time I conducted this research, the average Salvadoran household receiving remittances got between $100 and $200 per month.[16] It is likely, then, that most transnational Salvadoran families' economic outlook is similar to those of the families I categorize here as surviving. Out of 130 participants, forty-eight (37 percent of the sample) described conditions of survival for family members in El Salvador. In most of these cases, despite receiving consistent remittances, children in El Salvador attended school and ate regularly but did not have excess money for clothing or other expenses. In fact, most did not have sufficient funds to pursue a college education. Migrant parents in this category tended to remit between $100 and $250 monthly,[17] but these sums were generally too small or distributed among several people so sparsely that they allowed families only to cover their bare necessities. These families lived in precarious situations because inevitably, when unexpected problems and expenses arose, they had no savings or other funds to fall back on.

Seventeen-year-old Doris and her brother, for example, were surviving with the money their parents sent. Both her mother and father were in the United States—her mother in Houston and her father in Los Angeles. Her father remitted only inconsistently, and, when I spoke to Doris, he had not sent anything in over three months. Instead, they usually relied only on their mother, who had recently obtained LPR status:

> She sends money monthly, but she sends all, I mean, she sends exactly what we need to cover school expenses, just for what we have to use. . . . She sends $100 on a Saturday, and we know that those $100 has to stretch out for two or three weeks.
>
> *LA: Is that enough for you and your brother?*
>
> Well, look, not very much, I mean, but we always take care of the money, not waste it because otherwise we won't be able to pay for both of our tuition, and there are two of us. . . . I pay 245 [colones—the equivalent of $28] monthly, and my brother pays $11[18] . . . What my mom sends is for all of us because my grandparents don't work. They are home with us. . . . When what she sends is not enough, we have an aunt whom my mom tries to borrow from. My mom calls her, and she'll let us borrow $10.

When I asked Doris about her response to the common belief that children receive lots of money from migrant parents and they spend it irresponsibly, she explained that her case simply did not fit this assumption. To the idea that she might have extra money to spend on clothing or other items, she stated, "That is rare. It is rare." Instead, she and her brother were attending a private school because her family opted to use their limited funds on solid schooling, "I've always been in private schools. For my mom, that was her priority." Choosing education, however, meant that the family lived precariously from week to week, unable to save extra funds or spend freely on other things.

Seventeen-year-old Reina and her brother also relied on remittances from both of her parents, who lived together with their two U.S.-born children in Virginia. Although her parents were together, with two children to support in the United States, they had additional expenses. Moreover, they came from very poor families, had each suffered great trauma during their childhood, and had not found healthy ways to deal with the anger and pain of having been abandoned or beaten as children. During our conversation, Reina shared that remittances from her parents varied greatly from month to month based on all of their expenses in the United States—including, at times, the money for bail to get her father out of jail after incidents of domestic abuse. In those cases, her mother had sent only about $100 for the month, though most months she tried to send $250. In months when they received larger sums, her great-aunt who was raising her would pay off multiple months of tuition for Reina and her brother. This allowed them to stay in school continuously, even when their parents did not remit enough to cover monthly expenses sometimes.

Another strategy for families that were surviving was to opt for the less expensive public schools to leave sufficient funds for other needs. This was the case for sixteen-year-old Alfredo, whose undocumented father lived in New York. The typical monthly sum for his family was $120. His father sent this to Alfredo's grandmother, and she ultimately decided how it was to be used:

> Let's say that she is aware if I need shoes or clothes. We go shopping, and for food, we use that money for food . . . for my expenses and hers, too, because she needs medicine, so we use it for that.
>
> LA: And have you considered going to a private school?
>
> Well, yes, I used to go to [an expensive well-known private school in San Salvador], but it was too far away, and we had to pay for transportation, so my grandmother said, "It's better if you go to school here, locally." So I agreed. I figure they teach the same things here or there. There's probably more discipline in a private school, but I've been here since second grade, and it's fine.

Sending Alfredo to public school freed up some of their funds for other important needs, including his grandmother's medications. Later in the interview, he shared that his father also sends extra cash and other gifts whenever relatives come, usually about once a year, from the United States to visit. This way, their needs were met, even if they were not financially stable enough to save or regularly spend on luxury items.

Over the long term, one of the biggest challenges for families that were surviving was their inability to pay for a university education for the children. Even if they had managed to get children through high school with consistent food and in good health, the costs of pursuing higher education were prohibitive; the monthly sums were simply too small to allow for savings or extra expenses, even for more schooling. This was the case for twenty-six-year-old

Adrián and twenty-four-year-old Liliana. These siblings grew up knowing that their father, Milton, was in the United States, somewhere near Los Angeles. During our conversation they recalled that their father, who at one point had TPS and then became undocumented, would send them packages once per year. Adrián remembered:

> He would help us, sometimes. Based on what I can remember, he would help us once every three months or so. But he would send the money to my grandmother, so we really don't know how often or how much he sent. The only things we got that were tangible were the toys he would send. My grandmother didn't ever tell us directly that he sent us money. We really had no idea how much he was sending.

Although their father was not a consistent economic provider, their mother and grandmother worked as street vendors, selling ice pops to make up for the difference. Remittances combined with wages from informal work allowed the family to pay for school and for food. The siblings were grateful that, between their caregivers and their father's remittances, they were able to graduate from affordable private high schools. When I met with them, they were both hoping to go to college one day. They had been solid students through high school and felt confident about their ability to earn a college degree, but the infrequent remittances simply were not enough to pay for the more expensive college tuition, books, supplies, and transportation. As Liliana noted,

> In high school I opted to focus on commerce and business, and, yes, now I work in the commercial end of things, and I do sales and service to clients. Although now I'd be more interested in studying psychology, I have to say that I see that as unrealistic, that I'd keep studying. Right now it's not an option.

Without the support of greater remittances, even for a family that is surviving, a college education is still out of reach.

These cases demonstrate that even when households receive more than the sum of the *canasta básica*,[19] this does not guarantee economic stability for families. Transnational families, even the ones that are one financial step above barely subsisting, that are able to provide consistent food and schooling for children, are nonetheless struggling to fulfill the initial hopes of most families for higher education and greater upward mobility. Financially, these surviving families' experiences are most closely representative of the average Salvadoran transnational family. Their limitations, therefore, are significant and telling of the challenges of relying on migrants' remittances for national development.[20] In the following section, I detail the experiences of those whose families are closest to living up to the common assumptions about wealth and wastefulness.

Thriving: Food, Private Schooling, and Surplus Money

Petite and fashionably dressed, twenty-four-year-old María Elena was upbeat and confident about her future. She was doing well in school and expected to graduate in a couple of years with a degree in computer science from one of El Salvador's top private universities. María Elena admitted that she was often saddened by her father's absence but also conceded that his remittances helped the family tremendously. He had been lucky enough to get TPS and had a stable job. She described how much money her migrant father sent on a monthly basis and all the household expenses her family was able to cover with these:

> My father typically sends us $980. . . . We buy food, pay for water, electricity, the phone, the house, cable, and those things that are indispensable. We also pay for my [two] sisters' tuition. Personally, I use the money to pay for the university every month, for my books, and all the other expenses at the university. . . . The rest of the money my father sends, we try to invest it by saving . . . We save as much as we can so that when there is an emergency we can go to that and not have to ask him for extra money that month—because there are always unforeseeable expenses.

Clearly, María Elena's family was thriving economically. All three siblings attended private schools through high school, and María Elena still easily afforded attendance at an elite private university where she anticipated a bright future because her educational expenses were not a hardship. In stark contrast to those whose families were barely subsisting or surviving, María Elena covered a series of expenditures, including cable television as one of those things that she considered "indispensable" for families. Also notable was their ability to save money for all of those unplanned but common expenses in life. For example, they had recently paid for her grandmother's sudden medical costs. This ability to gain access to education, food, health care, and other amenities—whether foreseen or not—gave her a certain peace of mind that was largely absent in the experiences of members of barely subsisting and surviving families.

Although nationally María Elena's experience is not common, in this study sixty-two out of 130 participants (48 percent) described that their migration and family separation strategy was paying off. Importantly, there is great variation in this category. For some families, $300 per month helped them cover all their expenses and more, while others received as much as $1,500 per month. In line with this wide variation, parents' remittances allowed some thriving families to achieve or maintain a livable status, while in other cases remittances provided access to greater education and notable upward mobility into the middle and upper-middle classes of El Salvador. What families shared in common in this category is that they were able to pay for their children's schooling and meals continuously, with money left over for luxuries or sometimes designated for savings. On the furthest, most privileged end of this spectrum, with access to elite private schooling, ample school supplies, and the resources to participate in extracurricular activities, the children in this category most abundantly benefited from their parents' migration and economic support.

Among the families whose status had improved greatly since the parents' migration, the children often recognized their new economic privileges relative to their peers at school. For example, fifteen-year-old Camila tried to share some of her new resources with her friends. I met her at school, where we talked about life since both her parents migrated to Maryland four years prior. Her parents left her under her older sister's care; although they were both undocumented, together they remitted about $400 consistently every month. They had opted to keep her at the relatively inexpensive private school so as to stretch out their money:

> The money covers everything necessary for me and for my sister . . . We spend it on clothes for me and here at the private school. They give me $10 [monthly], and every day I get two or three dollars for transportation, food, and all that . . . The $10 I spend on food because sometimes those $2 or $3 are not enough. So, I mean, sometimes my classmates don't bring money, and they ask me if they can have a quarter, or I treat them to a soft drink or something. Because some classmates don't bring money, so I help them buy food.

Camila later stated what she perceived as the differences between families receiving remittances and those who did not: "Those classmates don't bring money to school, and they can't buy food." Her comments reaffirmed the notion that transnational families always fared better than others. Her explanation was that "things keep getting more and more expensive here, and they can't keep up with the price of things if the parents stay in this country." In her case, her parents' remittances helped her to merely keep up with the rising costs of life in El Salvador and to keep paying $35 for monthly tuition at her private school even after her father lost his job. Given her experience, her message to her peers was that their families, too, would only be able to maintain stability through migration. This is important because, again, although thriving families are nationally only a minority of all transnational families, their message of success is amplified through the public discourse on this topic.

One line of this discourse is that children are wasteful with the money their parents send. It is true that the practice of sending extra funds, separate from the budget for household and school costs and allocated individually for the children of migrants, was common among thriving families. High school and college students typically received $10, $15, $25, and even up to $50 per month to spend as they wished. Only a handful of people I spoke with, however, were spending money carelessly, as the common discourse presumes. In these limited number of cases, they admitted to spending their extra money frivolously. Fifteen-year-old Wilfredo, for example, received $10 monthly from his parents in Boston. This sum was in addition to the usual $300 to $500 that they sent for him and his sister's schooling and household expenses. He acknowledged that he squandered his share away on pizza, movies, and video games for him and his older cousin. Fifteen-year-old Nadia, whose parents had both lived in Chicago for over four years, often spent the $15 she got for the month very quickly: "Sometimes it's gone in two days." As she described, "Because sometimes I want a, I don't know, a shirt or some other silly thing I see, and my sister doesn't have any more money, or it's too expensive. So I spend it very quickly." Similarly, seventeen-year-old Yancy, whose father had been living in Houston with LPR status for fourteen years, described all the things she spent her funds on:

> My father always sends us whatever we ask him. He sends us $500, for the three of us. He sends my grandparents money separately for all the other expenses. . . . The thing is that people know that I get money from my father, so they ask me, "Look, can I borrow some money?" And I'll lend it to them, but I don't like to charge people, so it ends up being a gift to them. Or if you go out with a bunch of friends, they know that you have money that you get from over there, and you end up paying much more than they do.

And that's where the money goes. And then I spend it on all my things, like shampoo and things like that. I use that money to buy lotions and pads, and all kinds of things like that. . . . So we use that for tuition; my brother is in the university, so we pay for that, and for books, and everything that we use in school—uniforms, shoes. This year I've already bought three pairs of shoes just for school.

Very much in line with the common discourse on transnational families, these examples reveal that, in some cases, people do use remittances mainly for consumption.

Finally, and perhaps the most stereotypical example of frivolous consumption, is sixteen-year-old Mayra. Her father had migrated with an immigrant visa and had been able to buy property that he rented and managed in the United States. When I went in to Mayra's elite private school in San Salvador to ask for permission to recruit students there, several of the teachers and administrators mentioned her as someone I should speak with. Informally, they told me they were frequently shocked when she flaunted to all her peers that she was wearing the latest styles, new $60 shoes, or a $60 backpack. Along with her school uniform, Mayra wore a designer sweater, trendy earrings, and an expensive purse. During our conversation, Mayra confirmed her teachers' stories:

My father sends [me and my brother] $400 each. Another $400 for food. So it's $1,200 per month. . . . [She laughs when asked what she buys with that money.] I buy lots of things. Lots of personal things. . . . $400 is for all the expenses, and if there's anything left, my mom keeps that in case of an emergency later on. My money, most of it I spend on personal things. . . . I buy clothes, things for my hair, shoes, backpacks.

After paying $160 for tuition, Mayra typically had over $200 monthly to spend as she pleased. She enjoyed this privilege and had no reservations when admitting that she spent much of her money on "personal things."

Interestingly, Mayra was not the only student at that school with migrant parents. The teachers, however, referred me only to Mayra and had much to say about her wastefulness and disregard for money. As I interviewed others at the same school, their stories varied. And while all of them were thriving—after all, it was an expensive elite private school—not all received similar sums of money individually, nor did they spend money as frivolously as Mayra.

Because this type of consumption and financial privilege, particularly at the level of Yancy and Mayra, is so rare in El Salvador, it stands out to people and leads them to develop the incorrect assumption that all transnational families are similarly wasteful in their spending.

The more common experience among the youth I spoke with is that they tried very hard to be responsible about how they used the funds. They were aware of their parents' sacrifices, of their parents' educational and financial goals for the family, and they were working to fulfill those goals. For example, sixteen-year-old Beatriz received $800 to $900 per month in remittances from her father and older brother, who lived together in Maryland:

> First, my mother pays the electricity, water, telephone, tuition for my sister and me, and then she goes shopping for food every two weeks, and when there is something left over, she takes us out.
>
> LA: *And do you have cable or other things like that?*
>
> No, we don't have cable.
>
> LA: *And when you go out, what kinds of things do you do?*
>
> We go to the zoo; we go eat pizza or chicken. Sometimes, not that often, we go buy clothes. But we also try to save because we know that there will be emergencies, and we want to be prepared.

Similarly, sixteen-year-old Yanira relied on relatives who had LPR status. Monthly she received $350 from her father and another $150 from her three siblings, who lived in Los Angeles, but she was quick to emphasize that they were not wasteful:

> I think that we spend only on the necessary things. We pay for food, for the house bills, and tuition. We don't have cable or anything like that. We do live in our own house. We've used the money to fix up the house a bit. We painted it and built a roof on the outside part. When we got the house it was very deteriorated, so we did spend money on fixing it up.

In each of these cases, although they received large sums that were sufficient for food and schooling, they were careful to invest the surplus money on housing, or they saved it for long-term goals or emergencies. In fact, I interviewed Yanira in her modest home and was able to witness the bareness of the living room, the very small television set, and the overall humble approach to consumption.

Ultimately, recipients mostly used large sums of remittances on higher education. Take the case of twenty-three-year-old Javier. Both of his parents, who had LPR status, lived in Dallas and remitted no less than $600 per month. Javier and his siblings grew up and still lived in a plain brick home in a notoriously dangerous neighborhood in San Salvador. I interviewed him and his nineteen-year-old brother, Leonardo, there. Javier described how his family spent the money:

> We use it for food, the expenses of the house, expenses of the university, schooling. . . . For example, here, one book that is mandatory in my field, it's called the DCM4, it costs between 700 colones and up to $150, so I can't buy that, we can't have that luxury. So what do we do? At the university lots of students get together from the same economic background, and we buy one original book, we take it to the copiers and ask for copies. I know that is illegal in this country, but that's what happens if we want to further our schooling. . . . So they send $600, but my grandmother administers that money, on water, electricity, phone, food, and any debts we may have . . . After they buy what is necessary for the household, we each get about $50 for the month, sometimes $25, and that is for expenses that are apart from the *canasta básica* of the household. And that's the money I use to make copies of textbooks. Sometimes we have to ask for more for daily transportation.

Javier's brother, Leonardo, was also quick to add, "We don't go out much, like we don't party or anything like that. We know how hard our parents work to send us that money, and we want to honor them. We used some to build more rooms for the house, but, aside from that, we don't take advantage." Similarly, unlike Wilfredo in a previous example, who spent his mother's remittances on pizza and video games for himself and his cousin, his sister, Clara, saved her $10 share every month to pay for a university education when she completed high school. Stories like these were the most common among thriving transnational families, but perhaps because these students did not wear only brand-name clothing or because they were humble about their financial stability, these were not the stories most often associated with transnational families overall.

Thriving transnational families are meeting their stated goals for migration; the children have access to upward mobility or are guaranteed to maintain their high social class standing in El Salvador through elite private schooling and other luxuries and amenities. At the microsocial level, the examples of frivolous consumption, because they are so rare in a country of great poverty, stand out and form the basis of a more general and misguided understanding of these families.

These experiences of economic success are, in fact, also the most commonly noted or implicitly assumed by researchers who highlight the positive impact of these monies on local development.[21] As numerous campaigns are discussed throughout the world to tax remittances, require families to bank these monies, or otherwise draw on these funds for national development, proponents of these measures draw on examples of thriving families, as though they were the only or even most common kind of transnational family. For this reason, I want to reiterate that, although families that are thriving economically made up almost half of the people in this study, they are only a small minority of Salvadoran transnational families overall. Given the reality of the U.S. labor market, few migrants earn enough to cover their living expenses in the United States while also sending significant sums to their relatives in their homeland. More important, my goal is to bring readers' attention to the disparities. The juxtaposition of three pairs of shoes in a single school year for one person who is thriving versus the limited nutrition, poor health, and extreme sacrifices for schooling someone who is barely subsisting underscores the deep inequalities that exist across transnational families and should not be overlooked.

Children's Emotional Well-Being

Beyond their financial stability, emotional well-being is also crucial to how transnational families fare over long-term separations. Similar to findings in previous research on transnational families, there was much sadness and discontent among the children of migrants in this study. Many felt abandoned and lonely, and it was not uncommon for them to cry throughout the interview. In fact, not a single person expressed happiness about their family situation. The long-term separation was painful and difficult for all. People's experiences, however, varied from interview to interview, even for students attending the same schools. Each person handled the unhappiness in different ways, and it is likely that their feelings also shifted over time. Here, I am interested in capturing the variation as it became clear across the narratives.

More so than economic well-being, emotional well-being is subjective and therefore difficult to measure. To try to understand this variation, I closely examined the narratives of the children of migrants—focusing on the words they used to describe their situations and on their feelings about being apart from parents. I identified two important threads about how they were faring emotionally at the time of the interview. Because emotional well-being is about both the affective component of happiness and the more cognitive component of satisfaction,[22] I incorporated these different ways of thinking about transnational family members' emotional well-being in El Salvador.

Distraught to Composed

First, it is possible to think of children in transnational families as being on a continuum of emotional well-being from completely distraught to fairly composed. Following my arguments in the preceding chapters, this is most directly related to how U.S. immigration laws shape their migrant parents' lives or to their migrant parents' gendered opportunities and expectations. Children of migrants on one of the far ends of the spectrum were utterly distraught: both severely unhappy *and* dissatisfied with the family separation. This was the group who most directly experienced the far-reaching consequences of the U.S. production of illegality as it determined their parents' wages and prevented visits between families. As a result, they felt a deep sense of loss, even years after the family separation. They felt strongly that their parents' migration had been a failure and that they had nothing positive to say about being members of a transnational family; they suffered immensely through the separation—crying most profusely throughout the interview.

Sixteen-year-old Lucía was one such example of a distraught child of migrants. I met her at one of the poorest public schools I had visited throughout the department of San Salvador. From the moment she walked into the empty room where we conducted the interview, she had tears running down her face. Though I offered to let her forgo the interview and then to let her end it early several times, she wanted to share her thoughts, even through her sobs. Her mother had migrated to Los Angeles eight years earlier; she was still undocumented, and the family had little to show for the sacrifice. When I asked Lucía what had been the most difficult aspect of being in this family situation, she paused, cried, and provided this thoughtful response:

> You're going to think I'm crazy, but when I was little, I would hear people say that McDonald's was American food, so whenever we went downtown by that McDonald's, I would try to peer inside, just look inside the window for as long

as I could to see if I could see my mother there . . . [*crying*] Yes, my life has been pure suffering without her. One never really understands why a mother would abandon you, why she would leave you if nothing changes. Nothing is better. Everything is worse.

Lucía suffered severely the consequences of illegality. It pained her to share this story of her childhood understanding of her mother's absence because she knew it captured the depth of her distress and her sense of abandonment to the point of suggesting she may have been acting insanely. And it is important to note that Lucía's story was not unique. Others shared similar hopes of seeing their parents on television whenever a channel ran footage taken in the United States or in the city or state where their parents lived. Like her, others also cried and stated that the transnational family strategy was not worth the years of struggle and pain, especially when they had no financial stability to show for it. Although they did not locate the source of their suffering in U.S. immigration policies, their parents' inability to provide financial stability or to visit were often directly tied to the U.S. production of illegality. Indeed, one of the most insidious consequences of illegality in the contemporary moment is the internalization of implicit messages of U.S. immigration policy. In line with this process of internalization, children come to misrecognize their own parents as the cause of their suffering, thereby further extending the painful consequences of illegality beyond U.S. borders.[23]

In another example, and after being apart from her parents for thirteen years, sixteen-year-old Clara said that the sacrifice of family separation was "not worth it because I feel that I had the right to be with them, to be raised by my parents, and I didn't have that chance. And it's all because of the money, and what for? Nothing has changed." Her parents, who lived in Miami, Florida, made an effort to maintain a close relationship with her, but, for Clara, this was not enough. Tearfully she added, "They call me almost every week, but it's not the same." For Clara, illegality prevented a real relationship with her parents: "You can't reach out through the phone to hug them or to receive a kiss from them." Having spent most of her life without the physical contact she desired from her parents, Clara was frustrated with mere long-distance phone calls. She, too, cried throughout the interview and expressed anger and resentment toward her parents for having failed in this strategy. In these cases, the absence of a parent is especially difficult when coupled with severe economic hardship.

Moving along this spectrum of children's emotional well-being, even in cases of greater economic stability, some children seemed enveloped in a sense of constant longing to be reunited with their migrant parents. Often informed by deep-seated gender ideologies, they described a continued and intense emotional attachment to their mothers or fathers in the United States and the pain of separation colored the lens through which they viewed the world around them. Twenty-one-year old Xiomara, for example, missed her mother terribly. She was reserved but confident throughout our conversation, recognizing that her mother's migration had been necessary for her family to get out of debt, for her to continue attending a private school, and to pay for a college education. She stated that things were going well, but she missed her mother. Her mother's absence affected Xiomara emotionally to the point that she could not concentrate on various tasks, and she often found herself breaking down and crying unexpectedly:

> I would try to relax, talk about other things, but no, it's not the same . . . You could try to stay busy, but there comes a moment, when you're alone, and, I mean, I would sleep in her old bed, so there was that moment that I was alone, in her spot in the bed. Because I would make sure to sleep in her spot, even to this day, I sleep in her spot, with her pillow, sometimes I even wear her nightgowns . . . There are just all these moments. You hear a song that she liked or that she sang, and that's when it hits you . . . Like when she talks about Christmas, I tell her there is no such thing as Christmas since she left, no Christmas that I haven't cried. And the 31st [New Year's Eve], you know, you always hug your mother first, and she's not here.

In cases like Xiomara's, the financial advantages of receiving remittances from migrant parents do not make up for the emotional hardships of family separation.[24] Coming from a close-knit family, Xiomara felt challenged to lead a normal life in the absence of her mother. The details she used to describe the pain, her meticulous bedtime practices to try to fill the void—these all provide a window into the extent of the longing and distress of being a member of a transnational family, even when it was a successful financial strategy with concrete and direct benefits in their lives.

Further along on this spectrum, children of migrants described their emotions and experiences with a bit more distance, clarity, and understanding. Twenty-four-year old María Elena, for example, did not cry during the interview, even though she spoke at length and several times about how much she missed her father and how she hoped he'd return soon. She was used to having a close relationship with him, and her grades dipped a bit when he left, but she had risen to his expectations and had become a solid student in college. Her father's original plan was to live and work in the United States for three years to guarantee his daughters' educational and professional opportunities. After getting TPS, however, those three years had turned into five, and, at the time of my interview with María Elena, he had recently informed them that he would have to stay a few more years. This unexpected lengthening of the family separation is not uncommon for transnational families.[25] Life in the United States is much more expensive than migrants anticipate, and many must first pay off migration and other debts before they can make a difference in their families' lives. Prior to migration, María Elena's father had been her confidante and a driving force in her life. In her response to my question about whether her father's migration was worth it, however, she had a mixed view:

> Well, yes, because economically, we have everything. I mean, we're always missing something, but the needs are less now than before. Economically, we're doing well. But then the trust [*confianza*] and the knowledge that he's there physically, that part is hard. Economically, I can't complain because I'm very conscious that if he went, it was in search of a better life for us. So even though he's not physically here, he's always calling, and we're always communicating.

María Elena recognized the concrete privileges she and her siblings reaped as a result and was able to balance out the emotional hardships to accept that the strategy of separation had paid off for her family. Moreover, unlike Clara in a previous example, some of María Elena's pain was alleviated by the frequent phone conversations with her father. Notably, she never mentioned feeling abandoned—a detail that further distinguished her emotional experience of separation from those who were distraught. Instead, her narrative suggests that she was able to better cope with the separation because her father was living up to his traditional gendered expectations as a good provider.

Moving further along in this spectrum, getting closer to a state of composure, the narratives of children of migrants revealed stronger emotional well-being for some members of transnational families. Such was the case for seventeen-year-old Doris. Her father had been living in Houston for six years, and her mother had been living in Los Angeles for four years. She and her brother, however, were only surviving, often struggling financially. Despite their economic woes, she was very forthcoming and optimistic during the interview and generally composed about the family separation. Contrary to the sense of abandonment that plagued the children of migrants in distress, Doris tried to focus on her mother's goals, and she was more forgiving of her absence: "I think that, just because she left, that didn't take her love away from us; it's just that she couldn't hug us from a distance." Unlike Clara, who resented the coldness of long-distance phone calls because they could not replace hugs, Doris rejected the notion that the distance meant that her mother no longer loved her—even though she suggested that hugs in person would be better. The family separation was easier to accept because Doris had spent a month with her mother the previous year and was awaiting an immigrant visa in the foreseeable future. Not pained by the consequences of illegality, even economic hardships and a transgression of gender ideologies seemed manageable when she could count on a family reunification. Like Doris, other children of migrants closer to a state of composure also expressed similar views of their family separation. They tried to stay optimistic and balanced, even when they made it clear that they missed their parents and that they would have preferred to live with them under the same roof.

The most composed of the migrant children—those on the furthest, most positive end of the emotional well-being spectrum—expressed that, despite being unhappy about their parents' absence, they did feel satisfied with their living conditions. They did not cry during the interview, and each time they spoke of the emotional hardships of being away from their parents, they quickly underscored the benefits of this strategy. Mostly, they wanted to prove that they were not ungrateful and that they valued their parents' efforts. Sixteen-year-old Iván was one example of a child of migrants who was rather composed about his family's situation. Relying on a migrant father with LPR status who successfully lived up to one of the traditional gendered expectations as a provider, Iván was less burdened than most other children of migrants. He was a junior at a top private high school in San Salvador. He lived up to his computer science teacher's praises about his confidence level and eloquence. When I asked him, toward the end of the interview, whether his father's migration to the United States was worth it, he paused to collect his thoughts and responded in a very serious, almost distanced manner:

The sad reality in our country is that parents cannot give their children the lives they dream of giving them. In my father's case, he tells us that it was with all the pain in the world that he had to make the decision to leave for some years. And I'm not going to tell you that it has been easy because you see that a home always needs the love and firmness [strictness] of a father, but the sacrifice that he has made for us is very much appreciated. And it's because of that sacrifice that I am here, in this private school and my sister is in [a private university].

From his perspective, his father's absence had been difficult only to the extent that the distance between them impeded the fulfillment of the idealized nuclear family norm. He understood that the absence, while labeled a sacrifice, was also the reason for his and his sister's privileged educational opportunities. This reality and his interpretation of it allowed Iván to appreciate his father's migration as a strategy.

Like Iván, other children had also reached a state where they could step back and think through their situation from a standpoint filled with composure. In each case, this optimistic outlook was made easier when parents were fulfilling traditional gender ideologies and especially if they were unburdened by the difficult consequences of illegality. While they expressed that family separation was painful and had other negative repercussions in their lives, they also seemed to understand the need for their parents' absence; by being able to focus on what they got in return for it, they could appreciate the benefits of a transnational family strategy.

Looking Beyond Annual Remittance Figures

In 2004, when I conducted interviews in El Salvador, 22 percent of all households there reported receiving remittances that were estimated at $2.5 billion, or 16 percent of the gross domestic product.[26] By 2012, the sum had swelled to $3.9 billion. On a per capita basis, El Salvador also has one of the highest annual sums in the region, with an estimated flow of approximately $350 per year.[27] Nationally, remittances help decrease poverty, reduce inequality, increase children's schooling levels, and provide support to the retired elderly.[28] According to the U.N. Development Program, 26 percent of remittance-receiving households,[29] compared to 37 percent of households not receiving remittances, fall below the poverty line. And only 6 percent of remittance-receiving households, compared to 14 percent that do not receive remittances, would be classified as living in extreme poverty.[30]

The cases in this chapter, however, reveal great diversity in the well-being of transnational families. Although some families are thriving economically and some children learn to cope emotionally with their parents' absence, these are not the only experiences among transnational families. Despite common local discourses and development researchers' enthusiasm for the presumed excess remittances, these assumptions do not reflect the reality of many transnational families. On the contrary, for that significant fraction of people who are barely subsisting or who live in extreme distress, the strategy of migration has failed to live up to its initial promise. While remittances continue to be the mainstay of the Salvadoran economy and the economies of several other developing nations, it is important not to overlook the economic and emotional tolls of the separation necessary to attain these revenues.

7 The Consequences of Long-Term Family Separation

I haven't tried too hard here because my future is over there.
— Sixteen-year-old Gustavo

THE LEGAL AND GENDERED INEQUALITIES that migrant parents face not only determine their children's economic and emotional well-being, but they also shape how transnational family members adapt on a daily basis. Family separation contextualizes critical aspects of their lives, including how children perform in school, develop their goals, and integrate into society. Children's aspirations are especially important because they can serve as signposts to help youth navigate challenges and roadblocks of family separation. Realistic and clear aspirations, for example, give people a sense of purpose and motivation to persevere.[1] In the midst of long-term family separation, however, the consequences of illegality and persistent gender ideologies create instability and uncertainty that can prevent some from developing clear goals and aspirations. Indeed, as this chapter demonstrates, there are long-term consequences of family separation that matter individually for transnational family members and collectively because they have important implications for the societies in which they live.

Contexts and Processes Shaping Children's Aspirations

Initially, most families separate under the belief that they will be reunited within a few years—apart just long enough to wait out the war, to earn enough money to get on their feet, or until they can figure out how to reunite legally in the United States. As they adapt, however, migrants struggle with the high cost of living in their new home and must prolong their family separation.[2] Then, the longer they stay, the more difficult it becomes to plan for or even imagine a return to their country where, to date, the job situation has not improved. In the meantime, the paths to legalization or legal migration for their children continue to be blocked. This is an especially difficult situation for those migrants who are in tenuous legal statuses (undocumented or only temporarily protected).

School Performance

Children and youth are likely to develop aspirations that are closely tied to how well they do in school. Given that most parents justified their migration in large part as a necessary hardship to provide food and more schooling for their children, school performance is central in gauging the overall conse-quences of family separation. Although it takes months and years to ascertain the benefits of this strategy for children's education, the challenges certainly do not wait to set in and cloud transnational family members' lives. Indeed, children, caregivers, and school personnel consistently noted that signs of family separation were clear in children's behavior even in the initial stages of separation. Schoolteachers and administrators shared their observations of what they all saw as a common pattern. One school principal described:

> Oh yes, it's very obvious when the parents leave. You can tell immediately because, from one day to the next, the students change. All of a sudden their grades drop, and they become very quiet, as if they are closing themselves up. Sometimes they also become rebellious. And they remain that way for weeks, sometimes months. And then, if everything else goes well, if they have fam-ily that is caring for them well, then they start to improve, and they return to the people they were [before their parents left]. But that is not always the case.

Over and over, school personnel were familiar with these signs, and they all certainly hoped for the best for those children. Unfortunately, efforts fell short of their good wishes; none of the schools had a single program or curriculum in place to help students cope with their new situations—even as common as family separations were.

In effect, several of the children I met shared similar stories of diminished school performance. In the short term, many had a difficult time settling into new routines and adjusting to their loved one's absence. But this also varied by age.[3] Children whose parents left during their infancy or early childhood had few recollections of what it was like to live with their parents, so they

had forgotten any difficult transitions. It was only later in life, after notic-
ing and internalizing the social expectations for nuclear families, that they
consciously began to react more strongly to their parents' prolonged absence.
Children who were five and older when parents left, on the other hand, often
vividly recalled details of their parents' departure, and they had immediate
negative reactions. Maura, the grandmother and caregiver of three children
ages nine through twelve, described how her grandkids reacted when their
parents left:

> At first, the littlest one, he was in agreement [that his parents go]. He thought
> things would be good because his parents were going to send him toys. So he
> was happy. The other two, they were not well. From one day to the next, their
> grades dropped. If you had seen them, it would break your heart. The girl
> would sit over there, by the window, to see when her mother and father were
> going to come back. And the other boy stopped eating. He said he wasn't hun-
> gry, and I was so worried because he is a big eater [comelón].

By the time I spoke to her, years after her daughter and son-in-law migrated, the kids' grades had improved only a bit, and the youngest was chroni-
cally misbehaving in school: "He's always getting in trouble . . . in his studies. He just doesn't consider it important . . . they call me to meetings, and
they always tell me that he's doing so badly." Maura linked his behavior to his
parents' prolonged absence: "Even though his mother calls them and talks
to them every single day—she buys calling cards, and she calls them—he's
resentful. He wants them here already."

Like Maura's grandchildren, many children of migrants translated their
emotional and economic suffering into lowered school performance. Sometimes consciously, but often unconsciously, their frustration and hurt feelings
blocked them from excelling in school. Fourteen-year-old Yamilet, for example, recalled how terribly she reacted to her father's departure:

> He left when I was seven years old, when my youngest sister was about a year
> and a half . . . So I was the one who felt it the most because I was already big. So
> the little kids would just tell me, "Don't cry. Don't cry, Yamilet, because you'll
> see that Papi will send us things, and we'll be very happy." But I got sick for
> an entire week. . . . I didn't feel like going to school. I got like a cold and even
> a fever, and my friends would come visit me at home. . . . I didn't go to school
> for a whole week.

Such intense feelings were not uncommon among the people I interviewed in El Salvador, and they confirmed educators' observations about the sudden drops in school performance among children in transnational families. I found that, despite parents' initial hopes, the suffering associated with family separation often ended up reducing children's performance in school—at least temporarily but sometimes over the long-term as well.

As family separation was prolonged, children went through different phases that also affected their school performance and aspirations. In one phase, a few students became rebellious, acting in ways that hurt their grades and diminished their participation in school. According to teachers and principals, in the most severe of these cases, students had to be terminated from school.

When these behaviors came up during interviews, adolescents in El Salvador blamed their absent parents. Gilbert, for example, believed his young sister's pregnancy was his father's fault for not sending enough remittances and not communicating with them consistently: "If he had stayed, my sister would not have gotten pregnant, and we wouldn't be living like this." Similarly, Iris, an attractive fifteen-year-old girl who admitted to various problematic behaviors, linked some of her actions to her mother's absence. Filled with anger and resentment, Iris rarely stated outright that she was sad. However, she revealed her deep sense of loneliness:

> Yes, I guess you could say that I'm rebellious . . . I don't know why I behave badly, and then my mother calls just to scold me [regañarme]. She gets mad and tells me that she left for me, that's what she always says, but how can she say that if it's not true? . . . She left because my father had left us, too. But she left, and now we don't have anybody for support, anybody to count on. She could have stayed, and we would still be eating just beans as we do now.

Unable to confirm her mother's true intentions and with little to show for the family separation, Iris was angry and hurt. She misbehaved and threatened to leave school as the only form of punishment she could enforce against her mother. Mostly, though, she craved love and attention. When I asked her why she had been with her boyfriend since she was a preteen, she responded, "Well, he makes me feel as if I have support. I don't have support from anybody else. My mother and father abandoned me. At least I can confide in him." Feeling abandoned, many children found acceptance in sources that prevented them from excelling in school.

Teachers also suggested that many of the girls' troubling behaviors were rooted in a search for love that included romantic relationships at early ages, sometimes resulting in teen pregnancies. Jacqueline confirmed their observations. When I met the nineteen-year-old, she already had a three-year-old daughter. Her father, who had established another family prior to her mother's departure, was mostly out of the picture. Her mother migrated to the United States when Jacqueline was only six years old, and she remitted consistently to the family. Despite the new financial stability, Jacqueline ended up exiting high school for a couple of years in the tenth grade, when she got pregnant. Prior to that, she had always strived to stay out of trouble and make her mother proud. But she got involved in a relationship with an older boy whose attention made her feel special. Since having her child, she took her maternal responsibilities seriously while also trying to complete high school. Even as a young dedicated mother, however, Jacqueline continued to suffer. She cried through the interview and shared that she felt abandoned and hurt because she spent her childhood without her mother. Like her, so many young people harbored feelings of abandonment, pain, and resentment that prevented them from taking advantage of their new economic resources and from excelling in school.

A few children of migrants—particularly those who had little adult supervision—also admitted to another behavior that prevented their academic success: the use of drugs and alcohol. Fifteen-year-old Camila, for example, had lived under the care of her older sister since both her parents migrated to the U.S. state of Virginia. Although Camila adored her sister, she took advantage of the lack of supervision after her sister and brother-in-law had a baby:

> At that school I had bad influences, always pressuring me to drink, get high, smoke, and all that. So that's what happened. One time they invited me and I went; so, I don't know, I liked it, and I started doing those things because my parents wouldn't find out. But I decided it was best to get out . . . but I went back, and I didn't feel strong enough to say no to all that, so I fell in again. So in the end, it was better for me to leave that school.

What ultimately drew Camila away from the self-damaging behavior—and what worked most effectively for a lot of the children—was her strong and loving communication with her parents and her caregiver:

> I would think about my parents and their efforts, what they are doing over there and my sister advising me, because I made my mom cry so many times.

I could hear her on the phone; I could hear her clearly crying. And my sister cried. So I said, "No, this is unfair. What I'm doing to her is unfair." So I decided I should get out, and I thought about my future. Where will I end up? I don't want to be homeless and drunk. That's what I thought about.

El Salvador is now a country directly in the middle of the nefarious international drug trade.[4] Increasingly, and as with many other countries of the region, drugs are easily accessible, and youth are easy targets. Certainly children in transnational families are not the only ones to succumb, but, when they feel especially unsupported and unsupervised, it is an almost effortless move for children in transnational families to find drugs. In this process, their school attendance and performance drops drastically, and their aspirations are likely to follow.

In many of these cases, the children who were suffering economically—the ones who were barely subsisting—were also the most resentful and likely to rebel. In line with the consequences of U.S. production of illegality, these were often the children of undocumented migrant parents. Unable to justify their parents' absence through tangible gains, having gone years without seeing their parents, and not knowing with certainty that they would ever have a clear path to reunification, these youth were understandably especially hurt. Misbehaving and doing poorly in school were the only available ways to hurt their parents back, even if they had to lower their own aspirations in the process.

I want to be very clear that among the children who were falling behind in school, not all of them *chose* this behavior. That is, some children felt no desire to hurt their parents, but, overwhelmed by various sources of stress—both economic and emotional—they could not concentrate. Such was the case for sixteen-year-old Daniel, who went from being a stellar student to having to worry about whether he could pass his classes. He cared deeply about his migrant father and wanted to make him proud, but the financial stress and his added responsibilities were too heavy to brush off. His stress was so severe that he had even contemplated suicide. Similarly, sixteen-year-old Tanya was repeating the ninth grade and did not think she would pass on her second attempt because she worried constantly about how to pay for her mother's medical care when her father did not send remittances. Feeling trapped by her dire economic situation, she found it impossible to concentrate on school.

Though her situation was less severe because her mother remitted large sums consistently, twenty-one-year-old Xiomara also had a difficult time concentrating in school. Despite her financial stability, Xiomara felt unfocused sometimes because she missed her mother so deeply. Though she completed high school, her lack of concentration resulted in low grades and test scores that disqualified her for admission into a top university. Instead, she had to settle for lower academic aspirations and a less-selective college.

Whether or not they were faring well financially, lots of children of migrants also acted in ways that lowered their school performance and muddled their aspirations. Like Xiomara, children commonly missed their parents during widely observed cultural celebrations. In Salvadoran society, Mothers' and Fathers' Day, Holy Week, Christmas, and New Year's Day are important holidays centered around the notion of family unity and shared joy. For children in transnational families, however, the many and cyclical festivities were painful reminders of a parent's absence. As weeks turned into months and months into years, family separation decidedly affected children's well-being and, in turn, their ability to learn and participate in school productively.

Overall, in El Salvador (as in other countries), children receiving remittances are completing more and more years of schooling.[5] However, based on the narratives of the youth I interviewed, it is worth investigating further whether children in transnational families are actually learning and progressing on to the next grade level or merely repeating the same grades and classes. Even when the youth I interviewed received consistent remittances, the emotional hardships of family separation led them, sometimes purposely and other times involuntarily, to lose focus in school. As some of these behaviors became more common in some cases, they reinforced lower aspirations. These patterns should be particularly worrisome given that parents left precisely to provide their children with more schooling and more opportunities for upward mobility.

Community Ties

Beyond school performance, children also developed aspirations based on their feelings of belonging in their country and their community. In effect, the economic and emotional challenges of family separation also shaped how children participated in their communities—through extracurricular activities, membership in groups and organizations, or attendance at local events. In this realm, children who were thriving financially were much more likely to take advantage of their resources to learn new skills or join organized activities such as soccer leagues, exercise, and dance classes. As a result, they focused their attention on various projects rather than feeling constantly miserable about their parents' absence. Yancy and Mayra, for example, were both economically thriving. They used their extra money to pay for English lessons at a private institute. Yancy had gone to gymnastics classes throughout her childhood, and Mayra was enrolled in swimming. As Yancy described:

> I like to learn English, and I used to like gymnastics. I still have friends; in fact, some of my best friends are from there because we used to see each other every day and we got along well . . . Those activities allow me to meet more people, not just my classmates from school. . . . It's nice to feel as if you get to know San Salvador better through them.

By keeping children of migrants busy and enriching their lives, these activities helped them feel connected to their peers and their communities.

Participation in such activities was less common among the children who were barely subsisting or just surviving. Although the extra activities may have helped them better cope with the family separation, they simply could not afford to participate. Depending on their responsibilities and household situation, most of these children instead spent all their free time at home or on the street in their neighborhood. Twenty-four-year-old Ana, for example, lived in a dangerous neighborhood with her younger sister, in a house that was made available through government assistance.[6] As she finished up her senior year in high school, she looked forward to working and earning money to improve their living conditions:

> I hope that things will be different next year when I can start to work. Where [my sister] works now, they pay her one dollar per day. She helps them make tortillas; they pay her a dollar and they give her food . . . I prefer for her to be there even if they don't pay much because otherwise she would be by herself at the house, and she can't be there by herself. No one else would be with her, and that scares me . . . It is dangerous in our neighborhood . . . When I get home, we just shut the door and lock ourselves in. It is the safest thing to do.

The limited and infrequent remittances from their father prevented Ana and her sister from being able to afford other living arrangements. Extracurricular activities were also out of reach. Ana's daily life in El Salvador, therefore, consisted of worrying about how to spend the smallest sum possible on food, how to be able to afford to make it to school, how to keep her younger sister busy and safe, and how to avoid becoming a target of imminent violence in her own neighborhood. Church once per week was her only connection to others in her community, but it was too short to allow her to create lasting bonds: "I see some of the same ladies every week, but no, I don't really know them." Without the financial resources to afford to live in a safer neighborhood or to pay for enriching activities, Ana and others like her had few options but to close themselves off from their communities just to feel protected. Unable to develop a sense of belonging in their neighborhoods or their country, many children of migrants also had difficulty developing aspirations that would further tie them to El Salvador.

For many of the youth, it seemed that economic hardship, emotional distress, low school performance, lack of belonging, and low aspirations all worked cumulatively to prevent them from thriving. This was particularly evident in Gilbert's case. His father had stopped sending remittances a couple of years prior, so Gilbert was just waiting to be old enough to leave. In his view, there was little reason to get involved in local activities:

> There is nothing for me to do here. My mother already told us that my [twin] brother and I probably can't go to school anymore next year because it's too many expenses at the high school. She wants us to start working, but we will be able to make more money over there [in the United States], and we'll be able to live with my father.

Later in the interview, I asked Gilbert about his performance in school. He revealed that, like other adolescents whose families were barely subsisting, he was doing poorly because he had come to orient himself toward a future in the United States. In explaining why he was performing only "so-so," he said matter-of-factly:

> Well, I'm probably going to go to the United States to be with my father. I want to see him again, and I want to know what it feels like to live with him. And so I'll go to school there. People say that you can work and go to school at the same time. So I'll do that since I won't be able to go to school here anymore.

Driven by the certainty that their families would not be able to afford to send them to school much longer, these youth disassociated themselves from their local context in El Salvador by not performing in school or failing to develop realistic goals in their place of residence. Fueled by their difficult living conditions and the desire to reunite with their parents, children whose families were barely subsisting withdrew from their social environment and stopped participating fruitfully in their daily lives to, instead, focus on their dreams of migration.

Planning for the Future: Migration Aspirations and Suspended Lives

I met many youth and young adults who, through the years, had developed a lack of concern for the world around them. Constantly waiting for the day when they could be reunited with their parents, they had not bothered to make meaningful local connections.[7] Sixteen-year-old Tanya, for example, spent much of her free time fantasizing about leaving to the United States. Dressed in a heavily used uniform one size too big, she told me, "I have one close friend, and I tell him, God willing, this will be the year that I leave." Even though she was in school and had younger siblings and a boyfriend, the only real connection tying her to the country was "my mother. She's the only person holding me back here. There is nothing else. I have nothing else to do here." Her migration aspirations, in turn, prevented her from participating fully in any activities that might make her life more meaningful in El Salvador. She fiddled with her long skinny fingers as she explained, "What for? I have faith that I will make it [to the United States], so why dedicate time to things here if I will have to drop everything when I leave?"

Like Tanya, many others seemed to have suspended their lives while waiting for the day to leave. Fifteen-year-old Fabián, for example, could not think of anything to say when I asked about his plans over the next few years. After staring blankly at the ceiling for several seconds, he shrugged his shoulders and shyly stated, "It's because I don't know what will happen—whether my mom will come back, or maybe she'll send for me. So I don't want to get into anything." Sixteen-year-old Pablo felt similarly paralyzed. His migrant father stopped remitting after injuring himself at work. Meanwhile, Pablo's mother had suggested that he would likely have to drop out of school after the ninth grade because she could not afford even the nominal fees for his high school attendance. Although Pablo wanted to complete high school, he felt unsure about his future as he waited to hear from his father about the possibility of joining him in the United States. Both Fabián and Pablo attributed their lack of engagement in their communities to their uncertain situation. Feeling suspended and lacking control, they were not inclined to invest their energy in people and organizations around them because the chances of having to leave them in the foreseeable future were high.

Many of the youth who could not or opted not to develop meaningful ties in El Salvador also seemed lost regarding their possible future in the United States. Eighteen-year-old Enrique, for example, missed his mother terribly. Because she was undocumented and had an unstable job as a garment worker, she was able to remit only between $100 and $150 per month. She had been telling him over the last few years that she was hoping to save up enough money to pay for his unauthorized trip by land to reunite with her in Los Angeles: "Ever since she told me that she was going to send for me, well, let's say that I don't pay as much attention in school, in my studies. Because they say that it's easier to study and work over there at the same time. So that's what I'll do." When I asked him more specifically, however, what he would do and how he would manage to achieve his goals, he was at a loss: "Right now I would work in whatever, just to pay for school. I would work at the supermarket as a bagger." Although his mother had been living in the United States for years, he was ultimately unfamiliar with life there, so he could imagine only a vague future. With such foggy understandings of what life would be like in new surroundings, it was difficult for many children of migrants to develop clear goals.

And yet, many children of migrants hoped to one day live in the United States. In wrapping up the interviews, I asked each person about his or her plan over the next five years and found that those who were emotionally consumed by their parents' absence, who had difficulty talking about their situation without crying, were especially looking forward to their family reunification. Sixteen-year-old Rosaura, for example, could not stop crying as soon as we started the interview. Her father had left when she was only eight years old, and she missed him dearly. They talked on the phone often, and he highly encouraged her to excel in school, but she was willing to put it all on hold just to have a chance to see him again. Although she was a good student, the possibility of moving to Oregon to join him seemed to cloud her goals and make them less concrete. This was evident in her response to my question about her plans for the next five years:

> Finish high school and complete a couple of years at the university and start to work to help my mom with my younger siblings . . . But I also want to go to the United States, I do. Two years ago, they were going to take me, but I didn't get a visa . . . I was going to be a visitor, then six months later I would return, and I'd be going back and forth like that . . . But it was not possible.

As it turned out, when migration became a possibility, she would have given up her efforts in school and sacrificed her goals to reunite with her father.

Those who were not faring well financially often provided economic reasons for wanting to migrate: either to help support their relatives in El Salvador or to lend a hand to their migrant parents in the United States. Pablo, for example, lived with his mother in El Salvador, but they were struggling after his migrant father was injured at work. As Pablo thought about his uncertain future—not sure if he would stay and work in El Salvador or possibly migrate to be with his father—he explained why he aspired to migrate:

> No, it's not because it's nice there, really. People say that it's a luxury just to be there, but that's not why I'm going. I want to improve my life, hopefully, and to help my mom by working. . . . I would like to help [my father] also, but I want to help my mom. . . . I would like to go and have in mind how much my mother has helped me. She has it tough having to work to support my little brothers.

When things had not improved enough with parents' remittances, migration was one of the few realistic options for family survival—to improve their own lives and those of their caregivers and younger siblings.

Tanya, whose father had never made good on his promises to help her financially, was in a similar situation. Her ailing mother sold pirated CDs on a local sidewalk, and her stepfather earned very little money selling fruits at an outdoor market. Desperate to help pay for her mother's medical care, Tanya was one of very few children of migrants willing to make the dangerous trip by land:

> More than anything, I would leave to help my mother out. But really, imagine this, what would I do here anyway? I can't continue my schooling after this year, probably.[8] Over there, there are more possibilities. I may even be able to continue going to school, and I can work.

Like Tanya, many others felt the same desperation to migrate. In their thoughts about the future, they were not aware of any possibilities for upward mobility in El Salvador. Among those who wanted to stay in El Salvador, most had no clear idea what kind of work they could do to earn enough to cover their expenses. Eighteen-year-old Enrique's words captured what many others expressed: "In this country [El Salvador] you need to have connections to get a job. I don't have any connections, so I might as well go with my mom [to the United States]." If children of migrants were not faring well financially and they lacked social networks to help them enter desirable jobs, migration was certainly the most viable solution to their problems, especially because it would also lead to family reunification.

As they got older and faced the realities of the restricted labor market, it seemed that many of them also considered migration as an option. Twenty-nine-year-old Sonia, whose mother had migrated when Sonia was only eight years old, explained that she was planning to migrate as soon as her paper-work for an immigrant visa came through:[9]

> I have nothing here to stay for. If I work in a *maquila* here, I mean, I might as well work for a factory over there and make more money. Here, in a *maquila*, you make about $114 per month. That's not enough. I don't know what I'll work in over there—taking care of kids or something.

Although their mother had remitted consistently throughout many years and all her siblings had completed high school (something they would not have been able to afford had their mother not migrated), the Salvadoran econ-omy still did not provide them opportunities to thrive. In fact, at the time of the interview, most of her siblings had already migrated or planned to do so in the near future. Her older brother had migrated to the United States when he was just a teenager to go help out his mother. Two other siblings were plan-ning on migrating without visas in the coming months.

As it currently stands, the economic reality in El Salvador is pushing out another generation of people for whom there are no opportunities to match their potential or fulfill their dreams. Despite migrant parents' expectations and sacrifices, the global inequality that deprives most in El Salvador also re-sults in too many of their children being unable to rise up the socioeconomic ladder. Instead, this generation (like so many others before) must look abroad for solutions. Their future orientations toward the United States, however, are problematic.

In the face of deeply rooted, historically maintained inequalities in El Sal-vador, these youth are relinquishing any possibilities of upward mobility by not pursuing concrete educational or professional goals in El Salvador. More-over, because most would have to migrate in an unauthorized manner, they face the dangerous journey that now increasingly claims the lives of many migrants from Central America and Mexico.[10] Their lack of familiarity with life in the United States leads them to develop unrealistic expectations about the opportunities that await them. With an increasingly harsh political and legal context of reception, it is highly unlikely that they will be able to work and continue their education in the United States without great difficulty.[11]

All of these patterns have broader implications for El Salvador. Children of migrants who were already struggling with the economic or emotional challenges of their parents' migration were also often socially disengaged. Unable to develop meaningful ties with those around them, they seemed to be at risk of greater isolation. In the long term, such patterns of disassociation do not bode well for Salvadoran society, where transnational families are relatively common. Collectively, their energy—through intellectual, physical, and creative capacity—is being wasted when society fails to provide them opportunities to build meaningful connections and contribute positively to the nation's future. Meanwhile, these youth are growing up without the possibility of developing concrete goals because they are unfamiliar with the place, language, and opportunities of what they see as their only future in the United States.

Aspirations to Remain in El Salvador

However, not all of the people I interviewed in El Salvador aspired to migrate. There were several whose ties to their family and friends, to their communities, and their own concrete futures anchored them to the country. Those who aspired to stay had usually done well economically. They were able to use remittances to finance their education; they excelled in school and were experiencing some of the tangible benefits of their new higher socioeconomic status. But none of this came without a cost to their family.

In some instances, the different sets of aspirations arose even within single families. Such was the case for Sonia's family. Although she and three of her siblings had already migrated or aspired to so, one of her sisters did not. Her sister, who had taken on most of the household responsibilities when their mother left, was also the only one who had obtained a college degree and had a white-collar job in El Salvador. Sonia understood very clearly why her sister's aspirations were different than the others in her family: "She has a visa, and she can travel to visit our mother whenever she wants. She has no desire to migrate permanently. She has a good job here. And, you know, professionals here are fine staying here." This pattern became evident among several other people I met: When they had a path or found a way to support themselves and live comfortably, they preferred to remain in El Salvador.

Notably, the persistent inequalities I have highlighted throughout the book are also behind the patterns of children's aspirations. That is, those children in families that relied on parents with stable legal status, who received consistent and sufficient remittances, were also the most likely to have increased their socioeconomic status noticeably enough that they preferred to remain and enjoy their new situation. These youth had tangible rewards that made such a difference in their lives that they did not want to part with them. Twenty-four-year-old María Elena, for example, was doing well in college and was optimistic about a bright future in her chosen career in business: "No, I don't think about leaving. I have never thought about living in the United States. Maybe I would go visit [my father], but that situation of traveling without a visa is too difficult, so, no. My future is here. I want to work in my field here." Like her, several others felt tied to El Salvador and wanted to live and contribute to their country—but only when doing so actually seemed feasible and within reach.

Things, however, were never easy for transnational families. Even when structural factors had aligned to permit parents to live up to their own expectations, when children had responded positively and established clear goals, and when the family's socioeconomic position had improved drastically, aspirations conflicted, and tensions were likely to rise. In the following section, I detail the experience of the Mármol family who, compared to most other families, were living out what is arguably the best case scenario in the context of long-term separation. Their reflections reveal that even when all factors aligned to benefit transnational families, negotiations and aspirations were difficult to reconcile.

Best-Case Scenario: The Mármol Family

I met the Mármol family through one of their relatives in Los Angeles who was familiar with my project and helped me get in touch with them. After I spoke with them on the phone, they kindly offered to host me when I visited the city for a conference. Staying with them for a couple of days, I got to know them better than most of the other families in the study, and when I conducted research abroad, I made it a point to also meet their children and grandmother who cared for them in El Salvador. The Mármol family includes migrant parents, Cristina and Cirilo in Dallas, Texas; their three children, Maricela, Javier, and Leonardo; and their caregiver, Doña Laura, in San

Salvador, El Salvador.[12] Now in her late thirties, Cristina initially migrated by herself and without a visa twelve years prior to our interview. Her husband, Cirilo, unexpectedly decided to join her in the United States just one month after her departure—leaving their three children to be raised by Cristina's mother.

When she was entering the country, immigration authorities detained Cristina, and then both she and Cirilo were undocumented for several years, but she was lucky. Her father, who had migrated decades earlier but never provided for her financially, unexpectedly stepped in and filed an application for her legalization. Although current laws would no longer permit her to stay, immigration policies at that time, in the early 1990s, did not require her to leave the country as a penalty. Once she became a Legal Permanent Resident, she was able to file for legalization for her husband. Driven by their unyielding commitment to bring their children to live with them in the United States, Cristina and Cirilo trusted lawyers and notary publics who conned them out of thousands of dollars and years of precious time. After a long, drawn-out, and very expensive process, however, they were both set to become natural-ized U.S. citizens just months after our interview. With U.S. citizenship, it would be much easier and faster to get the petitions for their children's im-migrant visas approved.

As their legal status became more and more stable over the years, they felt closer to and more excited about achieving family reunification. When I met them, they proudly gave me a tour of their home, pointing out the bedrooms and spaces they had designated for each of their children. Beaming with joy, it was obvious that they thought about their children often and that they used the goal of family reunification as their inspiration to get through long and busy days at work.

Cristina and Cirilo had great reason to be proud. They had made the best of a difficult situation while waiting over a decade to bring their children to live with them. Although they initially worked for many years in poorly paid, ex-ploitative jobs, they took advantage of the fact that they did not have to worry about childcare arrangements on a daily basis. Not having to work around school schedules, homework, or sick children, they were able to attend night school, learn new skills, practice their English, and, by the time I met them, they were both earning livable wages—Cristina as a Certified Nurse's Assistant and Cirilo as an auto mechanic. They sent a sizeable percentage of their earn-ings to their children in the form of remittances—at least $600 per month.

They used the rest to cover their expenses in the United States and pay their mortgage. In El Salvador, Maricela, Javier, and Leonardo had also done their part to make the family separation worthwhile. Maricela was already a college graduate, Javier was in his fourth year of a psychology degree, and Leonardo had just completed his second year of a math degree at one of the most selective universities in the country. In a family where they were the first to complete high school and attend college, they all agreed that it was their parents' migration and remittances that made it possible, and they were supremely grateful.

On the surface, it seems that this is precisely the kind of outcome to which all transnational families aspire. When parents migrate, they are filled with hope that their sacrifices will help children achieve higher education and a comfortable lifestyle. In the United States, they are (often naively) optimistic about obtaining a stable legal status, finding a decent job with livable wages, and sending their families sizeable sums every month while having enough money to also purchase a home and pay for children's migration. For the vast majority of people I interviewed, this kind of outcome seemed not just unlikely, but impossible. And yet, the Mármol family had achieved it. What did it take to get there? And did they lose anything in the process?

As I talked in greater detail with most members of this family, it became clear that their aspirations did not entirely match up. The parents' aspirations made complete sense when viewed through the lens of their lives and their sacrifices. As Cirilo emphatically explained:

> We have deprived ourselves of everything. We are not the type to spend on clothes and new things, no. We only spend on what is necessary, always thinking that we have to save. First we saved to file the legal paperwork for them, but you see the bad luck we've had, that they've stolen our money twice. So we're saving to pay for this house and to prepare ourselves for when their applications are approved, so we can bring them right away. All of that requires money, and we are prepared.

Guided by their shared mission to have everything in place for the entire family's reunification, Cirilo and Cristina focused all their energy on establishing things as they should be for a family of five (plus what they hoped would be frequent visits from Cristina's mother). Because they never wavered from their commitment and because they built their hopes entirely around the idea of living in the United States with their children, they now expected their children to be equally excited about moving in with them.

This is why, when I interviewed them, it was so surprising to learn from their children that they were fully committed to remaining in El Salvador. The youngest of the siblings, nineteen-year-old Leonardo, was excelling in his math program at a top university. He had recently accepted a part-time job as an instructor and was excited about his possible future as a professor. He knew about his parents' intentions, but his response was, "Well, I plan to stay here. If I go over there, it would just be to vacation, but my plans are really to stay here." This is not to say that he did not miss his parents. On the contrary, he and his brother, Javier, shared with me their sad stories of spending Christmas locked up in their room, crying over photographs of their parents and sharing the few childhood memories they still had of living with them. Leonardo hoped to live with them, or at least in the same city, sometime in the near future: "My parents should be the ones to come back here. I might be just hallucinating, but I think I have a good future here, and I would do well in my field." Having worked hard to use his parents' remittances fruitfully, his efforts were paying off. His economic status had improved dramatically, and he enjoyed his new social position. At this stage in his life, he did not want to let go of everything he had worked so hard to achieve.

His twenty-three-year-old brother, Javier, had similar aspirations. He was close to completing the equivalent of a bachelor's degree in psychology at a private university, and he was very clear about why he would not choose to migrate. Stories about the stress of everyday life in the United States abound in El Salvador, and his own mother, who visited them every year or two and called them on the phone regularly, shared details of her life:

> My mom tells me, "Look, if you come here [to the U.S.], if you go to school, it's just from school to home and back. You won't go to the beach, to the pool, to the lake, to the volcano, to hang out with your friend." . . . Every once in a while, they go to a restaurant or they get invited to a party . . . So I start to think, damn, if I want to go out here to visit a friend, I go down there, I go up there, I go to Santa Tecla, to Merliot. I go to San Vicente, I go to Sonsonate, right? And over there, I mean, I think about it, and over there, the human being is like a machine. I don't know, but it seems like they work like eighteen hours a day, and they only rest one day out of the week, and they go in, some of them go in at 4 in the morning, and then they get out at 7 pm.

Javier had heard enough about typical daily life for Salvadoran immigrants in the United States to know that migration would mean losing the freedom he so valued in El Salvador. He enjoyed his sense of belonging and his ability to get around to different parts of the small country whenever he had free time. As he summed up, "Life over there might be good, right? That's why they say that people live like kings there, but they have to work like donkeys." With the completion of a college degree on the horizon, he had no desire to live the life of a load-bearing animal.

Although Javier and Leonardo had been honest with their parents about their aspirations to remain in El Salvador, Cristina and Cirilo did not seem to register their kids' wishes. As migrant parents, they had spent over a decade of their lives pursuing their dream to reunite with their children. At the outset, it certainly made sense. Leonardo was only seven, and the others were preteens. They would migrate in time to complete much of their education in the United States, and they could benefit from the ample opportunities that had not been available to Cristina and Cirilo as children in El Salvador, or as adult immigrants. After they were scammed and when they had to reinitiate their applications for immigrant visas, they realized that their children would have to work harder to catch up.[13] Most likely, they would have to commit to extra years of schooling to properly learn English, but they remained optimistic that together they could make it work. Never did they expect that it would take over twelve years, however. Their children were now adults, and they were leading their own lives, doing well in El Salvador. Regardless, in Cristina and Cirilo's minds, after years of pursuing their dream, life could only be acceptable if the entire family lived together in the United States. Perhaps it would now take their children a lot longer to thrive, but if the parents had adapted, so could their children.

Javier and Leonardo understood their parents. They fully grasped that their parents had worked hard, and they appreciated the sacrifices. Javier made it clear that he and his siblings "are not like others who might get their money and go party, go drinking. We haven't done that. We each get our monthly sum, and everything is accounted for in school, and you can see it in our grades." But, as grateful as they were to their parents, they did not think that Cristina and Cirilo really understood them or took their aspirations seriously:

> Well, I respect my father and mother, really, and I thank them for the sacrifice they've made. It is something we will never lose, but it is also something we won't ever recover. We won't lose it because we are taking advantage of their

sacrifice. And we won't recover because of all the time—our childhood, pre-adolescence, adolescence—they missed it. I mean, that remained an empty space, right? We have not seen them age, and they have not seen us grow up, develop. They have not seen us. They have not been present during our successes. They saw us finish elementary school, high school, that we're in the university, right? They see our successes, but only in a superficial way because they can't be with us day in and day out to see our actual efforts in doing homework and studying.

This is a family that has had the privilege of multiple visits from parents throughout the years, of certainty of legally sanctioned family reunification, and of economic stability. Unlike most families I came across, they maintained close contact, and no one harbored resentment for their parents. They understood each other's positions and loved one another deeply. As Javier confirmed, "Our family ties are close, and the day that they tell me, 'Okay, we can't support you anymore,' I will always care for them. I love them, not only because they send money, but because they are my parents." And yet, without the daily interactions within shared physical space that is more conducive to deeper connections, there was always something missing, an "empty space." Without that deeper understanding and actual witnessing of each other's daily contexts and struggles, it was difficult to get in sync with each other's aspirations.

Javier and his siblings had managed to accomplish exactly what their parents initially hoped for them. On the verge of becoming college graduates and after experiencing a drastic and prolonged improvement in their living conditions, however, they could not fathom having to give up their new status. They understood all too well that, for Salvadorans, "If a doctor emigrates to the United States, over there he won't work as a doctor, he'll be a dishwasher." Javier and Leonardo and several others in their situation had heard multiple stories of the downward shift in status and quality of life for professional Salvadoran migrants to the United States:

> So this lady, she graduated as a psychologist, and for whatever reason she could not find a job here, so she left to the United States to wash dishes, but she's earning practically, well, she says it in colones, like 15,000 colones [about $1,700] per month washing dishes. So my mom tells me that if I study psychology and I graduate and learn to speak English, a psychologist there earns

$120 per hour. So I'm like, wow, how cool! But the sad reality is that, if I go to that country, I don't think I'll be working as a psychologist. Maybe I can do that after ten years. Why? Because I don't speak English, and I don't have any connections.

On the surface, the idea of migrating and earning the salary of a professional in the United States was tempting. Given the vast inequalities that separate the United States and El Salvador, who wouldn't want to go from earning roughly $120 per *month* to earning the same amount per *hour*? But Javier was right. Even for well-educated Salvadorans who migrate with an immigrant visa, the chances of working in their field are slim. Aware that to achieve economic stability he would have to give up his newly earned social and occupational status (accomplished through education funded by remittances) made migration less tempting.

As the time passed and the younger members of the family got closer to the day when their residency would finally be approved, family tensions increased around the mismatch of their aspirations. Because they had each done their part to make the best of the long-term separation, no one was willing to alter his or her goals, nor were they willing to let go of the dream that they would one day be reunited. Cristina and Cirilo had everything in place for their children to join them in the United States, while their children wanted their parents to return after accomplishing the families' economic goals. Emotionally, reunification was the right answer for them, but financially it was impossible. The ever-increasing global inequalities that stratify workers' wages so extensively prevented the family from continuing their successful trajectory if they were all to be based only in El Salvador.

The Mármol family's predicament is very telling. Even in the best of cases, when parents are documented; have stable, well-paying jobs; have sent remittances consistently; have filed for residency for their children; and have visited regularly—even then, long-term separation is difficult. Their children also responded as best as they could under the circumstances. They focused on school and excelled academically, all the while being grateful, not letting their hurt emotions turn into resentment or anger toward their parents. The Mármols reveal, however, that even when everything on the surface seems ideal, transnational family members must navigate deep emotional hardships and shifts in aspirations at different life stages. Long-term separation prolonged over many years, as is often the case for Salvadorans, is likely to end similarly for others. As time goes on, transnational family members' goals change, and if children have done well, reunification in the United States may no longer be in their best interest.[14] But after so many years, understandably, it is often too difficult to let go of their dreams.

More broadly, the experiences of the Mármol family underscore the role of (il)legality and economic structures to determine what is possible for immigrants in the United States as well as for children in places like El Salvador and other developing nations. Cristina and Cirilo, when given legal status to remain permanently in the United States, committed to a future in their new home. They took advantage of learning opportunities and dove into several challenges that ultimately helped them improve their lot. They earned certificates, gained professional skills, and worked tirelessly to invest in a home and a community that could not kick them out as easily anymore. They believed that they had a future in the United States, and they worked to make it the best they could. Meanwhile, their children used the new funds to improve their lives as well. They went to school and excelled because they had opportunities that only few have access to in El Salvador. They witnessed the improvement in their lives and worked hard to maintain their new status by preparing themselves to be professional leaders and contributors to their country. Even though they missed their parents dearly, they had no aspirations to migrate, as they preferred to remain in El Salvador.

Contrary to common misconceptions in angry debates about immigration in the United States, the Mármol family demonstrates that structural factors make all the difference. If people have opportunities to get an education and work in their chosen fields while earning enough to guarantee basic living standards, on the whole, they will not want to migrate to the United States—with or without a visa. Instead, they would prefer to remain in a place where they feel a strong sense of belonging and the freedom to enjoy their surroundings. For those who are already in the United States, who came because they saw no other way to carve a path for survival and mobility for themselves and their families, structural opportunities also make all the difference. Stable legal status—a break from the persecution currently directed toward undocumented immigrants—opens channels for productive contributions to this country with the promise that they have a future to invest in here. Unstable legal statuses, criminalization of immigrants, and blocked paths to legalization only discourage that kind of investment.

Conclusion

Transnational families' unequal experiences and expectations powerfully shape how they live their lives from day to day. More importantly, inequalities across transnational families matter because they help determine how children acclimate, participate, and associate with the people and the social environments where they reside. Through these processes, transnational family members either develop or fail to establish a solid foundation for their future. (Il)legality, gendered structures, and gender ideologies directly determine children's day-to-day lives but also powerfully shape their long-term aspirations. Children who were struggling financially and emotionally had a more difficult time developing concrete goals and often envisioned their future (only in fuzzy terms) in the United States. On the other hand, children who had learned to cope emotionally and who were thriving financially were more likely to want to stay in El Salvador where they could enjoy their newly achieved higher social status.

These patterns of aspirations made sense. Children who were barely subsisting or surviving due to their migrant parents' minimal or complete lack of economic support were limited in what they could afford to eat on a daily basis. Educationally, many were getting too old for the grade they were in, and, even if they overcame the embarrassment, they could rarely afford to attend school consistently. And, to top things off, holidays further crushed their spirits by reminding them that their parents' migration, rather than turning out to be an effective survival strategy, simply left them in poverty and feeling abandoned. Eventually, the acute sense of abandonment constricted their aspirations, often pushing them to disengage from the Salvadoran context. Sometimes they acted out, or made problematic choices, that, without any kind of institutional support, led them to give up on their educational and occupational goals. At that point, it became easier to focus intently on reuniting with their migrant parents in the United States.

Children who were thriving also missed their parents terribly and longed for family reunification, but they had learned to cope—even through the painful reminders brought by holidays. With access to private schooling, ample school supplies, and the resources to participate in extracurricular activities, thriving children most abundantly benefited from their parents' migration and consistent economic support. Thriving children, therefore, were more likely to understand their parents' migration and subsequent long-term separation as a sacrifice. This understanding made it possible to appreciate the many benefits they received from remittances. Their gains also improved their emotional well-being. Given their experiences, they were more likely to feel encouraged to engage with local activities and excel in school (at least partially in an effort to please parents). And so, they were on a path toward upward mobility or economic stability in El Salvador. Although, in earlier stages of their lives, they still wanted desperately to reunite with parents in the United States, once they reached adulthood and if they achieved a higher socioeconomic status, they developed a strong desire to remain in El Salvador. Only there would they be able to maintain their newly acquired professional and social status.

In my study, I was not able to follow up with these families. It is possible, and even likely, that shifting legal and economic contexts and new life stages will coincide with shifts in aspirations and achievements. At this particular moment in time, however, these notable patterns in aspirations were clearly in line with children's economic and emotional well-being. Meanwhile, parents who left with so much hope were often still guided by their aspirations for family reunification and economic stability. In the current context of immigration laws and gendered job opportunities, it is unclear how many families will have a chance to succeed in reaching their aspirations. As the southern Mexican and U.S. borders are further militarized and immigration policies continue to tighten,[15] chances for reunification diminish considerably for most families. And those who qualify for legalization, like the Mármols, may find that the long bureaucratic process only allowed for reunification when it was already too late.

8 ¿Valió la pena? Is Family Separation Worth It?

Yes, it was worth it because we were all able to study as much, well, not as much as we wanted, but we're all high school graduates [at least]. And that's something.

—Sonia

As much as it hurts, it is better to have a stable family with a little bit of money than to be separated, even if you have more things, because what is the use if you can't enjoy those things with your family? It is useless.

—Rubén

[I]t was not worth it [for them to leave] because I feel that I had the right to be with them, to be raised by my parents, and I didn't have that chance.

—Clara

Well, yes [it was worth it], because economically we have everything. I mean, we're always missing something, but the needs are less now than before. . . . But then the trust [confianza] and the knowledge that he's there physically, that part is hard.

—María Elena

It was worth it because right now, if he were here, he wouldn't have a job . . . But over there, he is working . . . But for me it was very difficult. I lived with him many years, and I cared about him, and he cared for me. So I cried when he left.

—Nicolás

I don't want to sound ungrateful, but you do live with a hole in your heart.

—Sofia

EACH OF THESE QUOTES WAS A RESPONSE TO MY QUESTION about whether family separation was worthwhile (*¿valió la pena?*). I asked it of every person I interviewed. Unsurprisingly, the responses were mixed and often complex. When economic success had eluded them, children of migrants were mostly clear that the family separation strategy was not worth it. However, among those who were faring well, who completed more schooling and lived more comfort-ably—even they danced around the words, never affirming unequivocally that the strategy had been a success. Parents, on the other hand, held on tightly to their belief that things would have only been worse had they stayed—even when they had suffered tremendously. This conviction sustained them. But what are the repercussions when so many children are growing up away from one or both parents? How does long-term separation shape their well-being and, in turn, their ability to participate meaningfully in the world around them? And how do migrant parents' sacrifices and prolonged inability to re-unite with children mediate their integration into their new home? In short, is family separation worth it?

Learning from Salvadoran Transnational Families

Listening carefully to the stories of transnational family members—paying close attention to the patterns across all of their narratives—there is great complexity in their experiences, but some things are also very clear. Family separation across borders and over a long period of time is difficult. Parents left their children usually only under the most difficult set of circumstances and only because they could not find solutions to their problems where they lived. Filled with hope, they set out, often through a dangerous and costly journey, to the United States, where global inequalities ensured that their la-bor would be better rewarded. Their dreams were straightforward: With more money, they would support their children and improve their lives. Along the way, however, they faced structural barriers—particularly rooted in immigra-tion policies and their gender—that prevented many from reaching their eco-nomic goals. Whether parents did well or not, the results were quite evident in the daily lives of their children. Some certainly thrived, but others fared only slightly better, while others yet were barely subsisting. Emotionally, some children of migrants learned to cope with the family separation, but others never stopped feeling consumed by the sadness and sense of abandonment.

In El Salvador, among children who received remittances, those economic inequalities determined their daily decisions: whether to have three sepa-rate meals or spread out only one meal throughout the day; whether to go to school hungry or rack up another absence to use transportation money on food; and whether to hang out with friends or lock themselves up in their homes to avoid being victimized in their neighborhoods. In those daily deci-sions, remittance recipients may have different responses to the question: Is family separation worth it? If they slept in a bed for the first time or now had their own room; if they received the medication they needed; or if they were enrolled at a top private school—in these cases, they would likely say that at least for economic purposes, yes, the family separation was worth it. On the contrary, if they had little to show for their parents' prolonged absence, the answer was usually a quick "no."

But beyond those daily decisions, as days turned into months, and months into years, a wider context also developed, and in answering the question— Was family separation worth it?—they also considered all the time that had transpired. It was painful to recognize that parents had missed key milestones in their lives; that no matter how much some of them tried, it was impossible to develop, only over phone conversations, the kind of emotional bond they desired; and that it might still be many years before they could be together again. In that often painful emotional context, they had to make decisions about the future. Over the long term, those inequalities that influenced their daily decisions eventually also shaped how they thought about their future: whether to invest in their education and prepare to be leaders of their country or simply disengage from the world around them as they waited for the day when they would have an opportunity to leave to the United States. Some were in such bad shape that they also pondered whether to hang themselves out of desperation or keep going for another day.

Collectively, how these children answer the question—Is family separation worth it?—will have important consequences for Salvadoran society. After being separated for so long, not knowing when they might be reunited, many members of these families felt disconnected from their surroundings. While each imagined and prepared for a future elsewhere, many years had gone by in which they were either participating or not, associating or disassociating from the social, political, and economic reality around them. In this way, U.S. immigration laws along with gendered structures and norms not only stratified people's lives during separation, but they also set the stage for long-term integration of transnational family members in their local contexts.

The implications are also noteworthy in the United States. In answering the question—Is family separation worth it?—many immigrant parents felt they had made the right decision, but their assessment was not based on their own well-being. Instead, they mostly felt satisfied that they could at least provide food and more schooling for their children in El Salvador. To that end, many spent their energies and resources thinking about and contributing to their loved ones in another physical space. Thus, their daily decisions led them, over the long run, to disassociate from society, shaping how they integrated (or failed to integrate fully) in the United States. In effect, for many of these families who do not foresee a legal path to reunification, the long-term separation means that they will spend years unable to plan concretely for their future, and many will hold back from participating in meaningful ways where they reside. This kind of transnationalism, therefore, deters migrants and nonmigrants alike from social, economic, and political integration that is crucial for a healthy society.[1]

Remittances and Development

In El Salvador, as in many developing countries like it, political leaders, bankers, and members of the business elite have already answered the question—Is family separation worth it? In their policies and practices, they respond with a resounding "yes." After all, politically, economically, and socially, migration is pivotal in El Salvador, where an estimated 20 to 35 percent of the population emigrates. Effectively, every aspect of Salvadoran national life is, in one way or another, affected by migration, but because remittances now make up over 15 percent of the gross domestic product, national politicians focus almost exclusively on the economic aspects. People hear that remittances bring in over $3 billion each year, and they want to know how to use this sum to improve the economy overall.

The stories in this book reveal important details that we tend to miss when we hear that El Salvador received a record $3.8 billion in remittances in 2008; that there was a notable reduction in remittances for a few years during the global economic downturn; and that the sums rose up to $3.9 billion in 2012. Indeed, after the plunge, remittances were on the upswing in many places by 2011: $2.5 billion in Honduras; $4.2 billion in Colombia; $4.3 billion in Guatemala; and $22.7 billion in Mexico.[2] Keeping track of these funds is important; remittances represent significant financial transfers that collectively uphold the national economy of El Salvador and many other migrant-sending countries. But, as impressive as these figures sound, when they are the *only* information we hear about migration and transnational families, they also have the effect of erasing the individual stories of pain and sacrifice, success and failure, and unfulfilled aspirations of the people who earned and received each dollar.

It is precisely the single focus on dollar figures that allows politicians and development organizations around the world to scrutinize how the money is spent and how it might be put to more productive use. In El Salvador, public leaders have been quick to condemn what they perceive as "wasteful spending" of family remittances. With little regard for gains in human capital and health, they have criticized poor families for spending their money in ways that do not generate more funds.[3] In encouraging people to bank or invest remittances,[4] political leaders and development experts have mostly failed to think holistically about transnational families, their members in El Salvador and the United States, or the collective social effect of having such a large percentage of the population living in long-term separation from loved ones.

The criticism of how families spend remittances comes easily in a context that generally demonizes transnational families. Throughout the country, in neighborly conversations, newspapers, and political blogs, people blame transnational families for everything from national economic woes to the proliferation of gangs and crime. The facile assumptions are that migrant parents try to buy their children's love by sending home exorbitant sums of money, which the children then spend irresponsibly; or, on the contrary, that parents reach the United States only to begin new lives and forget about their children, who then join gangs to fill the emotional void. Although such things do happen, these simplistic scenarios miss a wide range of complex experiences among transnational families. Most notably, they ignore the profound emotional suffering of family separation, obscure the structural constraints that powerfully determine how transnational families fare, and misrepresent these families' various and unequal economic realities. Yet too often it seems that Salvadoran policy makers have crafted their policies while relying too closely on these popular assumptions. It is my hope that the salience of raw pain and emotion in the narratives in this book—the ones that reveal the human toll of family separation—will come to have a more prominent role in discussions of remittances and development.

Legal and gendered analyses of remittance practices, moreover, uncover the tenuous situation for undocumented and women migrants, respectively, who are often at great financial and personal risk when they remit large percentages of their total earnings. Asking these families to bear the burden of national development would, in many cases, wipe out the slim margin of economic security they have managed to eke out at high personal costs.

What To Do? Policy Implications in El Salvador and the United States

Not unlike several developing nations around the world, El Salvador's prin-cipal export is its workers, and its principal import, their remittances. This is possible and made acceptable only in the context of a shamefully unequal global economy. Salvadoran and other world leaders have too often failed to move beyond a single focus on remittances. For example, on the main web page for the Vice Ministry for Salvadorans Living Abroad, in the section that describes their work, they recognize openly that "El Salvador is only think-able, only viable, and only possible if we include Salvadorans abroad in our national development plans."[5] But, under the current administration, there has also been an attempt to begin to treat the issue of migration and family separation more holistically. Indeed, shortly after coming into office in 2009, Salvadoran President Mauricio Funes and his Vice Minister Juan José Gar-cía developed a proposal to present to U.S. President Barack Obama in which they called for comprehensive immigration reform in language that framed family reunification as a matter of human rights.[6] Reframing the language and taking up a new angle are important steps in solving the human tragedy of family separations through migration.

Given the current state of affairs in the United States, however, it could be many years before truly humane and inclusive comprehensive immigration reform passes. In the meantime, the tens of thousands of Salvadoran children growing up without one or both parents due to migration, as well as their parents, will need politicians and educators to learn more of the intricacies of their experiences of long-term separation. The stories of young people like Daniel and transnational mothers like Esperanza, even when they include economic and educational success, are often steeped in pain and longing. For them, it is imperative that their social context begin to change in El Salvador, even as U.S. immigration policies remain the same.

The people in this book have clear ideas about the economic and political context they would prefer in place of their family separation. Seventeen-year-old Mirna for example, whose father had lived in the United States for most of her life, summed up her hopes quite plainly:

> I'd say to all the people who will hear this that no, I don't feel it is good for families to be separated. The government needs to pay attention and help peo-ple so that families can move up, here in the country, and not have to go to

other places where they get mistreated. Because my father tells me that many people, when they get over there, they are discriminated and looked down on. That is not necessary. The opportunities should be here. The government should provide that for people—because if you watch the news, you know that many people go, and they show on the news that they lose their lives trying to get there.

Mirna gave voice to the frustration and demands of so many adolescents and young adults I interviewed. If given a viable alternative, most families would choose to remain together. If there were economic opportunities to permit all families to survive and thrive in El Salvador, few would opt for migration. Salvadorans, like Mirna, are calling for the right not to have to migrate.[7] Therefore the big, messy, impossible, but only correct answer is for global development to advance more fairly. New policies need to regulate wealthy nations and elite transnational corporations. The most recent economic downturn proves that the greatest beneficiaries of global inequalities will not hold themselves accountable. Only policies that reflect a dramatic shift in how we value humanity will hold governments and corporations responsible, rein in their greed, and press them to act more reasonably to stop exacerbating inequalities and benefiting from the poverty of developing nations and disenfranchised peoples. Only these changes will guarantee individuals the human right to not have to migrate.

Short of at least a partial redistribution of wealth, there are many other necessary steps to improve conditions for transnational families. The narratives I highlight in this book suggest a great need to engage these youth in El Salvador. To this end, new programs should provide the space for children and adolescents to develop relationships with others and feel connected to their communities and their country. Schools, parks, religious institutions, and community centers should have access to public funds earmarked for this work: to reach out more vigorously to these young people who are so often feeling abandoned and alone, even when their caregivers are doing their best to raise them.

Another step in improving transnational families' situation would involve a massive social campaign in El Salvador to more equitably redefine gender ideologies to better accommodate the lived experiences of motherhood and fatherhood in the oppressive global context of migration and family separation. Fatherhood needs to be understood as a lifelong responsibility to children, regardless of parents' relationship status. More specifically, social expectations should shift in such a way that transnational fathers feel more emotionally connected to their children, even across borders and over time. Notions of motherhood, on the other hand, need to be altered to more critically reflect on the economic limitations that can force mothers to leave their children and their homes. Mothers cannot be expected to be the only morally responsible members of families or the only ones who can provide care on a daily basis, particularly when the government and society fail to provide them with the resources they need to do the work of mothering. Speaking of motherhood only as the highest form of womanhood—exclusively exalting the selflessness and extreme sacrifices—ignores the pervasive exploitation of women workers and the lack of institutional support for meeting the tremendous responsibilities placed on mothers. As an added benefit, it is likely that these more critical and realistic social redefinitions would also encourage intact families in El Salvador to more fairly distribute household responsibilities. Radio and television commercials as well as print ads would go a long way to shift representations of mothers and fathers and transnational families more broadly and in a more equitable way.[8]

Beyond media, schools and municipalities also have important roles to play in normalizing transnational families so that children can understand their situation in a broader context and feel less emotionally stigmatized. Teachers should develop classroom curricula, and local cultural celebrations should also reflect the fact that so many parents were forced to leave children in search of survival. Otherwise, a failure to include transnational families' realities in the national political discourse, in school curricula, or in community events, only permits the energy and creativity of these young people—who do not always live luxuriously and whose parents have not, in most cases, chosen to abandon them—to be wasted.

This is all imperative because, although legalization in the United States will resolve many problems, migration policies alone cannot compensate for the notable disparities that put transnational families at risk. The legally violent consequences of current immigration laws and gendered opportunities and expectations especially place transnational mothers and their children in positions of long-term vulnerability. Despite their low wages, mothers are more likely than fathers to consistently send large percentages of their earnings to their children. To achieve this, they make extreme sacrifices. Putting their children's needs above their own, many transnational mothers send most of their resources to El Salvador. And although their children benefit economically and educationally from their sacrifices, these immigrant women have little left for themselves. Because they work hard and keep only the bare minimum that they need for survival, they do not have the time or the funds necessary to participate in U.S. society. They are not investing in their future in the United States, nor are they integrating socially or politically. Even if comprehensive immigration reform were to pass, it would be a significant challenge for them to save enough money to pay for their children's travel, visa, and settlement costs. Only long-term changes in how Salvadorans think about motherhood and fatherhood, and in the expectations they place—legally and socially—on parents, will help ease these disparities.

In the United States, immigration policy has taken central stage in multiple presidential debates and public opinion polls, with little improvement for immigrants. On the contrary, in the absence of federal immigration reform, state and local level politicians and authorities have increasingly pursued what they call "attrition through enforcement" strategies to decrease the number of undocumented immigrants in the country. In effect, they have made life as difficult as possible for undocumented immigrants, their families, and their communities in efforts to make them so miserable that they will return to their countries even if they are not detained and formally deported. Unable to work, rent an apartment, attend community college, or even have access to basic utilities like water or power in some states, the attrition through enforcement approach has devastating consequences for immigrants. What this book reveals, however, is that such inhumane tactics do not work. People, even when deeply pained by the distance that separates them from their children, will not voluntarily leave the United States. No matter how poorly they are treated, they cannot leave. Given the extent of global inequalities, to do so would be a form of surrender because they would be returning to a country where economic development has been suspended.

In the meantime, without comprehensive immigration reform,[9] families continue to suffer the devastating effects of long-term separation, and the United States loses out on the investment and integration of immigrant parents in transnational families—particularly the undocumented and temporarily protected. As easy targets for exploitation in the labor force, with little recourse when they become injured, and unable to visit their loved ones, immigrants with unstable legal statuses are victims. To be clear, some legal protections are better than none. Families relying on immigrants with TPS fare better financially than families with undocumented immigrant parents. This should not, however, lead to the conclusion that limited legal protections—in the form of temporary work permits and short-term protection from deportation—are sufficient or acceptable.

Transnational families relying on parents with TPS suffer profoundly the inability to be together, even during emergencies—parents cannot leave without losing their work permits, and children have no legal pathway to reunite with parents in the United States. Furthermore, unable to plan concretely for the future, their lives and aspirations are suspended—an experience that closely resembles that of families relying on undocumented parents. Therefore, at a time when politicians tout guest worker programs as possible solutions to the immigration deadlock, the narratives in this book should serve as a warning. For Salvadoran transnational families, TPS translates into a general uncertainty about the future and discourages both children and parents from participating more fully in the communities where they live. It is highly likely, then, that a guest worker program that limits protections for workers and separates them from their families will similarly lead to emotional suffering and insecurity for many more families.

Resources poured into immigration enforcement, moreover, could go a long way to instead protect the human and labor rights of migrants. There need to be grave repercussions for thieves, kidnappers, rapists, and murderers who currently prey with great impunity on migrants while en route to the United States. In the United States, workers' narratives underscore the rampant labor exploitation that goes unregulated in industries that rely on immigrant labor. Enforcement practices, then, should target abusive employers in domestic work, hotels, restaurants, construction companies, and warehouses.

Centering the Production of (II)legality and Gender

Although development researchers and policy makers have overlooked key aspects affecting remittances, international migration and family researchers have been paying close attention. Indeed, they have produced a growing body of scholarly work to accompany the increasing worldwide incidence in family separation due to migration. Research focusing on transnational families in which parents migrate to secure their nonmigrant children's survival has, at different times, emphasized benefits and coping mechanisms,[10] challenges to and enduring gendered practices,[11] the spatial fragmentation of caregiving,[12] and daily practices and survival strategies across borders.[13] Most recently, the tremendous emotional costs to family members have repeatedly surfaced as central components of the transnational family experience,[14] particularly for members of mother-away families. While all of these findings are inherently important for understanding the overall experience of family separation, given that the transnational family strategy is, at its core, a response to economic circumstances, families' economic outcomes also merit more systematic examination.

In this book, I have tried to contribute by exploring more directly whether all transnational families benefit equally from remittances and, if not, why not? Conversation after conversation with children of migrants immediately and unequivocally revealed that families were faring quite unevenly. Some were thriving, others were surviving, and some were only barely subsisting. Because their economic situation was based almost entirely on how their migrant parents fared in the United States, I expected to find answers in the immigrant integration literature. Researchers examining how well immigrants fare in the United States explain differences in experiences by citing human capital, social networks, and length of residency.[15] These factors, however, did not fully or consistently explain the inequalities across transnational families.

As I paid close attention to the families' stories and the emergent patterns, it became evident that it did not always matter how many people migrant parents knew, how long they had lived in the United States, or how much schooling they had attained. Instead, U.S. immigration policies—particularly through the production of illegality—and gendered opportunities and expectations more powerfully explained these transnational families' divergent experiences. The emphasis of immigration laws and gendered structures and norms bring into sharp relief the vast inequalities that permeate transnational families. Only through an examination of the production of gender did it make sense that children in mother-away families were often faring well, even though immigrant women generally had terrible job options in the United States. And only by centering immigration policies was it possible to see the cumulative advantages and disadvantages of legal statuses in the short- and long-term prospects of these family members in the United States as well as beyond its borders.

My contention is not that these factors—human capital, social networks, and length of residency—are unimportant. Rather, I argue that their explanatory power is complicated and weakened by illegality and gender—particularly for migrants who are undocumented or only temporarily protected.

In line with existing research, I show that female immigrants are especially vulnerable to structural barriers that block their economic success. My contribution, however, is to demonstrate that, despite the structural disadvantages, immigrant mothers' families can still thrive economically due to two key mechanisms, both of which are deeply informed by gender ideologies, idealized notions of motherhood, and masculinities in Latin America. First, driven by social expectations that deem mothers as selfless, morally superior members of the family, mothers approach parenting as a firm responsibility that requires them to prioritize their children's well-being above their own. Fathers, on the other hand, have multiple ways to achieve masculinities, allowing them the possibility of approaching parenting more loosely. Second, mothers stay committed to their children over longer periods, even when their relationship status changes, while fathers often associate fathering responsibilities with marital responsibilities so that, when partnerships end, they are likely to loosen ties with children as well. These gendered parental behaviors then determine how much and how often parents send in remittances, which in turn shape children's economic well-being.

Aside from determining children's economic well-being in El Salvador, immigrant parents' gendered remitting behaviors also suggest divergent paths to integration in the United States. Transnational mothers are vulnerable because they send most of their resources to their children. By keeping very little for themselves, they limit their socioeconomic integration and risk great long-term hardship much like other poor women in the United States.[16] Men, on the other hand, tend to send fewer remittances, and they do so less frequently. Unburdened by idealized notions of fatherhood, immigrant fathers are more likely than mothers to become inconsistent remitters. And, although some fathers admit to spending surplus money on entertainment and drinking, their greater earnings relative to women provide savings and investment opportunities in the United States, potentially improving their experiences of socioeconomic integration.

Along with gender, for migrants with unstable legal statuses, their lack of legal protections best explains their families' economic and emotional experiences. Not only are undocumented and temporarily protected parents limited to poorly remunerated, exploitative jobs, but they are also blocked from visiting their relatives or bringing them to live in the United States legally. In these ways, legal status, as conferred through immigration policies, channels migrants through integration processes in the United States while also structuring children's emotional well-being by determining how long families are separated and how certain they feel about their reunification.

Proponents and supporters of punitive immigration laws claim that these laws protect national security and are necessary to preserve the sovereignty of the nation. Targeted immigrants, however, experience these laws differently. The cumulative experiences associated with long-term family separation, under today's immigration regime, can trample on immigrant parents' rights so pervasively that the consequences are evident beyond U.S. territory where they profoundly shape the emotional and economic well-being, as well as the aspirations and sense of belonging, of children. At a time when "attrition through enforcement" is a popular approach to try to decrease the number of undocumented immigrants in the country, these stories should make it unequivocally clear that such tactics do not work. Even immigrants who long to be with their children, who suffer daily because they are missing their children's childhoods and special moments, even those immigrants cannot leave. In their situation, they are forced to put up with dehumanization and criminalization because, economically, it is not currently realistic to think that they could return and do any better. They want desperately to return, to be with their loved ones, but they know that returning will mean poverty and hunger and complete immobility financially. And they cannot, as good parents, do this to their children. It is my hope that as we recognize these inequalities and the sacrifices of transnational family members, family separation for the purpose of survival will no longer go unquestioned as a celebrated practice in the name of national development.

This book has been an attempt to move beyond dollar sums and facile assumptions. I talked to the human beings who made the decisions and those who bore the consequences of family separation. Their words and experiences suggest that there is a need to look more closely for the realities not captured in annual figures. The $3.9 billion in remittances in El Salvador last year did nothing to prevent parents from facing danger, even death, during their journey north. The sum did not bring about change in U.S. immigration laws to open paths for legalization or legally sanctioned family reunification. The $3.9 billion did not mean that undocumented workers and women immigrants were treated fairly on the job, nor that mothers and fathers would share their parenting burdens equitably. Most importantly, the sum did not guarantee that all families would benefit equally from long-term separation. On the contrary, knowing that collectively people in El Salvador received $3.9 billion last year hid the fact that some of those recipients were failing in school, over-whelmed by their emotions, and unable to participate in their society. The $3.9 billion did nothing to prevent some of them from considering suicide to escape their problems and their pain.

Families throughout the world are experiencing long-term separation across national borders. Limited economic opportunities—especially for women—along with human-made and natural catastrophes drive parents to opt for migration as their last hope—despite the financial, physical, and emotional risks. In recent years, many receiving countries have implemented increas-ingly restrictive immigration policies that include tighter border controls, more temporary worker permits, and greater restrictions on the ability to acquire permanent residence. Arguably, family separation is built into these immigration policies. Not only have immigration laws limited migration in multiple ways, but they also make life unbearable for immigrants already in receiving countries, blocking routes to obtain legal residency and diminish-ing the possibility for family reunification. Even for those who are eligible, bureaucracies create long waiting periods that can stall family reunification for over a decade. Rates of family separation, then, will only continue to in-crease. In the meantime, social expectations in much of the world continue to demand that children grow up with at least one parent, but global inequali-ties make this increasingly unlikely. Are we comfortable being a country that legally enables human rights abuses of migrants? What are we willing to do to stop the sacrificing of these families?

Reference Matter

Appendix

Table 1. Descriptive statistics of migrant parents interviewed in the United States
($n = 47$).[a]

	Mean or proportion	
	Female (n = 25)	*Male (n = 22)*
Age		
Average age in years (standard deviation)	39.4 (9.1)	41.5 (10.2)
Age range in years	25–55	26–57
Age 25–34	0.36	0.27
Age 35–44	0.32	0.27
Age 45–57	0.32	0.45
Length of residence in United States		
Average length of residence in United States in years (SD)	10.4 (5.9)	12.1 (7.8)
Range of length of residence in United States in years	3–20	3–27
Length of time in United States less than 10 years	0.44	0.45
Length of time in United States 10 or more years	0.56	0.55
Education		
Average level of education at migration (SD)	8.2 (3.1)	9.0 (3.3)
Range of level of education in years	2–16	0–14
Less than 9 years of education	0.32	0.41
9 or more years of education	0.68	0.59
Legal status at interview		
Undocumented[b]	0.36	0.23
Temporary Protected Status (TPS)[c]	0.20	0.18
In process of LPR[d]	0.08	0.00
Legal Permanent Resident[e]	0.36	0.55
U.S. citizen[f]	0.00	0.05
Weekly earnings at interview		
≤ $300	0.40	0.23
$301 to $499	0.40	0.14
≥ $500	0.20	0.64

Table 1. (continued)

	Mean or proportion	
	Female (n = 25)	Male (n = 22)
Social networks[g]		
Family	0.48	0.27
Friends	0.16	0.36
Family and friends	0.12	0.14
No one	0.24	0.23

[a] This table is also included in Abrego 2009 on page 1073.

[b] Undocumented immigrants are present in the United States without lawful status.

[c] Temporary Protected Status (TPS) grants beneficiaries the legal right to remain in the United States and to work during a designated period. It does not lead to legal permanent resident status.

[d] Migrants who are in the process of obtaining legal permanent residency may obtain a work permit but cannot travel internationally without permission. Some may be "in-process" for many years.

[e] Legal Permanent Residents (LPR) can reside and work in the United States permanently.

[f] Naturalized U.S. citizens are immigrants who previously had LPR status but, through an application process, gained full legal citizenship rights.

[g] Having friends or relatives who live in the United States does not guarantee that those people will help newly arrived immigrants (see Menjívar 2000).

Table 2. Descriptive statistics of children interviewed in El Salvador (n = 80a).[a,b]

	Mean or proportion		
	Mother away (n = 29)	Father away (n = 38)	Both away (n = 13)
Age			
Average age in years (standard deviation)	17.9 (3.4)	17.1 (2.8)	17.0 (3.2)
Age range in years	14–29	14–26	14–24
Age 14-17	0.55	0.79	0.77
Age 18-29	0.45	0.21	0.23
Length of parents' residence in the United States[c]			
Average years (SD)	9.7 (5.8)	9.5 (5.3)	9.0 (5.8)
Range in years	3–21	3–18	3–20
≤ 10 years	0.52	0.57	0.53
> 10 years	0.48	0.43	0.46
Parents' legal status at interview			
Undocumented	0.45	0.34	0.38
Temporary Protected Status (TPS)	0.21	0.34	0.31
In Process of LPR	0.14	0.00	0.08
Legal Permanent Resident	0.21	0.32	0.23

[a] This table is also included in Abrego 2009 on page 1074.

[b] Table excludes three caregivers who participated in the study.

[c] Missing information about length of their parents' residence for one respondent in a father-away family.

Table 3. Children's economic well-being by who is away.[a]

	Mother away (n = 49)		Father away (n = 58)		Both away (n = 23)		Total (n = 130)	
Barely subsisting	4	8%	12	21%	4	17%	20	15%
Surviving	18	37%	25	43%	5	22%	48	37%
Thriving	27	55%	21	36%	14	61%	62	48%

[a] This table is an expanded version of the one included in Abrego 2009 on page 1077. In this case, the figures include data from narratives of children and caregivers in El Salvador and migrant parents in the United States.

Notes

Preface

1. I asked my mother to reflect on her experience as a child in a transnational family to produce the image on the cover of this book. The painting reveals her childhood and the way she imagined her mother, as a larger-than-life, distant, but ever-present figure overseeing her small world in her small town of San Martín. The painful separation, evident in her tears and those of her sisters, grandmother, and mother, fill Lake Ilopango (at Corinto Beach), nearby. Her mother, meanwhile, is like the largest tree of the plaza—rooted in the town—even as she is physically absent. My mom hoped that she and her siblings and their daily lives always occupied her mother's mind. The cross represents her brother's tragic death. He drowned in that lake, just months before they got their immigrant visa to join their mother in the United States.

2. For more detailed information about the kinds of challenges children face during reunifications, see Artico 2003; Menjívar and Abrego 2009; and Pratt 2012.

3. Abrego 2011.

4. For information about efforts to demand human rights for LGBT people in El Salvador, see Davenport 2012.

5. Ponce 2012.

6. Menjívar and Abrego 2012.

Chapter 1

1. I use pseudonyms and have disguised details about places to protect the anonymity of people who participated in this project.

2. "Remittances are defined as economic transfers that follow unidirectional paths from a mobile worker to her or his sending household, community, and country" (Maimbo and Ratha 2005; cited in Cohen 2011).

3. Carolina Rivera, author of "Prosperity," performed the piece in May 2003 at the Highways Performance Space in Santa Monica, California, as part of a show with various other acts and performers collectively entitled "Epicentrico: Rico Epicentro," directed by Raquél Gutiérrez.

4. Fox Searchlight Pictures 2007.

5. Nazario 2007.

6. For a succinct and useful description of the history and multiple usage of transnationalism and various associated concepts, see Hernández-León 2008: 11. The literature on *transnationalism*—documenting and theorizing migrant–homeland ties—does not immediately reveal why inequalities exist across transnational families (Basch, Glick Schiller, and Szanton Blanc 1994; Glick Schiller, Basch, and Blanc-Szanton 1992; Guarnizo and Smith 1998; Levitt and Jaworsky 2007; Pessar and Mahler 2003; Portes, Guarnizo, and Landolt 1999; and Waldinger and Fitzgerald 2004). There is, however, a growing consensus that immigrants benefit in multiple ways from maintaining links to people and institutions in their home countries and, furthermore, that participation in transnational activities does not hinder incorporation into their new home (Fitzgerald 2004; Goldring 1998; Guarnizo, Portes, and Haller 2003; Itzigsohn and Giorguli-Saucedo 2005; Levitt 2001; Popkin 1998; Smith 2006; and Stephen 2007).

7. Dreby 2010; Dreby and Adkins 2010; and Schmalzbauer 2005.

8. Dreby 2006; Menjívar and Abrego 2009; and Parreñas 2005a.

9. Dreby 2007; and Orellana et al. 2001.

10. Boehm 2012; Ehrenreich and Hochschild 2002; Hondagneu-Sotelo and Avila 1997; and Landolt and Da 2005.

11. Zentgraf and Chinchilla 2012.

12. Dreby 2010.

13. For similar findings, see also Castañeda 2012.

14. Schmalzbauer 2008.

15. Portes and Rumbaut 2001: 46.

16. Boyd 1989 and Massey et al. 1987.

17. Myers 2007.

18. Alba and Nee 2003; Feliciano 2005; Menjívar 2006; and Portes and Rumbaut 1996.

19. Castañeda 2012.

20. Faist 2008; Nyberg-Sørensen, Van Hear, and Engberg-Pedersen 2002; and Piper 2008, 2009.

21. Taylor 1999; Kapur and Center for Global Development 2003; Ratha 2003; and World Bank 2006.

22. "Latin America: Despite the Crisis, Remittances Are Still Robust"; retrieved on February 8, 2013, from www.worldbank.org/en/news/feature/2012/11/20/remesas-america-latina.

23. For similar conclusions in the Mexican and Georgian cases, see Castañeda 2012.

24. Dreby 2010; Parreñas 2005b; and Schmalzbauer 2004.

25. Parreñas 2001, 2005a, 2005b; Pratt 2012; and Zentgraf and Chinchilla 2012.

26. Dreby and Stutz 2012 and Pratt 2012.

27. Boehm 2012.

28. Pratt 2012.

29. De Genova 2002 and Ngai 2004.

30. Boehm 2012; and Menjívar and Kanstroom forthcoming.

31. Abrego forthcoming; Abrego and Menjívar 2011; and Menjívar and Abrego 2012.

32. De Genova 2002 and Ngai 2004. Also, see descriptions of immigrants' experiences from the 1970s and 1980s in Chapter 4.

33. Menjívar and Abrego 2012.

34. The change in policy had especially notable consequences for Mexicans, who had a long history of circular migration between Mexico and the United States. See Hondagneu-Sotelo 1994 and Massey, Durand, and Malone 2002.

35. Donato and Armenta 2011.

36. Chacón 2010.

37. Coleman 2007: 58–59.

38. See Menjívar and Abrego 2012: 1393.

39. Chacón 2012; Hernández 2008; and Menjívar and Abrego 2012.

40. "Secure Communities," retrieved on February 18, 2013, from www.ice.gov/secure_communities/.

41. See Table 38 of the Department of Homeland Security's *Yearbook of Immigration Statistics: 2010*, retrieved on April 24, 2012, from www.dhs.gov/files/statistics/publications/YrBk10En.shtm, for a breakdown of the number of deportees with and without histories of criminal offenses.

42. Indeed, "widespread enforcement of criminal immigration laws is a relatively new phenomenon" (Chacón 2012: 614).

43. Chavez 2008 and Santa Ana 2012.

44. National Community Advisory 2011; retrieved on February 20, 2013, from http://trac.syr.edu/immigration/reports/310/.

45. Abrego forthcoming; Chavez 2008; and Menjívar and Abrego 2012.

46. Bacon 2008 and Gleeson 2012.

47. Abrego forthcoming; Calavita 1992; Coutin 2000, 2002; De Genova 2002, 2004; Donato and Armenta 2011; Goldring, Berinstein, and Bernhard 2009; Gonzales and Chavez 2012; Massey and Bartley 2005; Menjívar and Abrego 2012; Menjívar and Kanstroom Forthcoming; and Willen 2007.

48. Coutin 1996, 2000.

49. Motomura 2008.

50. Gleeson 2012.

51. Abrego 2006 and Painter, Gabriel, and Myers 2001.

52. Adler 2006 and Dreby 2012.

53. Donato and Armenta 2011 and Jiménez and López-Sanders 2011.

54. Gonzales and Chavez 2012 and Menjívar and Abrego 2012.

55. Menjívar and Abrego 2012.

56. Massey and Bartley 2005 and Menjívar and Abrego 2012.

57. Abrego forthcoming.

58. Coleman 2007.

59. Boehm 2012; Menjívar and Kanstroom forthcoming; and Pratt 2012.

60. Mahler and Pessar 2001 and Ortner 1972.

61. Abrego and Menjívar 2011; Alcalde 2010; Bejarano 2002; Davis and Greenstein 2009; Dore and Molyneux 2000; Hagan 1994; Hondagneu-Sotelo 2003; Lorber 1994; Mahler and Pessar 2001; and Thorne 1992.

62. Lorber 1994; and Menjívar 2011.

63. Chant and Craske 2003; Hume 2004; Melhuus and Stølen 1996; and Padilla 2012.

64. Hume 2004 and Madrigal and Tejeda 2009. For discussions of multiple masculinities in different contexts, see Connell 1987; Connell and Messerschmidt 2005; and Ocampo 2012.

65. Chant and Craske 2003; Hume 2004; and Padilla 2012.

66. Alcalde 2010; Chant 1992; Fauné 1995; Friedmann, Abers, and Autler 1996; Schirmer 1993; and Stephen 2001. Miguel Mármol, an important figure in Salvadoran history, describes that by 1905 it was not uncommon to be raised by a single mother who worked outside the home (Dalton 2000). The same was true in the United States in the eighteenth and nineteenth centuries when the public–private divide was blurred for poor women who could not fulfill the cult of domesticity (see Dill 1998).

67. Arriagada 2002.

68. Dreby 2009; Hagan 1994; and Menjívar 2000, 2011.

69. Dreby 2009 and Menjívar 2011.

70. Hume 2004: 67; Madrigal and Tejeda 2009; and Zinn 1982.

71. Indeed, motherhood is continually negotiated across class and ethnic boundaries in the United States, as well (see, for example, Dill 1998; Glenn 2002; and Segura 1994).

72. Hume 2004: 70.

73. Bannon and Correia 2006; Hume 2004; and Mahler 1999.

74. Dreby 2010; Dreby and Adkins 2010; Lutz 2010; Mckay 2007; Parreñas 2001; Schmalzbauer 2004; Suárez-Orozco, Bang, and Kim 2010; and Suárez-Orozco, Todorova, and Louie, 2002.

75. Contreras and Griffith 2012 and Lutz 2010.

76. Boehm 2012; Hirsch 2003; Hondagneu-Sotelo 1994, 2003; Pessar 2005; Smith 2006; and Stephen 2007.

77. Hondagneu-Sotelo 1994; Levitt 2001; and Mahler 1999.

78. Contreras and Griffith 2012; Lutz 2010; Parreñas 2005a; and Pessar 2005.

79. Gammage et al. 2005; Orozco 2006; and Semyonov and Gorodzeisky 2005.

80. UNFPA 2006 and Vanwey 2004.

81. Waldinger and Gilbertson 1994.

82. Hondagneu-Sotelo 2003 and Menjívar 1999.

83. Waldinger and Gilbertson 1994.

84. Importantly, all families are dynamic and highly contradictory social units that negotiate external economic conditions to distribute burdens and rewards in an internally stratified manner (González de la Rocha 1994, 2001).

85. UNFPA 2006.

86. Suro 2003: 4; see also Constable 2009; Mckay 2007; Skrbiš 2008; and Zelizer 2005.

87. Abrego 2009 and UNFPA 2006.

88. Padilla 2012.

89. Dreby 2006, 2007; Hondagneu-Sotelo and Avila 1997; McGuire and Martin 2007; Parreñas 2005b; Pratt 2012; and Suárez-Orozco, Todorova, and Louie 2002.

90. Walter, Bourgois, and Loinaz 2004.

91. Hamilton and Chinchilla 2001 and Menjívar 2000.

92. Almeida 2008; Barry 1987; Dalton 2000; and LaFeber 1993.

93. Pérez and Ramos 2007.

94. Viterna 2006 and Weitzhandler 1993.

95. García 2006.

96. This is the definition of a refugee or an asylee set forth in 101(a)(42) of the U.S. Immigration and Nationality Act (INA); retrieved on November 13, 2012, from www.uscis.gov/portal/site/uscis/menuitem.eb1d4c2a3e5b9ac89243c6a7543f6d1a/?vgnextoid=1f1c3e4d77d73210VgnVCM100000082ca60aRCRD&vgnextchannel=1f1c3e4d77d73210VgnVCM100000082ca60aRCRD.

97. Applicants for *refugee* status are located outside of the United States or at a U.S. port of entry, while *asylum* applicants apply after having already entered the country.

98. Hayden 2006.

99. Indeed, much of the activist work Salvadorans took on in the early 1980s was to demand a reclassification as "refugees" rather than economic migrants at the height of the violence in the country (Coutin 2000).

100. Given the sizeable nature of unauthorized migration, it is unclear exactly how many Salvadorans have moved to the United States in recent decades.

101. The 2011 U.S. Census Bureau's American Community Survey enumerates a Salvadoran immigrant population of 1,952,483. However, Salvadoran government sources place it at well over 2,000,000 (PNUD 2005).

102. Baker-Cristales 2004 and Motel and Patten 2013. In fact, a full 62 percent of immigrants from El Salvador arrived in the United States in 1990 or later (Dockterman 2011). Over one-quarter of all Salvadorans have arrived since 2000 (Terrazas 2010), more than a decade after the end of the civil war.

103. DeLugan 2012 and Moodie 2010.

104. Coutin 1998, 2000, 2007; Hernandez 2006a; and Menjívar and Abrego 2012.

105. Boehm 2012; De Genova 2002; Dreby 2010; Holmes 2007; and Zavella 2011.

106. Coutin 2000.

107. Weitzhandler 1993 and Coutin 2000. Salvadorans were the first recipients of Temporary Protected Status. Since then, TPS is most typically granted in response to political or natural disasters in the home country of migrants who are otherwise undocumented in the United States or who are seeking asylum.

108. At that point, Salvadorans qualified for Deferred Enforced Departure. This designation was extended until March 1996 (Coutin 2000).

109. TPS also applies to a few other national-origin groups. For more information, see "Temporary Protected Status," U.S. Citizenship and Immigration Services, retrieved on May 23, 2012, from www.uscis.gov/portal/site/uscis/menuitem.eb1d4c2a3e5b9ac 89243c6a7543f6d1a/?vgnextoid=848f7f2ef0745210VgnVCM100000082ca60aRCRD& vgnextchannel=848f7f2ef0745210VgnVCM100000082ca60aRCRD.

110. For Salvadorans, the designated period has typically been eighteen months, though TPS can be reapproved and extended for subsequent eighteen-month periods. Currently, TPS has been available continuously for Salvadorans since March 9, 2001, and at the time of this writing is set to expire on March 9, 2015.

111. Dockterman 2011; PNUD 2005: 67; and Terrazas 2010.

112. Coffino 2006 and Hernandez 2006a.

113. There are apparent discrepancies in these numbers across different sources. Some of the differences have to do with who is included. The Pew Hispanic Center, for example, includes all people of Salvadoran origin, including those who are U.S.-born. The Migration Information Source reports, on the other hand, include only Salvadoran immigrants born in El Salvador. According to figures from the Pew Hispanic Center, 55 percent of all people of Salvadoran origin in the United States are U.S. citizens, but this includes the 37 percent who are citizens because they were born in the United States. See "Hispanic Origin Profiles," Pew Hispanic Center; retrieved on August 7, 2010, from http://pewhispanic.org/data/origins/. According to Aaron Terrazas of the Migration Information Source, on the other hand, 29.6 percent of Salvadoran foreign-born were U.S. citizens in 2008.

114. Donato et al. 2011.

115. Andrade-Eekhoff 2006; Hernandez 2006b; and Repak 1995.

116. Fauné 1995; Hernandez 2006b; Hondagneu-Sotelo 2001; Menjívar 2000; and Milkman, Reese, and Roth 1998.

117. Menjívar 2000: 41.

118. Menjívar 2000: 41 and Segura 2010.

119. Menjívar 2000: 42.

120. Indeed, the famous Salvadoran revolutionary, Miguel Mármol, describes in great detail his own single mother's struggles in the labor market and her willingness to participate in political armed movements in the early 1900s (Dalton 2000).

121. Kampwirth 2002.

122. García 1999; García and Gomáriz 1989; Kampwirth 2002; and Menjívar 2000.

123. Kampwirth 2002 and Stephen 2001. Even as early as 1930, for example, before Salvadoran women were allowed to vote, Prudencia Ayala had already tried to run for president (Navas, Orellana, and Umaña 2007 and Oliva 2013).

124. Stephen 2001: 58.

125. Fauné 1995.

126. Ibid.

127. Repak 1995.

128. Hamilton and Chinchilla 2001.

129. Repak 1995.

130. Hernández 2002; PNUD 2005: 493; and Zentgraf 2002. There are notable variations in the rate of men's and women's migration from different towns in El Salvador (see Mahler 1999), with differences between rural and urban areas, as well.

131. Dockterman 2011.

132. For more information about my own position as a researcher in this project and my analytical practices, see Abrego 2009.

133. The Appendix contains descriptive statistics for the parents I interviewed.

134. There are fourteen geographic subdivisions in El Salvador, called departments.

135. Although I included the three caregivers' words in the text, I omitted their cases (one mother and two grandmothers) from the Appendix, where I display the descriptive statistics for the children I interviewed in El Salvador.

136. I arrived in El Salvador in August 2004, five months after the presidential election in which the right-wing party, ARENA, used scare tactics to win. Tony Saca, the conservative candidate, aired political ads stating that a win by his opponent, Shafick Handal, would make the U.S. government unhappy, leading to the deportation of Salvadorans back to the country and ending the flow of remittances. As Frontline World Reporter Joe Rubin documented:

> A typical pro-Saca television spot that aired repeatedly in the closing days of the campaign showed a middle-class Salvadoran couple receiving a phone call from their

son in Los Angeles. "Mom, I wanted to let you know that I'm scared," the young man says. "Why?" his mother asks. "Because if Schafik becomes president of El Salvador, I may be deported," her son answers, "and you won't be able to receive the remittances that I'm sending you." (Joe Rubin, "El Salvador: Payback, October 12, 2004; retrieved on May 8, 2013, from www.pbs.org/frontlineworld/elections/elsalvador/; and DeLugan 2012: 99)

Although these statements were false, months later when I arrived, some people I approached in neighborhoods around San Salvador were afraid to participate in the study. They worried that sharing information about their undocumented relatives would lead to their deportation. This initial response informed me of the significance of the production of illegality in the United States for people who lived in El Salvador. This was also the reason I began to approach educators for access to children of migrants in schools.

137. García 2012 and Martínez 2006.

138. Villacorta et al. 2011: 25.

139. Castañeda 2012.

140. Ariza 2002; Boehm 2012; Dreby 2010; López Castro 1986; Massey et al. 1987; Smith 2006; and Stephen 2007.

141. Indeed, as militarization of the border increases, even transnational Mexican families' separation is prolonged (Boehm 2012; Dreby 2010; and Stephen 2007). The same has been true for Guatemalan families (Moran-Taylor 2008).

142. Some scholars conceptualize transnational families as split households. For example, in *Servants of Globalization* (2001b), Rhacel Parreñas argues that transnational families occupy a single household over space because:

> Although transnational family members perform daily activities across vast geographical distances, they overcome spatial barriers through the rapid flow of money and information. Due to advancements in technology, information about family members can be received instantaneously, and money can be transferred to urban centers of Third World countries within twenty-four hours. (pg. 81)

On the other hand, Geraldine Pratt finds that among Filipina domestic workers in Canada, "Cyborg mothering is a fantasy for most poor migrant mothers who cannot access the technology . . . Communication with their children is often infrequent, and inevitably fragmented and stripped of the sensuality of day-to-day, face-to-face, embodied contact" (2012: 70).

143. Massey et al. (1987) and López Castro (1986) contend that migration and separation cause limited concern because they represent a strategy that benefits the entire family.

144. For an overview of European-based transnational families, see Bryceson and Vuorela 2002.

Chapter 2

1. In contemporary debates about immigration, mainstream media outlets and political pundits tend to portray undocumented immigrants as calculating actors who willfully leave their countries with the purpose of taking advantage of people and opportunities in the United States. Jorge's and Esperanza's stories, like so many in this study, reveal a more complicated reality of hesitation, fear, and pain associated with migration as an unwanted option.

2. Viterna 2006.

3. Indeed, those scenes of violence were created to instill fear in the population, as a way to communicate that any form of rebellion would not be tolerated (Moodie 2010).

4. Booth and Walker 1989 and Viterna 2006.

5. There are also the "atrocities of war" that anthropologist Ellen Moodie analyzes (2010), which force people to flee petty and organized crime in the country. Although I hear these stories now more frequently among recent immigrants (Martínez 2010), the people I interviewed did not mention them as reasons for migration.

6. Moodie 2010.

7. Ortez Andrade 2011.

8. Ibid.

9. Moodie 2010.

10. Although women and men claim to migrate for the same reasons, there are always underlying structures and inequalities that play out in gendered ways to determine the order and experience of migration (Hondagneu-Sotelo 1994). The same is true of LGTBQ (lesbian, gay, transsexual, bisexual, and queer) migrants who say they migrated for economic reasons; with prodding it becomes clear that generalized homophobia prevented them from securing stable employment in their country of origin (Cantú 2001).

11. In conversations with extended relatives, it seems that, during that era, acceptable forms of masculinity for working-class and university students required some level of engagement with the ongoing conflict. This, in turn, increased young working-class men's risk of repression.

12. Booth and Walker 1989 and Kampwirth 2002.

13. Although women also fought in the war, they were forcibly recruited less often than men (Kampwirth 2002; Viterna 2006; and Wood 2003).

14. More broadly in El Salvador, women were involved as combatants, making up 20 percent of the guerrilla forces (Luciak 2001 and Kampwirth 2002). There was only one woman in the study who fought in the war, and she migrated many years later.

15. Several families in this study cited medical expenses and lack of health care as the main reasons for their migration, suggesting a need to explore this further in migration studies more generally.

16. Unlike most men, Antonio shed many tears during the interview. It is possible that his long-term active membership in a church allowed him to negotiate his performance of masculinity to include such visible displays of emotion (see Lorentzen and Mira 2005), even if only in private.

17. These stories are reminiscent of the consequences of NAFTA for farmers in Mexico (Bacon 2008).

18. See Chapters 3 and 4.

19. This was prior to the change in national currency from colones to U.S. dollars.

20. Dill 1998 and Glenn 2002. In the United States, similar processes have taken place since the eighteenth and nineteenth centuries, when white middle-class women with race and class privilege were the only group with the resources to attain the idealized cult of domesticity. Poor women of color, however, had to practice mothering in ways that matched their own economic limitations.

21. As in other parts of the world with a long history of state violence and widespread repression of poor communities, El Salvador also suffers high rates of domestic violence and violence against women (Hume 2004, Menjívar 2011, and García 1999). Importantly, there are multiple and varied approaches in civil society to try to remedy and reverse these patterns (see Madrigal and Tejeda 2009).

22. Angela migrated twice: the first time in 1988 (she remained in the United States for two and a half years) and the second time in 1991. This story is about the time she migrated in 1988, when the war was still going on, but she did not face direct threats in her town.

23. Colones were the Salvadoran currency prior to dollarization. One U.S. dollar was equivalent to roughly 8.75 colones.

24. Varied reasons for migration are also common among Mexicans (Zavella 2011).

Chapter 3

1. Even though undocumented immigrants are protected under various labor laws, their fear of deportation prevents many from seeking justice in these cases (Gleeson 2010, 2012).

2. Menjívar and Abrego 2012.

3. Menjívar and Kanstroom forthcoming.

4. "More than two-thirds (67.3 percent) of the 19,659 Salvadorans admitted for permanent residence in 2008 entered as family-sponsored immigrants (6,802, or 34.6 percent) and as the immediate relatives of US citizens (6,428, or 32.7 percent). Small numbers of Salvadorans entered as employment-based immigrants (1,038, or 5.3 percent) or as refugees and asylees (590, or 3.0 percent)" (Terrazas 2010).

5. Hernandez 2006a.

6. Refusal rates hover around 50 percent for Salvadoran nationals who apply for nonimmigrant U.S. visas. See "Calculation of the Adjusted Visa Refusal Rate for Tourist and Business Travelers under the Guidelines of the Visa Waiver Program," retrieved on April 28, 2013, from http://travel.state.gov/pdf/refusalratelanguage.pdf.

7. Between 2003 and 2012, the U.S. embassy in El Salvador granted only between 19,000 and 36,000 nonimmigrant visas annually. In comparison, it is estimated that about 55,000 U.S.-bound Salvadorans leave the country without a visa every year. See "55 mil salvadoreños emigran hacia EE.UU. al año," at ElSalvador.com, retrieved on April 28, 2013, from www.elsalvador.com/mwedh/nota/nota_completa.asp?idCat= 47859&idArt=6616087.

8. Embassy of the United States, San Salvador, El Salvador, "Nonimmigrant Visa Application Process," retrieved on February 23, 2013, from http://sansalvador.usembassy .gov/how_to_apply.html.

9. See links to U.S. visa refusal rates from 2006 through 2012 at "Calculation of the Adjusted Visa Refusal Rate for Tourist and Business Travelers under the Guidelines of the Visa Waiver Program," retrieved on April 28, 2013, from http://travel.state .gov/pdf/refusalratelanguage.pdf.

10. "55 mil salvadoreños emigran hacia EE.UU. al año."

11. Nationals from Central American countries can travel legally and with few restrictions throughout much of Central America. However, few U.S.-bound Central American migrants have visas to travel through Mexico and must therefore travel clandestinely through that country (Ogren 2007). Due to pressure from the U.S. government, Mexican authorities heavily target Central Americans in transit for deportation (ibid.).

12. Travelers who have obtained a visa to go to the United States do not need a separate visa to go to Mexico. For more information about Salvadoran nationals' requirements to obtain a tourist visa to Mexico, see: "Embajada de México en El Salvador: Turista," retrieved on August 15, 2013, from http://embamex.sre.gob.mx/elsalvador/ index.php?option=com_content&view=article&id=144&Itemid=56 .

13. Behrens 2009 and Center for Economic and Policy Research, "Obama and the Militarization of the 'Drug War' in Mexico and Central America," retrieved on May 10, 2013, from www.cepr.net/index.php/blogs/the-americas-blog/ obama-and-the-militarization-of-the-drug-war-in-mexico-and-central-america.

14. Martínez 2010.

15. Amnesty International 2010.

16. Martínez 2010.

17. Multiple respondents confirmed the accuracy of these figures. See also "Nonimmigrant Visa Application Process."

18. This is similar to the gendered experiences of undocumented Guatemalan Mayans in Houston, Texas (Hagan 1994).

19. Migrants' families in El Salvador also suffer throughout the duration of the trip, wondering about the safety of their loved ones who often cannot call them while en route (Hammock, Letona, Pérez, and Isen 2005).

20. Amnesty International 2010. For more information about the widespread human rights abuses against migrants en route, see the documentaries, "De Nadie" (2005) produced by Tin Dirdamal, "Los Invisibles" (2010) produced by Marc Silver and Gael Garcia Bernal, "La Bestia" (2011) directed by Pedro Ultrera, "Maria en Tierra de Nadie" (2011) directed by Marcela Zamora, and "Which Way Home" (2009) by Rebecca Cammisa.

21. Martínez 2010.

22. The sexual trafficking of Central American migrants has also become common in Southern Mexico (Martínez 2010). See Falcón 2001 for a discussion of rape as a gendered form of torture.

23. See the documentary "Maria en Tierra de Nadie" (2011) for a closer examination of these experiences.

24. Although I did not systematically ask migrants if they had sought professional counseling, the few who seemed especially haunted by the memories of their trip claimed that they had not. They justified their decisions to deal with the trauma on their own by citing time constraints and a lack of knowledge about where to find such resources or how to pay for them.

25. Institute for War & Peace Reporting, "Mothers Search Mexico for Missing Children," retrieved on April 26, 2013, from http://iwpr.net/report-news/mothers-search-mexico-missing-children; Central American Issues and Controversies, "Central American Parents in Pursuit of Closure," retrieved on April 26, 2013, from http://miguelcarrillo795.wordpress.com/2013/02/25/61/; and Mexico Voices, "Central American Mothers Caravan Searches Mexico for Missing Sons and Daughters," retrieved on April 26, 2013, from http://mexicovoices.blogspot.com/2012/10/central-american-mothers-caravan.html.

26. Salvadorans and other Central American unauthorized migrants experience gendered violence throughout the length of the Mexican territory and, like Mexican women migrants, are also targeted at the U.S.–Mexico border (Falcón 2001 and Zavella 2011).

27. Martínez 2010.

28. Ibid.

29. Menjívar 2000.

30. Ibid.

31. Considering that Salvadoran migrants typically earn relatively low wages—about $22,500 per year for males (Gammage and Schmitt 2004: 81) and that, presumably, recently arrived immigrants earn even less than the average reflected in the U.S. Census figures, $6,500 is a rather large sum.

32. For more information about visa requirements for Salvadoran nationals wishing to travel to the United States, see Embassy of the United States, San Salvador, El Salvador, "Non-Immigrant Visas," retrieved on August 15, 2013, from http://sansalvador.usembassy.gov/nonimmigrant_visas.html

33. These migrants traveled with immigrant visas. Notably, however, the sums I mention here do not take into account the costs of legal and paperwork fees throughout the years to file for legal permanent resident status for family members.

34. Round-trip airfare from El Salvador to the United States ranges from about $300 during off-peak travel season to about $900 during peak travel season.

35. Hondagneu-Sotelo 2001.

36. Alcalde 2010; Bejarano 2002; Chant 1992; Chant and Craske 2003; Friedmann, Abers, and Autler 1996; Melhuus and Stølen 1996; and Schirmer 1993.

37. Martínez 2010.

38. This is especially true now that Salvadorans can rely on vast social networks to support further migration.

39. Abrego 2011.

Chapter 4

1. See Chapter 3 for more details about her experience.

2. For more details about these terms and their definitions, see the Department of Homeland Security website: www.dhs.gov/ximgtn/.

3. Few immigrants are eligible to apply for legal permanent residency; when they do, they may be "in-process" for an extended period of time. Immigrants who are in the process of obtaining legal permanent residency may simultaneously apply for a work permit, but they cannot travel internationally without undergoing a bureaucratic process to obtain permission.

4. As a result of the 1996 Illegal Immigration Reform and Immigrant Responsibility Act (IIRIRA), LPRs are increasingly targeted for deportation over past legal infractions, making this in practice less than a "permanent" status.

5. Golash-Boza 2013.

6. Menjívar and Abrego 2012 and Pratt 2012.

7. Abrego 2011, forthcoming; De Genova 2002; and Ngai 2004.

8. For more details, see U.S. Citizenship and Immigration Services, "Green Card through Family," retrieved on May 23, 2012, from www.uscis.gov/portal/site/uscis/menuitem.eb1d4c2a3e5b9ac89243c6a7543f6d1a/?vgnextoid=4c2515d27cf73210VgnVCM100000082ca60aRCRD&vgnextchannel=4c2515d27cf73210VgnVCM100000082ca60aRCRD and U.S. Citizenship an Immigration Services, "Green Card through a Job," retrieved on May 23, 2012, from www.uscis.gov/portal/site/uscis/menuitem.eb1d4c2a3e5b9ac89243c6a7543f6d1a/?vgnextoid=24b0a6c515083210VgnVCM100000082ca60aRCRD&vgnextchannel=24b0a6c515083210VgnVCM100000082ca60aRCRD.

9. Menjívar and Abrego 2012.

10. It should be noted, however, that the 1996 Illegal Immigration Reform and Immigrant Responsibility Act (IIRIRA) reduced the threshold for crimes and offenses that may be considered grounds for deportation and made legal permanent residents deportable. In effect, the laws have been eroding the rights of LPRs (Golash-Boza 2013 and Menjívar and Abrego 2012).

11. See Chapter 1 for a more detailed explanation of these factors and their influence.

12. Chavez 1998; Coutin 2000; Fortuny, Capps, and Passel 2007; Hagan 1994; Loh and Richardson 2004; Menjívar 2006; and Milkman, González, and Narro 2010.

13. Borjas and Tienda 1993 and Myers 2007.

14. In fact, this is a pattern among undocumented males (see, for example, Holmes 2007; Franklin 2008; Loh and Richardson 2004; Nissen, Angee, and Weinstein 2008; and Walter, Bourgois, and Loinaz 2004).

15. I am evaluating his level of education within the national context of El Salvador where, in 2004, the national average of educational attainment was 5.6 years—3.6 years for residents of rural areas and 6.9 years for residents of urban areas (PNUD 2005: 474). Among immigrants, moreover, a full 37.6 percent completed some or all of elementary school, another 26.5 percent completed some postelementary school, only 18.7 completed high school, another 12.9 completed some post-high school education, and only 4.4 achieved a college education or more (PNUD 2005: 493).

16. Cf. Valenzuela 2002.

17. Hondagneu-Sotelo 2001.

18. Having a "green card" means having LPR status.

19. CNA stands for Certified Nursing Assistant.

20. Gleeson 2012. It is also possible that, although undocumented immigrants have no choice but to fill the most dangerous jobs, those with legal protections choose to avoid dangerous jobs, knowing that their TPS or LPR status grants them better job opportunities (Franklin 2008).

21. Menjívar and Abrego 2012.

22. Mckay 2007 and Zelizer 2005.

23. The same is true of Filipina domestic workers in Canada, whose families in the Philippines also suffer the consequences of immigration policies (Pratt 2012).

24. Visiting children in person is only a possibility for immigrant parents with legal status who also work in flexible industries or with understanding employers. Not everyone who has legal permanent residency is able to travel frequently to El Salvador. Some people have jobs and employers who will not give them any time off to travel. Others simply do not earn enough to be able to pay for the costs of a trip, especially on a routine basis.

25. Indeed, children's reactions to family separation change as they get older (Dreby 2010).

26. This is reminiscent of the girls in Soto's work (2010) on Mexican transnational families.

27. Importantly, even with certainty that they are legally eligible to bring their children, many documented immigrants still had to wait over a decade for the paperwork to go through the slow bureaucratic process of INS and later USCIS. In those cases, the lengthy separations are still difficult, but the certainty of reunification helps to relieve much of the stress.

28. Abrego and Lakhani n.d.

29. Currently, the only countries whose citizens are eligible for Temporary Protected Status in the United States are El Salvador, Honduras, Liberia, Nicaragua, Somalia, Sudan, and Haiti.

30. Menjívar 2006.

31. For more details about the inability of TPS to signal full legality, see Abrego and Lakhani n.d.

32. "Individuals who have been granted TPS may work in the United States and may apply to U.S. Citizenship and Immigration Services (USCIS) to receive an Employment Authorization Document (EAD). An EAD is a plastic, credit card-sized document that shows proof of the individual's authorization to work in the United States and contains a photograph of the individual." This is cited in the USCIS Fact Sheet, "Documentation Employers May Accept and Temporary Protected Status Beneficiaries May Present as Evidence of Employment Eligibility," retrieved on August 15, 2013, from http://www.uscis.gov/USCIS/News/2010%20News%20Items/May%202010/tps-ead-fact-sheet.pdf.

33. This is a common emotion among children who have lived apart from their parents due to migration (Artico 2003 and Pratt 2012).

Chapter 5

Portions of Chapter 5 previously appeared in "Economic Well-Being in Salvadoran Transnational Families: How Gender Affects Remittance Practices." *Journal of Marriage and Family* 71(2009):1070–1085.

1. Gammage and Schmitt 2004 and Wright et al. 2000. Indeed, the labor market often also follows the logic of gender ideologies (Menjívar 1999).

2. It is not my sense that women internalized gendered disparities in wages as warranted or fair, but they certainly understood them as immutable.

3. Cf. Carroll et al. 2007 and Goodheart 2007.

4. Working conditions for lower-skilled immigrant women question early feminist optimism about the potential for women's emancipation through employment (for discussions of these debates, see Hondagneu-Sotelo 2000 and Menjívar 1999).

5. These are also among the top six most common occupations for Salvadoran migrant women in the United States overall (PNUD 2005: 496). See also Hernandez 2006b and Wright et al. 2000.

6. See also Hondagneu-Sotelo 2001.

7. Soldatenko 1999.

8. Women in unionized housekeeping jobs earned higher wages than those in nonunionized jobs.

9. Zavella 1991.

10. Gammage and Schmitt 2004 and Wright et al. 2000.

11. Andrade-Eekhoff and Silva-Avalos 2003: 22; and Walter, Bourgois, and Loinaz 2004.

12. See Chapter 6 and Appendix Table 3 for more information.

13. See Appendix Table 3 for more specific figures.

14. See Appendix Table 3. Although they are small and nonrepresentative numbers, a greater proportion of children in father-away families were barely subsisting compared to children in mother-away families (21 percent compared to 8 percent). Mothers, despite earning little, often contributed to thriving families in El Salvador. In fact, a full 55 percent of mother-away families were thriving, compared to only 36 percent of father-away families. And although this fact is not captured in the table, it is also noteworthy that children in families with both migrant parents typically received most or all of their remittances from migrant mothers.

15. Gammage and Schmitt 2004.

16. PNUD 2005: 500.

17. Alcalde 2010.

18. Chant and Craske 2003. I am certainly not suggesting that gendered behavior is inherent or natural. It is problematic to explain away patterns as merely cultural (see Volpp 2011). Rather, I want to emphasize the power of gender ideologies, as present in everyday life and common understandings of the world, in shaping women's and men's opportunities and decisions while simultaneously erasing structural inequalities (see Menjívar 2011).

19. See Ocampo 2012 for a discussion of multiple masculinities for disadvantaged and marginalized men.

20. Hume 2004: 67; and Madrigal and Tejeda 2009.

21. Mahler and Pessar 2001, 2006; and Pessar and Mahler 2003. Despite the possibility that transnational spaces offer to contest gender ideologies, and even when women and men succeed in some transgressions, other gendered expectations are difficult to overcome and continue to powerfully inform migrants' behaviors.

22. Traditional gender ideologies, in these cases, are doubly problematic when they limit women's work opportunities to exploitative sectors and simultaneously provide justifications that make structural and persistent abuse acceptable.

23. In these ways, although mothers had clearly transgressed gender ideologies that expected them to be physically present and nurturing of their children on a daily basis, they also continue to reaffirm gender ideologies that expected them to be self-less at any cost.

24. For more details about Felipe and his family, see Chapter 4.

25. Madrigal and Tejada 2009 and Hume 2004.

26. Fauné 1995 notes that El Salvador had the highest rate of female-headed households in Central America (31 percent).

27. Indeed, similarly powerful gender ideologies are at play around the world where women have been found to be more reliable at saving or investing their money on family (Seguino and Floro 2003). This is one of the reasons microcredit projects have targeted mostly women in developing nations, problematically ignoring gender ideologies and gendered structural barriers (Vonderlack-Navarro 2010).

28. See also Chapter 2 for more details.

29. See Fauné 1995 for more details about the high rates of female-headed households in Central America. This is due, in part, to masculine identities being tied to virility rather than to parental responsibilities.

30. There were a few cases in which the women migrated alone while still maintaining intact marriages. Among these cases, only one marriage was still intact at the time of the interview. More commonly, the nonmigrant father started a new relationship, but he raised the children while their migrant mother continued to support them.

31. For similar discourses and practices among Mexican and Guatemalan transnational families, see Dreby 2010; Nicholson 2006; and Stephen 2007.

32. See, for example, Gorman 2008.

33. It is not uncommon in El Salvador for multiple generations of families to celebrate New Year's Eve together. Parents and children hug each other at midnight before greeting friends and neighbors.

34. Emotional suffering due to a mother's absence is common in transnational families in various countries (Dreby 2010; Dreby and Adkins 2010; Lutz 2010; Mckay 2007; Parreñas 2001a; Schmalzbauer 2004; Suárez-Orozco et al. 2002; and Suárez-Orozco et al. 2010).

35. Miranda et al. 2005 and Schen 2005.

36. For an interesting point of comparison, consider the rates of child support among divorced parents in the United States. In 2009, parents paid only about 40 percent of child support due (Grall 2011).

37. These kinds of gendered patterns and expectations are similar to what happens elsewhere in the region (see, for example, Menjívar 2011).

38. Mahler and Pessar 2001, 2006.

Chapter 6

1. Dalton 2004; Fajnzylber and López 2007; Funkhouser 1997; Gammage 2006; Lungo, Andrade-Eekhoff, and Baires 1997; Rivera Funes 2003; and Sanabria 2003.

2. Suro 2003: 8.

3. Gammeltoft 2002 and Orozco 2002.

4. Salvadoran scholarly work, blogs, videos, and opinion pieces in all the most widely read newspapers related to migration provide evidence of the popularity of these lines of thought. See, for example, Andrade-Eekhoff and Silva-Avalos 2003. Moreover, throughout El Salvador, and in the United States among Salvadoran migrants, when I mentioned my study, people reacted by drawing on one of these three discourses about transnational families.

5. Abrego 2009.

6. Villacorta et al. 2011.

7. PNUD 2005: 16.

8. In comparison, nationally 37 percent of households in El Salvador not receiving remittances fall below the poverty level (PNUD 2005: 16). This suggests that transnational families still fare better than families who do not ever receive remittances.

9. PNUD 2005: 481.

10. This was the situation in El Salvador when I conducted the interviews. Later, in 2009, when FMLN President Mauricio Funes came into office, he started a Presidential Program for School Packages (*Programa Presidencial Paquete Escolar*) to provide each student with a brand-new school uniform, a new pair of shoes, and a few basic school supplies. This is likely to make a big difference for poor families in the country whose children would otherwise drop out when they could not afford these mandatory expenses. See "Presidente Funes entrega zapatos y uniformes escolares" on the official website of the Salvadoran Ministry of Education, retrieved on May 12, 2013, from www.mined.gob.sv/index.php/component/k2/item/6168-presidente-funes-entrega-zapatos-y-uniformes-escolares.html.

11. Edwards and Ureta 2003 and PNUD 2005: 20.

12. See Chapter 4 for details about the propensity of undocumented male workers to become injured at work.

13. Pupusas are a common food in El Salvador made out of cornmeal and typically stuffed with cheese and beans. Unlike the Los Angeles version of pupusas that ranges from five to eight inches in diameter, large enough for people to be satisfied with one per meal, pupusas in El Salvador are much smaller in comparison at about 2.5 inches. As I observed there, given the small size of pupusas, it is common for people to eat at least three per meal.

14. Across the spectrum of economic well-being, several families also mentioned illness as one of the driving factors for migration. In many of these cases, a child was

born with a medical condition that required expensive treatments the parents could not afford. In contrast to families that are barely subsisting, those who are surviving and thriving use remittances to purchase medication and consistent health care that, in turn, has greatly improved the health of the child and other family members.

15. The grading in El Salvador is based on a 10-point scale where 10 is equivalent to an A+.

16. Andrade-Eekhoff 2003 and PNUD 2005: 23, 487–490.

17. These sums are consistent with the Salvadoran national average for monthly remittances, which is somewhere between $107 and $219 per household on the spectrum from towns that receive the least and the most remittances, respectively (PNUD 2005: 23).

18. Because the currency had changed only a few years earlier, people still often referred to money in both colones and U.S. dollars, as Doris does in this example.

19. In 2004, the *canasta básica* was equivalent to $129.50 (PNUD 2005: 481). See Chapter 2 for more details.

20. Taylor 1999; Kapur and Center for Global Development 2003; Ratha 2003; and World Bank 2006. These narratives should give development practitioners pushing for development on the backs of transnational families some pause.

21. Acosta et al. 2007; Edwards and Ureta 2003; Gammeltoft 2002; Gutiérrez 2003; and Taylor 1999. Even among scholars who emphasize the negative effects of remittances on development (Binford 2002), their focus is on macroeconomic patterns of labor participation rather than on the social and emotional experiences at the level of the family.

22. Peiró 2006.

23. Menjívar and Abrego 2012.

24. Because women have a long history of being heads of household in El Salvador, Xiomara and others do not have a problem with mothers joining the paid labor force. Gender ideologies, however, do not yet excuse mothers from daily care work for their children, making family separation quite painful for children of migrant mothers.

25. Dreby 2010.

26. PNUD 2005: 15.

27. This is markedly higher than the estimated average in 2004 for twenty-eight low- and middle-income countries of $128 per capita per year (Fajnzylber and López 2007: 4).

28. Edwards and Ureta 2003; Fajnzylber and López 2007; PNUD 2005; and World Bank 2006.

29. PNUD 2005: 16. Falling below the poverty line is defined as having resources that fall below the cost of the *canasta básica*. See Chapter 2 for more details.

30. Ibid.

Chapter 7

1. MacLeod 1987.

2. Dreby 2010.

3. See, for example, Dreby 2007, 2010.

4. Martínez 2010.

5. Amuedo-Dorantes, Georges, and Pozo 2008; and Edwards and Ureta 2003.

6. Homes are made available to low-income families through the National Fund for Public Housing (*Fondo Nacional de Vivienda Popular—FONAVIPO*).

7. Lilia Soto finds a similar experience among girls in Mexican transnational families (2010).

8. She was in the ninth grade, and expenses were going to increase at the high school level. Many poor youth I interviewed talked about the looming reality of having to drop out after the ninth grade because their families would no longer be able to afford even nominal fees for high school.

9. For Salvadorans, an immigrant visa is usually the result of an approved petition of a family reunification application through the U.S. Citizenship and Immigration Services.

10. Martínez 2010.

11. Cf. Abrego 2006, 2008, 2011; and Menjívar and Abrego 2012.

12. I have already included several details about their lives in previous chapters.

13. These types of scams that target undocumented immigrants are also forms of legal violence (Menjívar and Abrego 2012). Their vulnerability, as legally produced through immigration policies, makes them easy prey while leaving them with little legal recourse to right these wrongs.

14. This is similar to what Pratt (2012) found among Filipino transnational families and Schmalzbauer (2004, 2008) found among Honduran children of migrants.

15. Macías 2006; Ogren 2007; and Thompson 2003.

Chapter 8

1. This is contrary to what some scholars have found in their work (Fitzgerald 2004; Levitt 2001; and Smith 2006).

2. Maldonado, Bajuk, and Hayem 2011.

3. In trying to find ways to use collective remittances more efficiently, the Salvadoran government began various matching funds programs run by the Social Investment and Local Development Fund (FISDL in Spanish) to channel money raised by hometown associations—groups of immigrants from the same hometown who raise funds for their town—to projects that are meant to generate more revenue for the state.

4. At a special day-long event on January 30, 2012, at UCLA to commemorate the twentieth anniversary of the signing of the Peace Accords, much of the discussion of

development experts and Salvadoran legislators was focused on the need to bank and invest family remittances. See the note about "20th Anniversary of El Salvador's Peace Accords" on the UCLA Latin American Institute's page; retrieved on September 18, 2012, from http://international.ucla.edu/lai/events/showevent.asp?eventid=9227.

5. See "Viceministerio para los Salvadoreños en el Exterior" on the official web page of El Salvador's Ministry of Foreign Relations; retrieved on September 18, 2012, from www.rree.gob.sv/index.php?/viceministerio-para-los-salvadorenos-en-el-exterio/viceministerio-para-los-salvadorenos-en-el-exterior.php. Author's translation.

6. Agencia EFE (San Salvador), "El Salvador presentará propuesta de reforma migratoria al Gobierno de EEUU," August 28, 2009.

7. Fuentes Rubio 2004.

8. In 2012, for example, Salvadoran independent artists created the parody "Capitán Centroamérica" (Captain Central America), in which the fictitious superhero of everyday life was raised by relatives because his mother migrated to the United States. The web series is available on YouTube or on their facebook page; retrieved on August 18, 2012, from https://www.facebook.com/puya.web.

9. Even the proposals for comprehensive immigration reform being debated in the United States in May 2013 suggest that changes will be slow and incomplete. The few undocumented immigrant parents to qualify for legalization will have to wait possibly over a decade before they can apply for their children's immigrant visas.

10. López Castro 1986 and Massey et al. 1987.

11. Dreby 2010; González de la Rocha 1989; Hondagneu-Sotelo and Avila 1997; and Parreñas 2005a.

12. Bernhard, Landolt, and Goldring 2008; Ehrenreich and Hochschild 2002; and Landolt and Da 2005.

13. Fletcher 1999; House 1999; and Schmalzbauer 2005.

14. Cohen 2000; Dreby 2007; Hondagneu-Sotelo and Avila 1997; McGuire and Martin 2007; Parreñas 2005b; and Suárez-Orozco, Todorova, and Louie 2002.

15. Alba and Nee 2003; Borjas and Tienda 1993; Boyd 1989; Feliciano 2005; Massey et al. 1987; Myers 2007; and Portes and Rumbaut 1996.

16. Dodson 1998 and Hays 2003.

References

Abrego, Leisy J. 2006. "'I Can't Go to College Because I Don't Have Papers': Incorporation Patterns of Latino Undocumented Youth." *Latino Studies* 4(3):212–231.

———. 2008. "Legitimacy, Social Identity, and the Mobilization of Law: The Effects of Assembly Bill 540 on Undocumented Students in California." *Law & Social Inquiry* 33(3):709–734.

———. 2009. "Economic Well-Being in Salvadoran Transnational Families: How Gender Affects Remittance Practices." *Journal of Marriage and Family* 71:1070–1085.

———. 2011. "Legal Consciousness of Undocumented Latinos: Fear and Stigma as Barriers to Claims Making for First and 1.5 Generation Immigrants." *Law & Society Review* 45(2):337–370.

———. Forthcoming. "Latino Immigrants' Diverse Experiences of Illegality," in *Constructing Illegality: Immigrant Experiences, Critiques, and Resistance*, edited by Cecilia Menjívar and Daniel Kanstroom. Cambridge: Cambridge University Press.

Abrego, Leisy J., and Sarah Morando Lakhani. n.d. "Incomplete Inclusion: Legal Violence and Immigrants in In-Between Statuses." Unpublished manuscript.

Abrego, Leisy J., and Cecilia Menjívar. 2011. "Immigrant Latina Mothers as Targets of Legal Violence." *International Journal of Sociology of the Family* 37(1):9–26.

Acosta, Pablo, Cesar Calderón, Pablo Fajnzylber, and Humberto Lopez. 2008. "What Is the Impact of International Remittances on Poverty and Inequality in Latin America?" *World Development.* 36(1):89–114.

Adler, Rachel H. 2006. "'But they claimed to be police, not la migra!': The Interaction of Residency Status, Class, and Ethnicity in a (Post-PATRIOT Act) New Jersey Neighborhood." *American Behavioral Scientist* 50(1):48–69.

Alba, Richard D., and Victor Nee. 2003. *Remaking the American Mainstream: Assimilation and Contemporary Immigration*. Cambridge, MA: Harvard University Press.

Alcalde, M. Cristina. 2010. "Violence across Borders: Familism, Hegemonic Masculinity, and Self-Sacrificing Femininity in the Lives of Mexican and Peruvian Migrants." *Latino Studies* 8(1):48–68.

Almeida, Paul. 2008. *Waves of Protest: Popular Struggle in El Salvador, 1925–2005*. Minneapolis: University of Minnesota Press.

Amnesty International. 2010. "Invisible Victims: Migrants on the Move in Mexico," edited by Amnesty International Publications. London: Amnesty International. Document Number: 41/014/2010. Available at www.amnesty.org/en/news-and-updates/report/widespread-abuse-migrants-mexico-human-rights-crisis-2010-04-27.

Amuedo-Dorantes, Catalina, Annie Georges, and Susan Pozo. 2010. "Migration, Remittances and Children's Schooling in Haiti." *The ANNALS of the American Academy of Political and Social Science* 630(July):224–244.

Andrade-Eekhoff, Katharine. 2003. *Mitos y realidades: El impacto económico de la migración en los hogares rurales*. San Salvador, El Salvador: FLACSO-El Salvador y FUNDAUNGO.

———. 2006. "Migration and Development in El Salvador: Ideals Versus Reality," in *Migration Information Source*. Available at www.migrationinformation.org/Feature/display.cfm?id=387.

Andrade-Eekhoff, Katharine, and Claudia Silva-Avalos. 2003. *Globalización de la periferia: Los desafíos de la migración transnacional para el desarrollo local en América Central*. San Salvador, El Salvador: Informe de la Facultad Latinoamericana de Ciencias Sociales Programa El Salvador.

Ariza, Marina. 2002. "Migración, familia y transnacionalidad en el contexto de la globalización: algunos puntos de reflexión." *Revista Mexicana de Sociología* 64(4):53–84.

Arriagada, Irma. 2002. "Cambios y desigualdad en las familias latinoamericanas." *Revista de CEPAL* 77:143–161.

Artico, Ceres. 2003. *Latino Families Broken by Immigration*. New York: LFB Scholarly Publishing.

Bacon, David. 2008. *Illegal People: How Globalization Creates Migration and Criminalizes Immigrants*. Boston: Beacon Press.

Baker-Cristales, Beth. 2004. *Salvadoran Migration to Southern California: Redefining El Hermano Lejano*. Gainesville: University Press of Florida.

Bannon, Ian, and Maria Correia (Eds.). 2006. *The Other Half of Gender: Men's Issues in Development*. Washington, DC: World Bank Publications.

Barry, Tom. 1987. *Roots of Rebellion: Land and Hunger in Central America*. Boston: South End Press.

Basch, Linda G., Nina Glick Schiller, and Cristina Szanton Blanc. 1994. *Nations Un-bound: Transnational Projects, Post-Colonial Predicaments, and Deterritorialized Nation-States.* Langhorne, PA: Gordon and Breach.

Behrens, Susan Fitzpatrick. 2009. "Plan Mexico and Central American Migration." in *North American Congress on Latin America.* Retrieved on May 1, 2013, from https://nacla.org/news/plan-mexico-and-central-american-migration.

Bejarano, Cynthia L. 2002. "Las Super Madres de Latino America: Transforming Motherhood by Challenging Violence in Mexico, Argentina, and El Salvador." *Frontiers: A Journal of Women Studies* 23(1):126–150.

Bernhard, Judith K., Patricia Landolt, and Luin Goldring. 2008. "Transnationalizing Families: Canadian Immigration Policy and the Spatial Fragmentation of Care-Giving among Latin American Newcomers." *International Migration* 47(2):3–31.

Binford, Leigh. 2002. "Remesas y subdesarrollo en México." *Relaciones: Estudios de Historia y Sociedad* 23(90):115–158.

Boehm, Deborah A. 2012. *Intimate Migrations: Gender, Family, and Illegality among Transnational Mexicans.* New York and London: New York University Press.

Booth, John, and Thomas W. Walker. 1989. *Understanding Central America.* Boulder, CO: Westview Press.

Borjas, George J., and Marta Tienda. 1993. "The Employment and Wages of Legalized Immigrants." *International Migration Review* 27(4):712–747.

Boyd, Monica. 1989. "Family and Personal Networks in Migration." *International Migration Review* 23(3):638–670.

Bryceson, Deborah, and Ulla Vuorela (Eds.). 2002. *The Transnational Family: New European Frontiers and Global Networks.* Oxford, UK, and New York: Berg.

Calavita, Kitty. 1992. *Inside the State: The Bracero Program, Immigration, and the I.N.S.* New York: Routledge.

Cantú, Lionel. 2001. "A Place Called Home: A Queer Political Economy of Mexican Immigrant Men's Family Experiences," pp. 112–136 in *Queer Families, Queer Politics: Challenging Culture and the State,* edited by Mary Bernstein and Renate Reimann. New York: Columbia University Press.

Carroll, David, Dylan H. Roby, Jean Ross, Michael Snavely, E. Richard Brown, and Gerald F. Kominsky. 2007. "What Does It Take for a Family to Afford to Pay for Health Care?" Los Angeles: UCLA Center for Health Policy Research.

Castañeda, Ernesto. 2012. "Living in Limbo: Transnational Households, Remittances and Development." *International Migration.* doi:10.1111/j.1468-2435.2012.00745.x

Chacón, Jennifer M. 2010. "Border Exceptionalism in the Era of Moving Borders." *Fordham Urban Law Journal* 38:129–153.

———. 2012. "Overcriminalizing Immigration." *Journal of Criminal Law and Criminology* 102(3):2013–2091.

Chant, Sylvia (Ed.). 1992. *Gender and Migration in Developing Countries*. London: Belhaven Press.

Chant, Sylvia, and Nikki Craske. 2003. *Gender in Latin America*. New Brunswick, NJ: Rutgers University Press.

Chavez, Leo R. 1998. *Shadowed Lives: Undocumented Immigrants in American Society*. Fort Worth, TX: Harcourt Brace.

———. 2008. *The Latino Threat: Constructing Immigrants, Citizens, and the Nation*. Palo Alto, CA: Stanford University Press.

Coffino, Eli. 2006. "A Long Road to Residency: The Legal History of Salvadoran & Guatemalan Immigration to the United States with a Focus on NACARA." *Cardozo Journal of International and Comparative Law* 14:177–207.

Cohen, Jeffrey H. 2011. "Migration, Remittances, and Household Strategies." *Annual Review of Anthropology* 40:103–114.

Cohen, Rina. 2000. "'Mom is a Stranger': The Negative Impact of Immigration Policies on the Family Life of Filipina Domestic Workers." *Canadian Ethnic Studies Journal* 32(3):76–88.

Coleman, Matthew. 2007. "Immigration Geopolitics beyond the Mexico–US Border." *Antipode* 39(1):54–76.

Connell, Robert W. 1987. *Gender and Power*. Oxford, UK: Polity Press.

Connell, Robert W., and James W. Messerschmidt. 2005. "Hegemonic Masculinity: Rethinking the Concept." *Gender & Society* 19(6):829–859.

Constable, Nicole. 2009. "The Commodification of Intimacy: Marriage, Sex, and Reproductive Labor." *Annual Review of Anthropology* 38:49–64.

Contreras, Ricardo, and David Griffith. 2012. "Managing Migration, Managing Motherhood: The Moral Economy of Gendered Migration." *International Migration* 50(4):51–66.

Coutin, Susan B. 1996. "Differences within Accounts of U.S. Immigration Law." *PoLAR: Political and Legal Anthropology Review* 19(1):11–19.

———. 1998. "From Refugees to Immigrants: The Legalization Strategies of Salvadoran Immigrants and Activists." *International Migration Review* 32(4):901–925.

———. 2000. *Legalizing Moves: Salvadoran Immigrants' Struggle for U.S. Residency*. Ann Arbor: University of Michigan Press.

———. 2002. "Questionable Transactions as Grounds for Legalization: Immigration, Illegality, and Law." *Crime Law and Social Change* 37(1):19–36.

———. 2007. *Nations of Emigrants: Shifting Boundaries of Citizenship in El Salvador and the United States*. Ithaca, NY: Cornell University Press.

Dalton, Juan José. 2004 (January 26). "Remesas de salvadoreños rebasan ingresos por exportaciones de café." *La Opinión* (Los Angeles).

Dalton, Roque. 2000. *Miguel Mármol: Los sucesos de 1932 en El Salvador*. San Salvador, El Salvador: UCA Editores.

Davenport, Allison. 2012. "Diversidad Sexual en El Salvador: Un Informe Sobre la Situación de los Derechos Humanos de la Comunidad LGBT." Report produced by Clínica Legal de Derechos Humanos Internacionales, UC Berkeley Law School.

Davis, Shannon N., and Theodore N. Greenstein. 2009. "Gender Ideology: Components, Predictors, and Consequences." *Annual Review of Anthropology* 35:87–105.

De Genova, Nicholas P. 2002. "Migrant 'Illegality' and Deportability in Everyday Life." *Annual Review of Anthropology* 31:419–447.

———. 2004. "The Legal Production of Mexican/Migrant 'Illegality.'" *Latino Studies* 2(2):160–185.

DeLugan, Robin Maria. 2012. *Reimagining National Belonging: Post-Civil War El Salvador in a Global Context.* Tucson: The University of Arizona Press.

Dill, Bonnie Thornton. 1998. "Our Mother's Grief: Racial Ethnic Women and the Maintenance of Families." *Journal of Family History* 13:415–431.

Dockterman, Daniel. 2011. "Hispanics of Salvadoran Origin in the United States, 2009." Washington, DC: Pew Hispanic Center.

Dodson, Lisa. 1998. *Don't Call Us Out of Name: The Untold Lives of Women and Girls in Poor America.* Boston: Beacon Press.

Donato, Katharine M., Joseph T. Alexander, Donna R. Gabaccia, and Johanna Leinonen. 2011. "Variations in the Gender Composition of Immigrant Populations: How They Matter." *International Migration Review* 45(3):495–526.

Donato, Katharine M., and Amada Armenta. 2011. "What We Know about Unauthorized Migration." *Annual Review of Sociology* 37(1):529–543.

Dore, Elizabeth, and Maxine Molyneux (Eds.). 2000. *Hidden Histories of Gender and the State in Latin America.* Durham, NC, and London: Duke University Press.

Dreby, Joanna. 2006. "Honor and Virtue: Mexican Parenting in the Transnational Context." *Gender & Society* 20(1):32–59.

———. 2007. "Children and Power in Mexican Transnational Families." *Journal of Marriage and Family* 69:1050–1064.

———. 2009. "Gender and Transnational Gossip." *Qualitative Sociology* 32:33–52.

———. 2010. *Divided by Borders: Mexican Migrants and Their Children.* Berkeley: University of California Press.

———. 2012. "The Burden of Deportation on Children in Mexican Immigrant Families." *Journal of Marriage and Family* 74:829–845.

Dreby, Joanna, and Timothy Adkins. 2010. "Inequalities in Transnational Families." *Sociology Compass* 4:673–689.

Dreby, Joanna, and Lindsay Stutz. 2012. "Making Something of the Sacrifice: Gender, Migration and Mexican Children's Educational Aspirations." *Global Networks* 12(1):71–90.

Edwards, Alejandra Cox, and Manuelita Ureta. 2003. "International Migration, Remittances, and Schooling: Evidence from El Salvador." *Journal of Development Economics* 72(2):429–461.

Ehrenreich, Barbara, and Arlie Russell Hochschild (Eds.). 2002. *Global Woman: Nannies, Maids, and Sex Workers in the New Economy*. New York: Metropolitan Books.

Faist, Thomas. 2008. "Migrants as Transnational Development Agents: An Inquiry into the Newest Round of the Migration-Development Nexus." *Population, Space and Place* 14:21–42.

Fajnzylber, Pablo, and J. Humberto López. 2007. "Close to Home: The Development Impact of Remittances in Latin America (Conference Edition)." Washington, DC: The International Bank for Reconstruction and Development/The World Bank.

Fauné, María Angélica. 1995. "New, Wider Households in Women's Hands." *Envío* 169. Available at www.envio.org.ni/articulo/1881.

Falcón, Sylvanna. 2001. "Rape as a Weapon of War: Advancing Human Rights for Women at the U.S.–Mexico Border." *Social Justice* 28(2):31–50.

Feliciano, Cynthia. 2005. "Educational Selectivity in U.S. Immigration: How Do Immigration Compare to Those Left Behind?" *Demography* 42(1):131–152.

Fitzgerald, David. 2004. "Beyond 'Transnationalism': Mexican Hometown Politics at an American Labor Union." *Ethnic and Racial Studies* 27(2):228–247.

Fletcher, Peri L. 1999. *La Casa de Mis Sueños: Dreams of Home in a Transnational Mexican Community*. Boulder, CO: Westview Press.

Fortuny, Karina, Randy Capps, and Jeffrey Passel. 2007. "The Characteristics of Unauthorized Immigrants in California, Los Angeles County, and the United States." Washington, DC: The Urban Institute. Available at www.urban.org/UploadedPDF/411425_Characteristics_Immigrants.pdf.

Franklin, Stephen. 2008. "Uncertain Safety for Latino workers: Construction Job Fatality Rates Exceed Those for Other Groups, and Many Are Reluctant to Complain." *Chicago Tribune*. March 2. Available at www.chicagotribune.com/features/lifestyle/health/chi-sun-latino-worker-deathsmar02,1,1652511.story.

Friedmann, John, Rebecca Abers, and Lilian Autler (Eds.). 1996. *Emergences: Women's Struggles for Livelihood in Latin America*. Los Angeles: UCLA Latin American Center Publications.

Fuentes Rubio, José Mario. 2004. "La Regulación Internacional del Flujo Migratorio y el Respeto a los Derechos Humanos." *Emigración* 1(1):99–122.

Funkhouser, Edward. 1997. "La migración internacional salvadoreña y las remesas: Un perfil," pp. 43–94 in *Migración internacional y desarrollo: Tomo I*, edited by Mario Lungo. San Salvador, El Salvador: Fundación Nacional para el Desarrollo.

Gammage, Sarah. 2006. "Exporting People and Recruiting Remittances: A Development Strategy for El Salvador?" *Latin American Perspectives* 33(6):75–100.

Gammage, Sarah, Alison Paul, Melany Machado, and Manuel Benítez. 2005. *Gender, Migration and Transnational Communities*. Washington, DC: Inter-American Foundation.

Gammage, Sarah, and John Schmitt. 2004. "Los inmigrantes mexicanos, salvadoreños y dominicanos en el mercado laboral estadounidense: las brechas de género en los años 1990 y 2000," in *Serie Estudios y Perspectivas*. México, D.F.: Comisión Económica para América Latina y el Caribe (CEPAL), Unidad de Desarrollo Social.

Gammeltoft, Peter. 2002. "Remittances and Other Financial Flows to Developing Countries." *International Migration* 40(5):181–211.

García, Ana Isabel (Ed.). 1999. *La situación de las mujeres en Centroamérica: una evaluación en el umbral del siglo XXI*. San Jose, Costa Rica: Fundación Género y Sociedad (GESO).

García, Ana Isabel, and Enrique Gomáriz. 1989. *Mujeres centroamericanas*. San Jose, Costa Rica: FLACSO.

García, Juan José. 2012. "From Peace Accords to Voting Abroad." Presented at the "20th Anniversary of El Salvador's Peace Accords and Implications for Transnational Development and Voting Abroad," a Conference organized by the UCLA North American Integration and Development Center. January 30. Los Angeles, CA.

García, Maria Cristina. 2006. *Seeking Refuge: Central American Migration to Mexico, the United States, and Canada*. Berkeley: University of California Press.

Gleeson, Shannon. 2010. "Labor Rights for All? The Role of Undocumented Immigrant Status for Worker Claims-Making." *Law & Social Inquiry* 35(3):561–602.

———. 2012. *Conflicting Commitments: The Politics of Enforcing Immigrant Worker Rights in San Jose and Houston*. Ithaca, NY, and London: Cornell University Press.

Glenn, Evelyn Nakano. 2002. *Unequal Freedom: How Race and Gender Shaped American Citizenship and Labor*. Cambridge, MA: Harvard University Press.

Glick Schiller, Nina, Linda G. Basch, and Cristina Blanc-Szanton (Eds.). 1992. *Towards a Transnational Perspective on Migration: Race, Class, Ethnicity, and Nationalism Reconsidered*. New York: New York Academy of Sciences.

Golash-Boza, Tanya. 2013. "Forced Transnationalism: Transnational Coping Strategies and Gendered Stigma Among Jamaican Deportees." *Global Networks*. DOI: 10.1111/glob.12013.

Goldring, Luin. 1998. "Power and Status in Transnational Social Fields," pp. 165–195 in *Transnationalism from Below*, edited by Michael P. Smith and Luis E. Guarnizo. New Brunswick, NJ: Transaction.

Goldring, Luin, Carolina Berinstein, and Judith K. Bernhard. 2009. "Institutionalizing Precarious Migratory Status in Canada." *Citizenship Studies* 13(3):239–265.

Gonzales, Roberto G., and Leo R. Chavez. 2012. "'Awakening to a Nightmare': Abjectivity and Illegality in the Lives of Undocumented 1.5 Generation Latino Immigrants in the United States." *Current Anthropology* 53(3):255–281.

González de la Rocha, Mercedes. 1989. "El poder de la ausencia: mujeres y migración en una comunidad de los altos de Jaliscos," pp. 317–342 in *Coloquio de Antropología e Historia Regionales: Las realidades regionales de la crisis nacional*. Zamora, Michoacán: El Colegio de Michoacán.

———. 1994. *The Resources of Poverty: Women and Survival in a Mexican City*. Cambridge, MA: Blackwell Publishers.

———. 2001. "From the Resources of Poverty to the Poverty of Resources? The Erosion of a Survival Model." *Latin American Perspectives* 28(4):72–100.

Goodheart, Jessica. 2007. "Poverty, Jobs and the Los Angeles Economy: An Analysis of U.S. Census Data and the Challenges Facing Our Region." Los Angeles: Los Angeles Alliance for a New Economy Partnership for Working Families.

Gorman, Anna. 2008. "Deportee Torn between Two Countries." *Los Angeles Times*, February 29; available at www.latimes.com/news/local/la-me-deport 29feb29,0,4779483.story.

Grall, Timothy S. 2011. "Custodial Mothers and Fathers and Their Child Support: 2009." Washington, DC: U.S. Department of Commerce, U.S. Census Bureau. Document Number: P60-240; available at www.census.gov/prod/2011pubs/p60-240.pdf.

Guarnizo, Luis E., Alejandro Portes, and William Haller. 2003. "Assimilation and Transnationalism: Determinants of Transnational Political Action among Contemporary Migrants." *American Journal of Sociology* 108(6):1211–1248.

Guarnizo, Luis E., and Michael P. Smith. 1998. "The Locations of Transnationalism," pp. 3–34 in *Transnationalism from Below*, edited by Michael P. Smith and Luis E. Guarnizo. New Brunswick, NJ: Transaction Publishers.

Gutiérrez, Rolando. 2003. "Remittances and the Inter-American Foundation." *Grassroots Development* 24(1):39.

Hagan, Jacqueline Maria. 1994. *Deciding to Be Legal: A Maya Community in Houston*. Philadelphia: Temple University Press.

Hamilton, Nora, and Norma Stoltz Chinchilla. 2001. *Seeking Community in a Global City: Guatemalans and Salvadorans in Los Angeles*. Philadelphia: Temple University Press.

Hammock, John, María Elena Letona, Gilma Pérez, and Ana Micaela Isen. 2005. "Testimonios de Familias Migrantes Salvadoreñas: Pobreza y Trabajo." Boston: Centro Presente. Available at http://fletcher.tufts.edu/faculty/hammock/pdf/Testimonios%20de%20familias%20migrantes%20salvadore%F1as-1.pdf.

Hayden, Bridget. 2006. "What's in a Name? The Nature of the Individual in Refugee Studies." *Journal of Refugee Studies* 19:471–487.

Hays, Sharon. 2003. *Flat Broke with Children: Women in the Age of Welfare Reform*. New York: Oxford University Press.

Hernández, David Manuel. 2008. "Pursuant to Deportation: Latinos and Immigrant Detention." *Latino Studies* 6(1–2):35–63.

Hernandez, Ester. 2002. "The Power in Remittances: Remaking Family and Nation among Salvadorans." PhD dissertation in *Social Sciences*. Irvine, CA: University of California, Irvine.

———. 2006a. "Relief Dollars: U.S. Policies toward Central Americans, 1980s to Present." *Journal of American Ethnic History* 25(2-3):225–242.

———. 2006b. "Confronting Exclusion in the Latino Metropolis: Central American Transnational Communities in the Los Angeles Area, 1980s–2006." *Journal of the West* 45(4):48–56.

Hernández-León, Rubén. 2008. *Metropolitan Migrants: The Migration of Urban Mexicans to the United States*. Berkeley: University of California Press.

Holmes, Seth M. 2007. "'Oaxacans Like to Work Bent Over': The Naturalization of Social Suffering among Berry Farm Workers." *International Migration* 45(3):39–68.

Hondagneu-Sotelo, Pierrette. 1994. *Gendered Transitions: Mexican Experiences of Immigration*. Berkeley, CA: University of California Press.

———. 2000. "Feminism and Migration." *Annals of the American Academy of Political and Social Sciences* 570(1):107–102. doi: 10.1177/000271620057100108

———. 2001. *Doméstica: Immigrant Workers Cleaning and Caring in the Shadows of Affluence*: Berkeley: University of California Press.

——— (Ed.). 2003. *Gender and U.S. Immigration: Contemporary Trends*. Berkeley: University of California Press.

Hondagneu-Sotelo, Pierrette, and Ernestine Avila. 1997. "'I'm Here, but I'm There': The Meanings of Latina Transnational Motherhood." *Gender & Society* 11(5):548–570.

House, Krista Lynn. 1999. "'Absent Ones Who Are Always Present': Migration, Remittances, and Household Survival Strategies in Guatemala," in *Geography*. Kingston, Ontario: Queen's University.

Hume, Mo. 2004. "'It's as If You Don't Know, because You Don't Do Anything About It": Gender and Violence in El Salvador." *Environment and Urbanization* 16(2):63–72.

Itzigsohn, Jose, and Silvia Giorguli-Saucedo. 2005. "Incorporation, Transnationalism, and Gender: Immigrant Incorporation and Transnational Participation as Gendered Processes." *International Migration Review* 39(4):895–920.

Jiménez, Tomás R., and Laura López-Sanders. 2011. "Unanticipated, Unintended, and Unadvised: The Effects of Public Policy on Unauthorized Immigration," pp. 3–7 in *Pathways*. Stanford, CA: The Stanford Center for the Study of Poverty and Inequality.

Kampwirth, Karen. 2002. *Women & Guerrilla Movements: Nicaragua, El Salvador, Chiapas, Cuba*. University Park: The Pennsylvania State University Press.

Kapur, Devesh, and Center for Global Development. 2003. "Remittances: The New Development Mantra?" Presented at the XVIII G-24 Technical Group Meeting.

LaFeber, Walter. 1993. *Inevitable Revolutions: The United States in Central America.* New York and London: W. W. Norton & Company.

Landolt, Patricia, and Wei Wei Da. 2005. "The Spatially Ruptured Practices of Migrant Families: A Comparison of Immigrants from El Salvador and the People's Republic of China." *Current Sociology* 53(4):625–653.

Levitt, Peggy. 2001. *The Transnational Villagers.* Berkeley: University of California Press.

Levitt, Peggy, and B. Nadya Jaworsky. 2007. "Transnational Migration Studies: Past Developments and Future Trends." *Annual Review of Sociology* 33:129–156.

Loh, Katherine, and Scott Richardson. 2004. "Foreign-Born Workers: Trends in Fatal Occupational Injuries, 1996–2001." *Monthly Labor Review* June: 42–53.

López Castro, Gustavo. 1986. *La casa dividida: Un estudio de caso sobre la migración a Estados Unidos en un pueblo michoacano.* Zamora, Michoacán: Colegio de Michoacán y Asociación Mexicana de Población.

Lorber, Judith. 1994. *Paradoxes of Gender.* New Haven, CT: Yale University Press.

Lorentzen, Lois Ann, and Rosalina Mira. 2005. "El milagro está en casa: Gender and Private/Public Empowerment in a Migrant Pentecostal Church." *Latin American Perspectives* 32(1):57–71.

Luciak, Ilja A. 2001. *After the Revolution: Gender and Democracy in El Salvador, Nicaragua, and Guatemala.* Baltimore and London: The Johns Hopkins University Press.

Lungo, Mario, Katharine Andrade-Eekhoff, and Sonia Baires. 1997. "Migración internacional y desarrollo local en El Salvador," pp. 47–86 in *Migración internacional y desarrollo: Tomo II,* edited by Mario Lungo. San Salvador, El Salvador: Fundación Nacional para el Desarrollo.

Lutz, Helma. 2010. "Gender in the Migratory Process." *Journal of Ethnic and Migration Studies* 36(10):1647–1663.

Macías, Patrisia. 2006. "Criminalizing Migration in an Era of Rights: Ethnographic Observations from the U.S.–Mexico Border." Presented at the Annual Meeting of the American Sociological Association. Montreal, PQ, Canada.

MacLeod, Jay. 1987. *Ain't No Makin' It: Aspirations and Attainment in a Low-Income Neighborhood.* Boulder, CO: Westview Press.

Madrigal, Larry, and Walberto Tejeda. 2009. "Facing Gender-Based Violence in El Salvador: Contributions from the Social Psychology of Ignacio Martín-Baró." *Feminism & Psychology* 19(3):368–374.

Mahler, Sarah J. 1999. "Engendering Transnational Migration: A Case Study of Salvadorans." *American Behavior Scientist* 42(4):690–719.

Mahler, Sarah J., and Patricia R. Pessar. 2001. "Gendered Geographies of Power: Analyzing Gender across Transnational Spaces." *Identities: Global Studies in Culture and Power* 7(4):441–459.

———. 2006. "Gender Matters: Ethnographers Bring Gender from the Periphery toward the Core of Migration Studies." *International Migration Review* 40(1):27–63.

Maimbo, Samuel Munzele, and Dilip Ratha (Eds.). 2005. *Remittances: Development Impact and Future Prospects*. Washington, DC: World Bank.

Maldonado, René, Natasha Bajuk, and María Luisa Hayem. 2011. "Remittances to Latin America and the Caribbean in 2010: Stabilization after the Crisis." Washington, DC: Multilateral Investment Fund, Inter-American Development Bank.

Martínez, Lilian. 2006. "El rostro joven de las remesas." in *El Diario de Hoy*. April 28. San Salvador, El Salvador. Available at www.elsalvador.com/noticias/2006/04/28/nacional/nac13.asp#.

Martínez, Óscar. 2010. *Los migrantes que no importan: En el camino con los centroamericanos indocumentados en México*. Barcelona: Icaria.

Massey, Douglas, Rafael Alarcon, Jorge Durand, and Humberto González. 1987. *Return to Aztlan: The Social Process of Migration from Western Mexico*. Berkeley: University of California Press.

Massey, Douglas, and Katherine Bartley. 2005. "The Changing Legal Status Distribution of Immigrants: A Caution." *International Migration Review* 39(2):469–484.

Massey, Douglas, Jorge Durand, and Nolan Malone. 2002. *Beyond Smoke and Mirrors: Mexican Immigration in an Era of Economic Integration*. New York: Russell Sage Foundation.

McGuire, Sharon, and Kate Martin. 2007. "Fractured Migrant Families: Paradoxes of Hope and Devastation." *Family and Community Health* 30(3):178–188.

Mckay, Deirdre. 2007. "'Sending Dollars Shows Feeling': Emotions and Economies in Filipino Migration." *Mobilities* 2(2):175–194.

Melhuus, Marit, and Kristi Anne Stølen (Eds.). 1996. *Machos, Mistresses, Madonnas: Contesting the Power of Latin American Gender Imagery*. London and New York: Verso.

Menjívar, Cecilia. 1999. "The Intersection of Work and Gender: Central American Immigrant Women and Employment in California." *American Behavioral Scientist* 42(4):595–621.

———. 2000. *Fragmented Ties: Salvadoran Immigrant Networks in America*. Berkeley: University of California Press.

———. 2006. "Liminal Legality: Salvadoran and Guatemalan Immigrants' Lives in the United States." *American Journal of Sociology* 111(4):999–1037.

———. 2011. *Enduring Violence: Ladina Women's Lives in Guatemala*. Berkeley: University of California Press.

Menjívar, Cecilia, and Leisy Abrego. 2009. "Parents and Children across Borders: Legal Instability and Intergenerational Relations in Guatemalan and Salvadoran Families," pp. 160–189 in *Across Generations: Immigrant Families in America*, edited by Nancy Foner. New York: New York University Press.

———. 2012. "Legal Violence: Immigration Law and the Lives of Central American Immigrants." *American Journal of Sociology* 117(5):1380–1424.

Menjívar, Cecilia, and Daniel Kanstroom (Eds.). Forthcoming. *Constructing Illegality: Immigrant Experiences, Critiques, and Resistance*. Cambridge, UK: Cambridge University Press.

Milkman, Ruth, Ana Luz González, and Victor Narro. 2010. "Wage Theft and Workplace Violations in Los Angeles: The Failure of Employment and Labor Law for Low-Wage Workers." Report published through the UCLA Institute for Research on Labor and Employment, Los Angeles.

Milkman, Ruth, Ellen Reese, and Benita Roth. 1998. "The Macrosociology of Paid Domestic Labor." *Work and Occupations* 25:483–510.

Miranda, Jeanne, Juned Siddique, Claudia Der-Martirosian, and Thomas R. Belin. 2005. "Depression among Latina Immigrant Mothers Separated from Their Children." *Psychiatric Services* 56(6):717–720.

Moodie, Ellen. 2010. *El Salvador in the Aftermath of Peace: Crime, Uncertainty, and the Transition to Democracy*. Philadelphia: University of Pennsylvania Press.

Moran-Taylor, Michelle J. 2008. "When Mothers and Fathers Migrate North: Caretakers, Children, and Child Rearing in Guatemala." *Latin American Perspectives* 35(4):79–95. DOI: 10.1177/0094582X08318980

Motomura, Hiroshi. 2008. "Immigration Outside the Law." *Columbia Law Review* 108(8):2037–2097.

Motel, Seth, and Eileen Patten. 2013. "Statistical Portrait of Hispanics in the United States, 2011." Washington, DC: Pew Hispanic Center. Retrieved on March 1, 2013, from www.pewhispanic.org/2013/02/15/statistical-portrait-of-hispanics-in-the-united-states-2011/.

Myers, Dowell. 2007. *Immigrants and Boomers: Forging a New Social Contract for the Future of America*. New York: Russell Sage Foundation.

National Community Advisory. 2011. "Restoring Community: A National Community Advisory Report on ICE's Failed 'Secure Communities' Program": retrieved on February 10, 2013, from http://altopolimigra.com/s-comm-shadow-report/.

Navas, María Candelaria, Nancy Orellana, and Nidia Umaña. 2007. "Hacia una Sociología de Género en El Salvador." *Alternativas para el Desarrollo* 102:27–35. Available at www.repo.funde.org/463/1/APD-102-III.pdf.

Nazario, Sonia. 2007. *Enrique's Journey: The Story of a Boy's Dangerous Odyssey to Reunite with His Mother*. New York: Random House.

Ngai, Mae M. 2004. *Impossible Subjects: Illegal Aliens and the Making of Modern America*. Princeton, NJ: Princeton University Press.

Nicholson, Melanie. 2006. "Without Their Children: Rethinking Motherhood among Transnational Migrant Women." *Social Text* 24(3):13–33.

Nissen, Bruce, Alejandro Angee, and Marc Weinstein. 2008. "Immigrant Construction Workers and Health and Safety: The South Florida Experience." *Labor Studies Journal* 33(1): 48.

Nyberg-Sørensen, Ninna, Nicholas Van Hear, and Poul Engberg-Pedersen. 2002. "The Migration-Development Nexus: Evidence and Policy Options State-of-the-Art Overview." *International Migration* 40(5):3–47.

Ocampo, Anthony C. 2012. "Making Masculinity: Negotiations of Gender Presentation among Latino Gay Men." *Latino Studies* 10(4):448–472.

Ogren, Cassandra. 2007. "Migration and Human Rights on the Mexico–Guatemala Border." *International Migration* 45(4):203–242.

Oliva, Karina. 2013. "Voicing Indigenous Womanist Poetics through Salvadoran, Salvi, Chicana, Chingona Xnationalist Migrations." Presented at the Annual Meetings of the National Association of Chicana and Chicano Studies. March 21. San Antonio, TX.

Orellana, Marjorie Faulstich, Barrie Thorne, Anna Chee, and Wan Shun Eva Lam. 2001. "Transnational Childhoods: The Participation of Children in Processes of Family Migration." *Social Problems* 48(4):572–591.

Orozco, Manuel. 2002. "Globalization and Migration: The Impact of Family Remittances in Latin America." *Latin American Politics and Society* 44(2):41–68.

———. 2006. "Gender Remittances: Preliminary Notes about Senders and Recipients in Latin America and the Caribbean," in *United Nations Commission on the Status of Women*. New York: United Nations.

Ortez Andrade, Orestes. 2011. "La realidad socioeconómica y política de El Salvador: Los retos en la construcción de un modelo económico alternativo durante una crisis global." Presented at the University of California, Los Angeles. October 14.

Ortner, Sherry B. 1972. "Is Female to Male as Nature is to Culture?" *Feminist Studies* 1(2):5–31.

Padilla, Yajaira M. 2012. *Changing Women, Changing Nation: Female Agency, Nationhood, and Identity in Trans-Salvadoran Narratives*. Albany: State University of New York Press.

Painter, Gary, Stuart Gabriel, and Dowell Myers. 2001. "Race, Immigrant Status, and Housing Tenure Choice." *Journal of Urban Economics* 49:150–167.

Parreñas, Rhacel. 2001a. "Mothering from a Distance: Emotions, Gender, and Intergenerational Relationships in Filipino Transnational Families." *Feminist Studies* 27(2):361–390.

———. 2001b. *Servants of Globalization: Women, Migration, and Domestic Work*. Palo Alto, CA: Stanford University Press.

———. 2005a. *Children of Global Migration: Transnational Families and Gendered Woes*. Palo Alto, CA: Stanford University Press.

———. 2005b. "Long Distance Intimacy: Class, Gender and Intergenerational Relations between Mothers and Children in Filipino Transnational Families." *Global Networks* 5(4):317–336.

Peiró, Amado. 2006. "Happiness, Satisfaction and Socio-Economic Conditions: Some International Evidence." *The Journal of Socio-Economics* 35:348–365.

Pérez, Rossana, and Henry A. J. Ramos (Eds.). 2007. *Flight to Freedom: The Story of Central American Refugees in California*. Houston, TX: Arte Público Press.

Pessar, Patricia R. 2005. "Women, Gender, and International Migration across and beyond the Americas: Inequalities and Limited Empowerment," in *Expert Group Meeting on International Migration and Development in Latin America and the Caribbean*. Mexico City: Population Division, United Nations Secratariat. Available at www.un.org/esa/population/meetings/IttMigLAC/P08_PPessar.pdf.

Pessar, Patricia R., and Sarah J. Mahler. 2003. "Transnational Migration: Bringing Gender In." *International Migration Review* 37(3):812–46.

Piper, Nicola. 2008. "The 'Migration-Development Nexus' Revisited from a Rights Perspective." *Journal of Human Rights* 7(3):282–298.

———. 2009. "The Complex Interconnections of the Migration-Development Nexus: A Social Perspective." *Population, Space and Place* 15:93–101.

PNUD. 2005. *Informe sobre desarrollo humano de El Salvador 2005: Una mirada al nuevo nosotros, Impacto de las migraciones*. San Salvador, El Salvador: United Nations Development Program.

Ponce, Albert. 2012. "Racialization, Resistance and the Migrant Rights Movement: A Historical Analysis." *Critical Sociology*. DOI: 10.1177/0896920512465210

Popkin, Eric. 1998. "In Search of the Quetzal: Guatemalan Mayan Transnational Migration and Ethnic Identity Formation." PhD dissertation in Sociology. Los Angeles: University of California, Los Angeles.

Portes, Alejandro, Luis E. Guarnizo, and Patricia Landolt. 1999. "The Study of Transnationalism: Pitfalls and Promise of an Emergent Research Field." *Ethnic and Racial Studies* 22(2):217–237.

Portes, Alejandro, and Rubén G. Rumbaut. 1996. *Immigrant America: A Portrait*. Berkeley: University of California Press.

———. 2001. *Legacies: The Story of the Immigrant Second Generation*. Berkeley and New York: University of California Press and Russell Sage Foundation.

Pratt, Geraldine. 2012. *Families Apart: Migrant Mothers and the Conflicts of Labor and Love*. Minneapolis: University of Minnesota Press.

Pribilsky, Jason. 2004. "'Aprendemos a convivir': Conjugal Relations, Co-Parenting, and Family Life among Ecuadorian Transnational Migrants in New York City and the Ecuadorian Andes." *Global Networks* 4(3):313–334.

Ratha, Dilip. 2005. "Workers' Remittances: An Important and Stable Source of External Development Finance." *World Bank, Global Development Finance 2003*, pp. 157–175. Retrieved on August 25, 2013, from http://repository.stcloudstate.edu/cgi/viewcontent.cgi?article=1009&context=econ_seminars&sei-redir=1&referer=http%3A%2F%2Fscholar.google.com%2Fscholar%3Fq%3Dratha%2Bdilip%2Bworkers%2527%2Bremittances%26btnG%3D%26hl%3Den%26as_sdt%3D0%252C5#search=%22ratha%20dilip%20workers%20remittances%22.

Repak, Terry A. 1995. *Waiting on Washington: Central American Workers in the Nation's Capital*. Philadelphia: Temple University Press.

Rivera Funes, Oscar Francisco. 2003. "International Migrations and Their Economic Effects in El Salvador (Translation of Spanish Version)," in *Conference of The Population of the Central American Isthmus in 2003*. California Center for Population Research. University of California, Los Angeles.

Sanabria, Salvador. 2003. "Remittance Forum: Players and Programs in El Salvador." *Grassroots Development* 24(1):34–38.

Santa Ana, Otto. 2012. *Juan in a Hundred: The Representation of Latinos on Network News*. Austin: University of Texas Press.

Schen, Cathy R. 2005. "When Mothers Leave Their Children Behind." *Harvard Review of Psychiatry* 13(4):233–243.

Schirmer, Jennifer. 1993. "The Seeking of Truth and the Gendering of Consciousness: The Comadres of El Salvador and the Conavigua Widows of Guatemala," pp. 30–64 in *"Viva": Women and Popular Protest in Latin America*, edited by Sarah A. Radcliffe and Sallie Westwood. New York: Routledge.

Schmalzbauer, Leah. 2004. "Searching for Wages and Mothering from Afar: The Case of Honduran Transnational Families." *Journal of Marriage and Family* 66:1317–1131.

———. 2005. *Striving and Surviving: A Daily Life Analysis of Honduran Transnational Families*. New York and London: Routledge.

———. 2008. "Family Divided: The Class Formation of Honduran Transnational Families." *Global Networks* 8(3):329–346.

Seguino, Stephanie, and Maria Sagrario Floro. 2003. "Does Gender Have any Effect on Aggregate Saving? An Empirical Analysis." *International Review of Applied Economics* 17(2):147–166.

Segura, Denise. 1994. "Working at Motherhood: Chicana and Mexican Immigrant Mothers and Employment," in *Mothering: Ideology, Experience, and Agency*, edited by Evelyn Nakano Glenn, Grace Chang, and Linda Rennie Forcey. New York: Routledge.

Segura, Rosamaría. 2010. *Central Americans in Los Angeles*. Charleston, SC: Arcadia Publishing.

Semyonov, Moshe, and Anastasia Gorodzeisky. 2005. "Labor Migration, Remittances and Household Income: A Comparison between Filipino and Filipina Overseas Workers." *International Migration Review* 39(1):45–68.

Skrbiš, Zlatko. 2008. "Transnational Families: Theorising Migration, Emotions and Belonging." *Journal of Intercultural Studies* 29(3):231–246.

Smith, Robert Courtney. 2006. *Mexican New York: Transnational Lives of New Immigrants*. Berkeley: University of California Press.

Soldatenko, María. 1999. "Made in the USA: Latinas/os? Garment Work and Ethnic Conflict in Los Angeles' Sweat Shops." *Cultural Studies* 13(2):319–334.

Soto, Lilia. 2010. "The Preludes to Migration: Anticipation and Imaginings of Mexican Immigrant Adolescent Girls." *Girlhood Studies* 3(2):30–48.

Stephen, Lynn. 2001. "Gender, Citizenship, and the Politics of Identity." *Latin American Perspectives* 28(6):54–69.

———. 2007. *Transborder Lives: Indigenous Oaxacans in Mexico, California, and Oregon*. Durham, NC, and London: Duke University Press.

Suárez-Orozco, Carola, Hee Jin Bang, and Ha Yeon Kim. 2010. "I Felt Like My Heart Was Staying Behind: Psychological Implications of Family Separations and Reunifications for Immigrant Youth." *Journal of Adolescent Research* 20(10):1–36.

Suárez-Orozco, Carola, Irina Todorova, and Josephine Louie. 2002. "Making up for Lost Time: The Experience of Separation and Reunification among Immigrant Families." *Family Process* 41(4):625–643.

Suro, Roberto. 2003. *Remittance Senders and Receivers: Tracking the Transnational Channels*. Washington, DC: Multilateral Investment Fund and the Pew Hispanic Center.

Taylor, J. Edward. 1999. "The New Economics of Labour Migration and the Role of Remittances in the Migration Process." *International Migration* 37(1):63–88.

Terrazas, Aaron. 2010. "Salvadoran Immigrants in the United States." Washington, DC: Migration Information Source.

Thompson, Ginger. 2003. "Crossing with Strangers: Children at the Border; Littlest Immigrants, Left in Hands of Smugglers." *The New York Times*, November 3, A-1.

Thorne, Barrie. 1992. "Feminist Thinking on the Family: An Overview," in *Rethinking the Family: Some Feminist Questions*, edited by Barrie Thorne and Marilyn Yalom. Boston: Northeastern University Press.

UNFPA. 2006. *A Passage to Hope: Women and International Migration*. New York: United Nations Population Fund.

Valenzuela, Abel Jr. 2002. "Working on the Margins in Metropolitan Los Angeles: Immigrants in Day-Labor Work." *Migraciones Internacionales* 1(2):6–28.

Vanwey, Leah. 2004. "Altruistic and Contractual Remittances between Male and Female Migrants and Households in Rural Thailand." *Demography* 41(4):739–756.

Villacorta, Alberto Enriquez, Nayelly Loya, Victor Tablas, Maria Elena Moreno, and Carlos Sáenz. 2011. *Migración internacional, niñez y adolescencia en El Salvador.* San Salvador, El Salvador: Fundación Dr. Guillermo Manuel Ungo and Ministerio de Relaciones Exteriores a través del Vice Ministerio para los Salvadoreños en el Exterior. Available at www.rree.gob.sv/index.php?/alphaindex/descargas/m.php.

Viterna, Jocelyn S. 2006. "Pulled, Pushed, and Persuaded: Explaining Women's Mobilization into the Salvadoran Guerrilla Army." *American Journal of Sociology* 112(1):1–45.

Volpp, Leti. 2011. "Framing Cultural Difference: Immigrant Women and Discourses of Tradition." *Differences: A Journal of Feminist Cultural Studies* 22(1):90–110.

Vonderlack-Navarro, Rebecca. 2010. "Targeting Women Versus Addressing Gender in Microcredit: Lessons From Honduras." *Affilia: Journal of Women and Social Work* 25(2):123–134. DOI: 10.1177/0886109910364356

Waldinger, Roger, and David Fitzgerald. 2004. "Transnationalism in Question." *American Journal of Sociology* 109(5):1177–1195.

Waldinger, Roger, and Greta Gilbertson. 1994. "Immigrants' Progress: Ethnic and Gender Differences among U.S. Immigrants in the 1980s." *Sociological Perspectives* 37(3):431–444.

Walter, Nicholas, Philippe Bourgois, and H. Margarita Loinaz. 2004. "Masculinity and Undocumented Labor Migration: Injured Latino Day Laborers in San Francisco." *Social Science & Medicine* 59:1159–1168.

Weitzhandler, Ari. 1993. "Temporary Protected Status: The Congressional Response to the Plight of Salvadoran Aliens." *University of Colorado Law Review* 64:249–275.

Willen, Sarah S. 2007. "Toward a Critical Phenomenology of 'Illegality': State Power, Criminalization, and Abjectivity among Undocumented Migrant Workers in Tel Aviv, Israel." *International Migration* 45(3):8–38.

Wood, Elisabeth Jean. 2003. *Insurgent Collective Action and Civil War in El Salvador.* Cambridge, UK: Cambridge University Press.

World Bank. 2006. "Global Economic Prospects: Economic Implications of Remittances and Migration 2006." Washington, DC: The World Bank. Retrieved on February 11, 2013, from www-wds.worldbank.org/external/default/WDSContentServer/IW3P/IB/2005/11/14/000112742_20051114174928/Rendered/PDF/343200GEP02006.pdf.

Wright, Richard, Adrian Bailey, Inés Miyares, and Alison Mountz. 2000. "Legal Status, Gender and Employment among Salvadorans in the US." *International Journal of Population Geography* 6(4):273–286.

Zavella, Patricia. 1991. "Reflection on Diversity among Chicanas." *Frontiers: A Journal of Women Studies* 12(2):73–85.

———. 2011. *I'm Neither Here nor There: Mexicans' Quotidian Struggles with Migration and Poverty.* Durham, NC, and London: Duke University Press.

Zelizer, Viviana. 2005. *The Purchase of Intimacy.* Princeton, NJ: Princeton University Press.

Zentgraf, Kristine. 2002. "Immigration and Women's Empowerment: Salvadorans in Los Angeles." *Gender & Society* 16(5):625–646.

Zentgraf, Kristine, and Norma Chinchilla. 2012. "Transnational Family Separation: A Framework for Analysis." *Journal of Ethnic and Migration Studies* 38(2):345–366.

Zinn, Maxine Baca. 1982. "Chicano Men and Masculinity." *Journal of Ethnic Studies* 10(2):29–44.

Index

9 780804 790512